Final Test

Also by Peter Schrag

Final Test

*The Battle for Adequacy
in America's Schools*

TOURO COLLEGE LIBRARY
Kings Hwy

PETER SCHRAG

THE NEW PRESS

NEW YORK
LONDON

KH

Published in the United States by The New Press, New York, 2003
Distributed by W. W. Norton & Company, Inc., New York

LIBRARY OF CONGRESS CATALOGING-IN-PUBLICATION DATA

Schrag, Peter.
    Final test : the battle for adequacy in America's schools / Peter Schrag.
        p.   cm.
    Includes bibliographical references and index.
    ISBN 1-56584-821-7 (hc.)
    1. Public schools—United States.   2. Education—Aims and objectives—United States.
3. Educational law and legislation—United States.   4. Education—United States—
Finance.   I. Title.

LA217.2.S38 2003
371.01'0973—dc21

                                                                2003051382

The New Press was established in 1990 as a not-for-profit alternative to the
large, commercial publishing houses currently dominating the book publishing
industry. The New Press operates in the public interest rather than for private
gain, and is committed to publishing, in innovative ways, works of educational,
cultural, and community value that are often deemed insufficiently profitable.

The New Press
38 Greene Street, 4th floor
New York, NY 10013
www.thenewpress.com

In the United Kingdom:
6 Salem Road
London W2 4BU

Composition by Westchester Book

Printed in the United States of America

2   4   6   8   10   9   7   5   3   1

10/25/04

For David and all his children

Contents

Final Test

Introduction

I

The U.S. Supreme Court's unanimous school desegregation decision in *Brown v. Board of Education*, handed down on May 17, 1954, is far better known for what it did than what it didn't do. Ever since *Brown*, America has been officially committed to the provision of decent educational opportunities for all children, regardless of class or race. For much of that half century, those efforts rested primarily on the pursuit of school desegregation, on programs of compensatory education for disadvantaged children, and on efforts to achieve equity among schools, particularly in school funding. Most of us believed, or pretended to believe, that if children of all races and classes sat in the same classrooms or if schools in different communities and neighborhoods received equal financing, regardless of the local community's wealth and thus its ability to tax itself, the gaps in educational outcomes among children of different races, classes, and cultures could be closed. Now, as the nation approaches the fiftieth anniversary of *Brown*, it may well also be approaching a crucial turning point in public education and in the effort to achieve the things that *Brown* seemed to promise.

Brown, which decreed that where states provide public schooling, they must offer it in legally non-segregated schools, never evolved into what some reformers had hoped: a legal doctrine that in essence would have made education into a federally guaranteed constitutional right. On the contrary, in 1973, the sharply divided justices held that, despite the implications of *Brown,* public education was not a right protected by the U.S. Constitution. Even where children in different parts of a state were getting flagrantly inferior resources in funding, in the quality of their teachers, and in books and physical facilities, there was no federal constitutional violation. The 1973 decision, *San Antonio v. Rodriguez,* one veteran school activist said, "thwarted the reality and impact of *Brown....* The right under *Brown* without the resources to make it a reality is a hollow promise."[1]

That assessment, however, is far too gloomy, for not only did *Brown* signal the beginning of the end of legal segregation in all sectors of American life, it reenergized the nation's historical hope in public schools as the essential instruments of a great democracy. What *Rodriguez* did was to throw the promise of and the hope for genuine educational opportunity to the states, most of which had their own equal protection clauses and, more important, had state constitutional mandates requiring their legislatures to provide public education for all their children. The language of those constitutional provisions varies, as have the interpretations of the many judges that have ruled on them. But they have provided the base for two overlapping waves of reforms that have changed—and continue to change—American education in ways not imagined since *Brown.* Prompted in many cases by their own courts, a growing number of states are now dropping the shoe that the U.S. Supreme Court refused to drop in 1973.

The first of those waves of reform was the search for equity. Where there were major disparities in the property tax base among different school districts, which is where the lion's share of school revenues used to come from, some state courts ordered legislatures to equalize funding enough so that equal local tax efforts by different communities would produce roughly equal revenues for each pupil.[2] The second and more recent wave of reform, and by far the more important, is based on those state constitutional mandates requiring legislatures to maintain public schools. It seeks judicial orders and legislation defining what's necessary to provide a constitutionally sufficient education for each child—in teachers, books, facilities, and programs—and to require that funding be appropriated accordingly. The common label for this is "adequacy." It's an awful word, and susceptible to many definitions, but it is one that, for lack of a better alternative, we are now stuck with. By whatever name, however, the adequacy principle embodies a potentially revolutionary set of ideas, not only for creating better schools for the country's neediest children but perhaps for other social policy as well.

The new strategy sprang in part from the fact that the drive for school integration effectively reached a dead end (and, in fact, has given way to resegregation); in part from the many studies and reports showing that the ethnic gaps in measured outcomes—test scores, high school graduation rates, and college attendance—while narrowing considerably in the 1970s and 1980s, had not been eliminated; and in part from the gradual erosion, through either the courts or voter initiatives, of affirmative action in school placement and college admissions. In a growing list of states, race-based college admissions preferences are prohibited, thus throwing yet more emphasis on the ability of schools to provide quality preparation to students of all classes and races.[3] Equally important, there's the growing conviction among parents, educators, activists, and in many places community and business leaders, that equity, as measured in school funding, is often insufficient.

What's numerically equal may, in fact, not be adequate to meet the requirements of a high-tech economy, the varying social and educational needs of different kinds of students, or the complex social and civic demands of contemporary society. Because the least qualified and thus the lowest-paid teachers tend to be concentrated in the schools serving the poorest children, and because of other funding distortions, education may not be equal even *within* districts, even those that claim equal basic per-pupil funding in similar schools. A day's visit to schools in almost any American city—some handsomely staffed and equipped and offering challenging programs, others with dirty and unheated classrooms, leaking roofs and filthy rest rooms, a chronic lack of qualified teachers, shortages of books and other materials, and the endemic chaos resulting from a constant turnover of staff—makes clear how huge the gaps and how inadequate the resources still are.

II

The polls show that most Americans are satisfied with their schools—and in many instances they have every right to be. Two decades of reform and heightening awareness among parents and community leaders of the link (at least) between education and economic success have had significant impact on many of the nation's schools. The result has been more stringent course requirements in English, math, science, and social studies, and regular testing that in many cases can decide whether a student is promoted or allowed to graduate. Some states use substantial cash bonuses to reward teachers, principals, and sometimes even janitors in schools with high average or improving test scores. They sanction low-performing schools with a range of "interventions," including state takeovers and/or reassignment of principals and teachers, sanctions that will inevitably affect their future careers.

Through the boom years of the late 1990s, the tougher standards were often accompanied by significant increases in funding and legislation to reduce class size and impose (at least on paper) more demanding teacher certification standards. But for a variety of reasons those reforms have had only marginal impact on the neediest schools and in some cases have made the gaps between have and have-not schools even greater. As state mandates have driven down class sizes (for example), increasing the demand for teachers, schools serving low-income children have had an even more difficult time finding qualified people and space to house those classes. So lunchrooms, gyms, and libraries are cannibalized into classrooms, and many more classes are taught by substitutes and novices. Where schools are overwhelmed with underqualified teachers and inexperienced administrators, there's neither the time nor the talent for effective orientation and mentoring of new people. And since school enrollment has often grown fastest in inner-city neighborhoods, where the schools are the oldest and where land for new facilities is scarce and expensive, it's those schools that are the most overcrowded and run-down, where there are double sessions or multitracking and all the academic compromises, accommodations, and dilutions that come with them.

The great difference in resources has left many children from poor families attending have-not schools at an even greater disadvantage in meeting the new state standards and competing with those in better schools. Middle-class parents have the resources and time to shop for schools and teachers and advocate for children in the new age of high-stakes schooling, increasingly competitive elite college admissions, pricey cram courses, and even pricier private nursery schools.[4] Most poor parents have no such resources, even in negotiating with or pressuring the public school system. One set of schools has been or is being fixed; the other is not. One set of schools has the curricula, the labs, the materials, the playing fields, the teachers; the other does not. Twenty years of school reform, said Arthur Levine, president of Columbia University's Teachers College, have produced decent schools for the middle class: "The only people who have to send their kids to failing schools are the poor."[5] On the official ledgers, school funding might be equal. But in thousands of overcrowded classrooms with unqualified and demoralized teachers, insufficient books, and decrepit equipment, the picture is entirely different. And in most states, even the official ledgers show that schools with high proportions of poor pupils, the students who presumably need the most help, get less money—in many states a lot less—than the schools attended by the children of the affluent.

All that should be mostly old news. What's changed, and what prompted the new strategy, was the great wave of academic reforms and new curricular standards that began in the early 1980s and continues to the present day.[6] Those standards provide the legal justification, and to some extent the criteria, for the adequacy lawsuits that in the past decade have become an increasingly important force— perhaps the major force—in the attempt to provide better schools for poor (and sometimes middle-class) children. Accountability, in the words of one California report, has "put a bright light on the achievement gap among groups of students and among schools as a critical issue to address if the state is to adequately educate all its young people."[7]

Described most simply, the suits merely demand that the states, which have the ultimate responsibility under their own constitutions for public education, meet their constitutional duties. If the states are making the schools and students accountable, then surely the states have a reciprocal duty to make certain that the students have an opportunity to learn and thus a chance to succeed. Instead of allocating school funding in the great annual political contest among competing claimants on state resources, the adequacy principle asks the states to determine the actual cost of providing decent educational resources for each child and to use that as the gauge for school spending.

Even where there are no suits, adequacy has become a powerful weapon. High-stakes tests themselves are still being challenged as unfair or discriminatory, but in recent years the demand for the necessary resources to enable students to pass those tests and meet the standards has become the primary weapon for poor and minority children. Rather than attacking the tests, advocates are using them as weapons to improve the educational opportunities children are getting.

The adequacy cases are born of two levels of frustration. The first reflects the long-standing political weakness of the poor and minority communities that are disproportionately dependent on schools and other public services. But more important, the suits are also attempts to cut through the various layers of government, the red tape and buck passing, the jumble of agencies, and the often incoherent and contradictory programs that are involved in funding, management, and policy making in local schools. Who's responsible when there are only substitutes in the classroom, or there are no books, or the buildings are in continual disrepair? Is it the state or the local district? Is the problem in the principal's office or downtown? If extra resources for handicapped students aren't provided, which program and which administrator has failed? If the schools are filthy and hopelessly overcrowded, where do you turn? If the district mismanages its money and threatens to shut down its schools in March, or if programs are curtailed, where do you go for relief? Many states have never bothered to figure out what it costs to properly educate a student—neither the average student nor the student with special needs—much less discovered how districts spend the money the state gives them. Ultimately, the suits contend, the state is responsible for everything because state constitutions say so: the buck stops in Albany, in Concord, in Trenton, in Columbus, and in Sacramento.

But what's simple in the abstract raises thorny questions in practice. What is adequacy anyway? Who can define it and how can it be calibrated? To what extent do courts have the authority to tell a legislature how much to spend on schools and, in some cases, even how to spend it? The very foundation of the legislative budgeting process is in the ability of elected representatives to establish priorities among competing demands for public services. Legislatures have frequently raided state school appropriations in recessions when revenues go down; the school funds, which represent the largest single share of the budgets of most states, make a convenient target. That became dramatically clear again in the recession that began in the year 2000 and it may well dampen, if not jeopardize, all efforts to improve the schools. Conversely, if the courts can set minimums for state spending on schools, do they inevitably endanger other, equally urgent social services? Although virtually all state constitutions require their legislatures to support public education, thereby giving it a legally preferred place, that doesn't alter the realities of the budget process.

III

Those questions notwithstanding, courts in a growing list of states—Arkansas, Kentucky, Massachusetts, New Hampshire, New Jersey, North Carolina, South Carolina, Ohio, West Virginia, Wyoming—have ruled in favor of plaintiffs in adequacy suits. Most of those suits are brought by parents demanding better schools for their children or local districts seeking increased state funding on the ground that they can't provide education equal to state or other standards with the resources they have. In each of those cases, the courts have ordered state legislatures to provide the funding and the other remedies necessary to bring schools into compliance with what the courts regard as the constitutional requirements. In some states, lower court decisions upholding plaintiffs are still on appeal; in some, such as California, the suits have yet to come to trial. In Alabama, the Supreme Court, after upholding a lower court ruling that the state's funding system was inadequate and ordering legislative remedies, flatly reversed itself.

Even in states with court orders, there's no certainty that the resulting legislation, if any, will in any way be commensurate with what the court seemed to decree. In Kentucky, the legislature responded promptly to a sweeping decision striking down the existing school funding and governance structure with sweeping reforms covering every aspect of the educational system. In other states, adequacy-based reforms were initiated by the legislature even in the absence of any court order. In still others, the legislature moved only grudgingly, leading to a set of judicial flip-flops in Ohio and to a thirty-year duel between the court and the state's political leaders in New Jersey. In some states, the suits are being vehemently resisted by governors and other politicians, partly on the theory that the maintenance of classrooms and the provision of textbooks are the responsibility of local school districts and not of the states, and partly on separation-of-powers arguments that school funding is exclusively the responsibility of the legislature and governor, not of the courts. As in other lawsuits, the fact that the two sets of arguments tend to contradict one another hasn't stopped the states from advancing them.

There are still other questions. The new state academic standards and testing requirements have themselves shifted control from local districts to the states. If the states become responsible for the conditions in each local school, even if they don't become the officially designated rat catchers and toilet bowl cleaners, is local responsibility even further undermined? Conversely, if states are compelled to fund certain schools at a very high minimum level—as New Jersey now is—who will hold the schools accountable if they still fail to provide a decent education? To what extent are state takeovers of local schools and districts, generally regarded as the neutron bombs of academic reform, effective devices in shaping up failing or dysfunctional schools? And how should schools be judged anyway? There is no agreement among educators and child development experts about the validity of tests—and particularly fill-in-the-bubble multiple-choice standardized tests—in judging student academic achievement and school success. But for the moment, both state and federal policy makes those tests one of the prime instruments in such judgments, and thus the basis on which much of the adequacy case rests.

Advocates of the adequacy idea argue, quite correctly, that, unlike equity, adequacy can be a winner for all schools. It does not require redistribution of local tax wealth, as the Texas courts have ordered, in what are often described as Robin Hood schemes. But adequacy decisions nonetheless tend to constrain legislatures in their ability to make choices and establish policy and budgetary priorities, functions that are among their prime constitutional responsibilities. In times of tight revenues, if the courts have made some or all school spending legislatively untouchable, it either requires higher taxes or it makes other spending—particularly on health and social welfare programs, which tend to benefit the same families—even more vulnerable to cuts. That generates resistance from the legislatures and governors who regard court adequacy decisions as unconstitutional meddling in powers and responsibilities constitutionally delegated to them. As the courts rely on adequacy formulas based not just on equity but on calculations that sometimes require considerably more per-pupil spending in districts and schools serving high concentrations of at-risk children, backlash in judicially less favored districts is likely to grow. That is particularly true in tough economic times.

But none of those problems has prevented adequacy, combined with the states' new academic standards, from growing into the major force, morally, legally, and politically, that it's become in driving states toward the provision of better resources to previously neglected children, schools, and districts. And inevitably, adequacy goes beyond money. It touches on virtually every fundamental issue in American education and a good many beyond. How much does money matter? As this book will show, there are deep scholarly disagreements on that question, and considerable evidence to support skeptics in their contention that a large part of the additional money that's gone into schools in the past generation has provided only marginal improvements in student achievement and, in some cases, has been wasted or even stolen in districts that lack the capacity to spend it effectively. And assuming that money does make a difference, how should that money be spent? What's the trade-off, for example, between small classes and higher pay to attract and retain first-class teachers? What does it take to get good teachers into schools that most need them, and why, after a decade of trying, are states and school districts still unable to do it? Why can't kids learn if there are rats and roaches in the classrooms (a question actually asked by defense lawyers in California) or if they have no books to take home to study and do homework with?

Adequacy also touches on the whole range of debates about curricula and teaching strategies. How should handicapped children and students who come to school speaking little or no English be treated? In both cases teachers with special skills are often required. Where will they come from and how should they be trained? Do the tests on which much school success is now gauged really measure anything of educational importance? Do the tests, which focus narrowly on basic academic skills, force all teaching into a narrow mold? Is it fair to deny anyone a diploma on the basis of a single test? If so, how high should the threshold be?

More fundamentally, can the schools overcome the socioeconomic handicaps that poor and minority children bring to school, and, if so, at what cost? And as the percentage of children from poor families and from families speaking little or no English increases, does that burden become ever more difficult? Currently about one child in five lives below the official poverty line. But more than one-third of all American schoolchildren are needy enough to qualify for free or reduced-price school lunches; in New York City it's 70 percent, in Los Angeles 73 percent, in Detroit 78 percent.[8] Beneath those questions there lurks the widespread if often unstated question of whether the social (and, more darkly, the genetic) handicaps of poor and minority children— unmotivated students from overstressed families and unsupportive parents particularly—are so great that it can't be done at all. And if socioeconomic background is such a powerful element in determining success in school, why isn't the system spending whatever extra money it can find on the social service system—on housing, on health and child care, on family counseling—rather than in the classroom? Is there any way to get parents of poor children, stressed as they are, to read to their children? And why is it that even the children of successful black doctors and lawyers lag behind their white peers?

All these issues profoundly touch on the lives of millions of American children and parents and on the condition of thousands of schools—not just schools in the cities, but rural schools in Appalachia and elsewhere serving mostly white children, schools in the old inner suburbs—and the teachers, principals, and other people who work in them. Some of those schools are very ordinary but just not very good; some are horrendously dysfunctional places where the endemic chaos and constant turnover make even the rats and the lack of books seem like minor nuisances. Adequacy has major consequences at all levels: in the schools, in the districts and the states, and for the governors, school board members, legislators, superintendents, and principals who are supposed to run them.

This book tries to tell that story—the story of parents trying to provide better education for their children and of students who are stuck in those wretched schools. It describes the new legal strategies and the policy makers, scholars, and lawyers who developed—and are still developing—those strategies. It's about governors who pay tens of millions of dollars for expensive corporate litigators to stop them. It's about the struggles of the judges who have been thrust into this new and often uncharted territory and the budding industry of consultants and scholars who are brought on to guide the judges through that territory. Finally, it's about the increasingly significant consequences— in funding and in the classroom—of the adequacy strategy.

The book is divided into five chapters. The first, "What Alondra Learned," focuses on the students, teachers, and schools that this whole struggle is about. This section is not designed to describe ordinary schools or average schools. It focuses on troubled schools, on the people who try to teach and learn there, and on the administrative systems and policies that help make them what they are—and are not.[9]

The second, "Kentucky Landmark," is the story of *Rose v. Council for Better Education,* the sweeping 1989 Kentucky Supreme Court decision and the reforms following it that many judges and lawyers regard as the paradigm of adequacy-based policy, and uses that story to trace the broad outlines, politics, and history of the adequacy issue and to evaluate its successes and failures to this point.

The third, " 'A Right to the Privilege of Education,' " the core of this book, focuses on seven states—California, New Jersey, Ohio, Alabama, North Carolina, Maryland, and New York—that, in addition to Kentucky, span much of the national economic, demographic, and regional spectrum. In each, adequacy has been a major issue either in litigation or in legislative reform or both. The record in those states, in some cases going back more than two decades, spans an equally wide spectrum of outcomes but seems to indicate that wherever the issue comes up, either in court or in the political process, adequacy has had a significant impact.

The fourth, "Does Money Matter?" deals briefly with the major resource controversies—bitter scholarly debates in many cases—that underlie a great many of the disputes about school reform. What difference does money make, and how should it be spent? How likely is it that a state appropriation that increases per-pupil funding—say, from $6,500 to $7,500 per child (roughly the national average in 2001–2)—will make any difference in the classroom? What's the evidence that smaller classes are categorically better than larger classes? How much difference do good teachers make? What are the characteristics of good teachers, and how can they best be trained? How do you get them into the classrooms where they're needed most?

The last, "Final Test," is a summary and analysis of the issues and of the classroom impact of the new adequacy standards, and an assessment of the social and economic stakes. In a nation that can protect its economy and democracy only with an educated citizenry, in which 40 percent of all public school students are already nonwhite, and in which 20 percent are officially classified as poor and many more are near poor, a high level of education for all children is an absolutely essential task. Despite all the doubts and uncertainties in the adequacy-based struggle for decent schools for all of America's children, what other alternatives do we have if the traditional public school system is to be preserved? What happens if we fail again?

When I began this project, I thought it would be mostly about courts, legislatures, politics, and awful schools. But I soon discovered that it had to be about much more. It had to tell stories of teachers and students in schools that even forty years of writing about education hadn't prepared me for. And since adequacy touches on most of the ongoing controversies about teaching styles and curricular effectiveness, about school bureaucracies, about teacher union power, and particularly about finding the leadership able to create schools in which teachers want to work and children want to learn, it had to discuss them as well. It thus had to raise difficult questions that are uncomfortable for the passionate advocates on one or another side, and sometimes on several sides, of the nation's educational debates. And of course it had to deal with the children who are at the center of this story. Lawsuits and decisions expressed only in dollar formulas are not asking enough. The test ultimately will be in the classroom, not in the controller's office.

Yet there's no doubt that, after two generations of promises and professions of concern about inner-city schools and poor children, the suits are moving the states closer to defining education itself as a civil right, which is precisely what the Supreme Court's *Brown* decision seemed to promise but never delivered. At the same time, the implicit coupling of accountability and adequacy has started to bring some of the elements of the educational left and right together in common policies trying to link higher standards, especially for children in high-poverty schools, to increased resources.

We've had no end of debate about high-stakes testing—tests such as high school exit exams, whose results have major consequences for students and/or schools. Adequacy is the high-stakes test for the nation. "We know what to do," said Teachers College president Arthur Levine. "We're just not willing to do it." The adequacy strategy could well turn out to be both the most promising as well as the last attempt to disprove or change that gloomy assessment.

What Alondra Learned

I

By the time she was a seventeen-year-old high school student, Alondra Jones was a fully qualified survivor. She was then staying with two roommates in a publicly supported "transitional home" about a mile from her San Francisco school. In the prior eighteen months she'd lived with her cousin, who was her legal guardian, and the cousin's two teenage sons; she'd had to share a room with one of them. Before that she'd lived with her great-aunt, where she shared a room with the great-aunt's grandchildren, ages eighteen and sixteen. She had also lived for a month in Oklahoma with her grandmother and her father, and before that for another few months (in San Francisco) with her father and another cousin and her two minor children. Between her stay in Oklahoma and her stay with Cousin II, she said, "I went back and forth between my sister and my father's first wife." During part of that time she was out of school, once because her father hadn't enrolled her and once because she had, as she said, "family responsibilities" taking care of her cousin's kids.[1]

Given that history, little should have fazed her. She's a smart, feisty, even flamboyant young woman. But after three years at Balboa High School, she'd discovered that she was getting the short end of the educational stick and was angry enough to sue as a plaintiff in the ACLU's adequacy case against the state. Balboa is a once-grand seventy-five-year-old Spanish-style building in San Francisco's Mission District that now houses roughly twelve hundred students, of whom about one-fourth are black, another fourth Latino, another fourth Filipino, 4 percent white, and the rest Chinese and Samoan. Its ranking on the state's test-based Academic Performance Index was near the very bottom, even in comparison to other high-poverty schools.[2]

Some of her complaints were common enough, not only in such urban schools but in many rural schools, and they came from other students as well. There were, as is often the case in schools serving poor students, not enough textbooks—because there was often only one set per teacher for several classes, no one could take a book home—and so teachers struggled to copy enough pages to hand out to their classes. (Lawrence Poon, another Balboa senior, said that during his three years there, he'd never had any books to take home for homework).[3] There were the strings of substitute teachers. There were the dirty and often inaccessible bathrooms, one with yellow caution tape across the door "that police use when somebody gets shot or killed," and ones that, when they were open, had "that smell, that horrible, horrible smell." The stalls, one visitor observed in the fall of 2000, "are covered with graffiti, the toilets and floors caked with scum, and the walls are smeared with crusty, hardened spitballs made from wads of toilet paper."[4] There were labs without equipment and classrooms where, at least in the first weeks of school, there weren't enough seats or desks for the forty or fifty students who had been assigned there. (At Mission High School in San Francisco, where Alondra Jones had gone in her freshman year, classrooms were, she said, sometimes jammed because when the roof leaked the whole third floor was flooded and "there would be different subjects taught in one classroom.") At Balboa, there were classrooms that were too hot in the fall and spring, especially on the sunny side of the building, and too cold in winter.

There were, of course, the mouse droppings—"we joke back and forth about who's seen the most rats at their schools"—and the bird "doodoo" in the gym where the birds had come in through the broken windows: "We used to try to hit the birds with a basketball. We made that a game in gym." The gym teachers tried to clean it up after the windows were repaired. "It's still bird stuff on the floor," she said. "But it's not like centimeters apart.... Now if you are in gym class and playing basketball, you can like avoid the spots by zigzagging."[5]

But that was just the beginning: There was the class called Modern World where the teacher got sick in the fall "and we had a bunch of substitutes instead. Sometimes they would stay just for one day, and sometimes they would stay for one week.... We'd get a new assignment from a new substitute ... before we'd finished on a project from a substitute we'd had before the new one came. We had so many teachers that year that the report card didn't list a teacher's name—it just listed teacher F." There was the constant turnover of teachers, as in her Spanish class in eleventh grade, where the teacher left school in November and there was a different sub every day until finals. "We played games in class," she said, and the subs showed films. "We saw *Rush Hour, Entrapment, Amistad, Liar Liar,* and *Halloween....* People would just bring movies from their houses and we would watch them in class."

One of the substitutes, she said, caught her reading and told her to close the book and watch the movie. Finally, "one girl who'd transferred to our school ... tried to teach class sometimes because she'd learned some things at the other school. But she's not a teacher and she didn't really know much more Spanish than we did.... [But] we still had to take a final exam at the end of the semester even though we hadn't had a teacher or learned any Spanish. Everybody failed the final.... I asked the assistant principal how I could get a grade after all we had was substitutes.... I told the assistant principal it would be okay if they tested on the movies we watched in class, but they shouldn't have tested us on the Spanish we didn't learn. The assistant principal just told me they had to give us a test."[6] The same thing happened to Lawrence Poon in two English classes in his sophomore year. (The previous year, he said, he also had a full semester of Spanish without a regular teacher.) And because Balboa, in a budget-cutting move, suddenly truncated its schedule from seven to six periods, Poon found it nearly impossible to take all the courses he needed to get into college. So he planned to take physics at a community college on his own.

But what most angered Alondra Jones was her discovery of what things were like on the other side of the tracks. A young, socially engaged social studies teacher named Shane Safir had taken her and some fifty other Balboa students on exchange visits—including a weekend retreat—to Marin Academy, an expensive private school just north of San Francisco, where the tuition is $21,000 a year, plus books and various other fees. Marin had a "director of diversity" named Lisa Arrastia who had a special interest in issues of educational equity and who, as part of a midwinter mini-course, had sponsored exchange visits with an inner-city Chicago high school whose "ultimate goal was to empower all students to affect change in the economic imbalances that maintain current inequities in the U.S. education system."

The Balboa exchanges were part of Safir's broader effort to raise the social awareness of her students. Safir took her students to the state capitol in Sacramento to lobby for better school conditions. She assigned them to read Jonathan Kozol's book *Savage Inequalities,* a polemic about urban schools, which Safir had bought with money from an outside grant she and another teacher had secured. She gave them Richard Wright's *Native Son* and Lorraine Hansberry's *Raisin in the Sun,* a perennial school favorite, described in one teacher trot as being about "unfulfilled dreams, human motivation, and racial prejudice ... dreams that are shaped by society's superficial standards."[7] She talked to them about bipolar societies and social pyramids, and, most significantly, had them read parts of the Brazilian educator Paolo Freire's *Pedagogy of the Oppressed,* a document of social reform widely quoted in the late 1960s and early 1970s about curricula and materials that make "oppression and its causes objects of reflection by the oppressed" in the hope that "from that reflection will come their necessary engagement in the struggle for their liberation. And in the struggle this pedagogy will be made and remade."[8] Freire, who died in 1997, saw education as the path to liberation; the book elaborated an ongoing dialectic among an awareness of oppression, education, and liberation. Safir, who's too young to recall the sixties, says she learned about the book when she was training to be a teacher at Stanford in the 1990s.

But as the participants tell it, it was mainly from the visits to other schools—both to Marin and to better San Francisco public schools— that Alondra and her classmates got the message and outraged sense of injustice that came with it. "The really good thing about this experience," said a student who'd gone on an earlier Marin visit, "was that we didn't know how screwed we were getting; now we understand." Later, when the district cut its mismanaged budget and Balboa faced staffing cuts—Shane Safir was one of those whose jobs were threatened—they went to a school board meeting to protest both the cuts and the general conditions and mistreatment of the school, and were further insulted when Bill Rojas, then the superintendent, kept walking out to take phone calls as they were trying to make their case. "He's a jerk," said one afterward. They tried hard not to break down as they read their statements to the board.[9]

After she became a named plaintiff in the American Civil Liberties Union's adequacy suit against the state of California, Alondra, giving a deposition, was asked by one of the state's lawyers why she'd done it.

"It's the unfair conditions," she answered, "the fact that we didn't have . . . enough textbooks to take home to do like homework, whereas Marin Academy does, and that's unfair to us." She had seen the new performing arts center, the science and computer facilities, the multimedia workrooms, the theaters, and all the rest. At Balboa, Safir said, "the science labs are a joke," lacking enough materials to do more than one or two experiments a year.[10] Even the old art room had been closed down; teachers, working in makeshift rooms, scratched to find enough materials for projects. Students had to share textbooks, and sometimes, as in chemistry, they spent the whole period reading or copying notes from an overhead projector because the books couldn't go home. And since they didn't have books at home, they never could look anything up when they did their homework. "Our chemistry class and the other period's chemistry class," said Alondra Jones, "shared the same book, like my health ed class. And so when I got the book to use—and chemistry, it was kind of like a capitalist society; it was dog eat dog—I had my book. That was all I was worried about."[11]

Some of Alondra Jones's complaints, and those of some other students as well, were tinged with adolescent hyperbole. Some sounded like echoes from Kozol's book. Some probably stretched the length of time when their classrooms were without enough desks or chairs from days into weeks, enlarged mice into rats, and recalled rooms as being in even worse shape than they actually were.

Patricia Gray, the most recent in a series of principals at Balboa, said a lot of it was exaggerated: she'd never heard many of the complaints registered by students like Alondra Jones. The charges that there weren't enough books were mostly false, the bathrooms were cleaned daily, there weren't nearly as many substitutes in classes as the students said, and she rarely heard complaints about heat or cold. She also said that, as one of her first acts after she became principal, she wrote a "movie policy," banning all films not related to the courses in which they were shown. Gray also spoke proudly about a couple of recent graduates who'd gone to Berkeley and were doing well, and when she was asked whether Balboa students were receiving a good education, she said yes. But Alondra Jones was hardly the only one who complained about subs, toilets, filth, and lack of books. She had company among both teachers and other students.

What's certain is that when Patricia Gray was named principal in 1999, the place was in chaos—the school, in her words, "hadn't stabilized." In the three years before she came, teacher turnover at the school exceeded 100 percent, and although it was now lower than it had been before she arrived, it was still substantial. Nearly 40 percent of her staff lacked full regular teaching credentials. On orders from downtown, moreover, she had to "consolidate" classes to help solve a district budget problem, meaning that she lost seven of her sixty-six teachers.

With the exception of ninth-grade English and math classes, which were limited to twenty under state law, Gray said, the average Balboa class had thirty-four or thirty-five students. (At Marin Academy, the average class had fifteen students. For its 385 students, Marin had nearly as many teachers, forty-nine, as Balboa had for its 1,200.) It was tempting for her best teachers to leave, she said; the pay was higher in San Mateo, just south of San Francisco, and hers was a tough school in which to teach. In places such as the Bay Area and Los Angeles, high housing costs made it particularly tough to attract teachers to inner-city schools. Like a lot of others, she believed that there should be combat pay for schools like hers. "You don't treat cancer like you treat the common cold."[12]

Gray also acknowledged that for security reasons, as in hundreds of other schools, bathrooms were unlocked only during lunch and (appropriately enough) "passing periods," the five or six minutes when students change classes. Students who needed to go at other times had to find a security guard to let them in.[15]

But by themselves none of the specifics, from the strings of subs to the bird droppings, were really so significant. What mattered, as the ever-articulate Alondra Jones said in a deposition, was the cumulative message: it was an insult to students—they were, as someone at Balboa said, "throwaway kids"—and Alondra Jones was smart enough to get it:

> You know what, in all honesty, I'm going to break something down to you. It makes you feel less about yourself, you know, like you sitting here in a class where you have to stand up because there's not enough chairs, and you see rats in the buildings, the bathrooms is nasty.... Like I said, I visited Marin Academy, and these students, if they want to sit on the floor, that's because they choose to. And that just makes me feel less about myself because it's like the state don't care about public schools.... It really makes me feel bad about myself.
>
> Probably you can't understand where I'm coming from.... And I'm not the only person who feels that.... And I already feel that way because I stay in a group home because of poverty. Why do I have to feel like that when I go to school?
>
> Also, like the standards, they set real low standards for us. They have to. If we don't—if our test scores are the lowest, the standards are not set as high. So set standards like private schools have. Set high standards that Lowell has. Set high standards that Marin Academy has. You know, set high standards for me.
>
> Don't sit there and expect me to fail and then pass me old used-up textbooks and expect me to achieve from that. I have achieved that because I can persevere, obviously. I've been through a lot so I can persevere.[14]

Some of that was probably acquired from adults—a mix of ed-policy talk and homeboy language. Some probably also reflected the feelings of adults, many of whom appeared to be just as depressed and demoralized by the circumstances in which they worked. But by the time she finished her little outburst she was in tears.[15] Patricia Gray would say that Alondra Jones's record at Balboa was "erratic." But she had indeed persevered; she was about to graduate, had been admitted to a number of universities, including the University of California, and was preparing to go to Howard University in Washington, D.C., to begin her freshman year.

II

Like Tolstoy's unhappy families, dysfunctional schools are sometimes unhappy in their own fashion, depending on place, circumstances, and culture. More often, however, their troubles are variations on common themes. The adequacy lawsuits filed since the late 1980s resonate with those themes and with iterations of the financial inadequacies, inequities, and mismanagement that plaintiffs, and many others, associate both with the current shortage of classroom resources and with the low performance of students in failing schools, and which contribute to their perpetuation. One of the difficulties those suits face is that between the time they're brought and the time they come to trial the specific complaints they allege—a shortage of books and leaky ceilings in school A, the lack of Advanced Placement courses and laboratory equipment in school B—are dealt with, often as a result of the suit, only to pop up in other schools. It's like "whack-a-mole," said Michael Jacobs, an attorney with the San Francisco firm of Morrison and Foerster, who is working on one major adequacy suit in California. The reference is to the old carnival game in which the player uses a mallet to hit a succession of moles that pop out of holes; each time one is whacked, another pops up. Unless there is systemic reform, the game would go on forever. The same problem, of course, confronts the parent, the reporter, and the official evaluation team. The specific conditions at any given school are addressed, sometimes in whole, more often just in part, only to be replaced by identical failures at another school or by different problems at the original school.[16] Whack-a-mole.

In Ohio, after a survey in 1993 of the condition of the state's school buildings, Superintendent of Public Instruction John Theodore Sanders declared some students were "making do in a decayed carcass from an era long passed"—"dirty, depressing places." Another official, Jack D. Hunter, supervisor of school facilities with the Ohio Department of Education, testified that some 75 percent of Ohio's public school facilities "have asbestos that should be abated . . . either immediately or near-term." In one school in Wayne County, three hundred students were hospitalized after breathing carbon monoxide fumes leaking out of defective heaters and furnaces. In another district students were "breathing coal dust which is emitted into the air and actually covers the students' desks after accumulating overnight. Band members are forced to use a former coal bin for practice sessions where there is no ventilation whatsoever, causing students to complain of headaches."[17]

It makes for a long list. In one Ohio school there were maggot infestations behind the particleboard that had been installed to cover the peeling plaster; at another, raw sewage backed up onto the school playing fields from the school's ancient sewer system. At Miller Junior High in Shawnee, the principal and custodians "deliberately knocked plaster off the ceilings so that the plaster would not fall on the students during the day." And at Straitsville Elementary School in Perry County, as former student Christopher Thompson recalled it, "plaster was falling off the walls and cockroaches crawled on the restroom floors." The building gave him a "dirty feeling"; he would not use the bathroom at school because of the cockroaches. Later, according to the Ohio Supreme Court, Chris Thompson "had to contend with a flooded library and gymnasium, a leaky roof where rainwater dripped from the ceiling like a 'waterfall,' an inadequate library, a dangerously warped gymnasium floor, poor shower facilities, and inadequate heating. In fact, due to construction and renovation of the heating system, when Chris attended high school, there was no heat from the beginning of the fall of 1992 until the end of November or beginning of December. Students had to wear coats and gloves to classes and were subjected to fumes from the kerosene heaters that were fired up when the building became very cold."[18]

It's mostly banal stuff. You can compile such lists anywhere you look—in New York City, in Los Angeles, in rural Alabama or North

Carolina, in Philadelphia, in Chicago. Many of the situations are so familiar that they're hardly noticed anymore except by the people who are stuck in those schools: falling ceiling tiles, leaking roofs, insufficient lighting, cafeterias and hallways converted to classrooms and corridors into makeshift lunchrooms, filthy or nonfunctional toilets, windows that don't open or don't shut, buildings where teachers and children freeze in the winter and swelter in the spring and fall (and sometimes both, depending on what part of the building they're in) and, where schools run year-round, as they do in many urban districts, in the summer as well.

In New York in 1998, after the teachers' union sued the district over the dangerous conditions of the buildings its members were required to teach in, "the court [in the words of a subsequent complaint] ordered the parties to agree to a judgment providing for a safety plan. The plan adopted involved the extensive use of temporary scaffolding to safeguard people but did not involve the actual repair of defective conditions. As a result of this judgment close to one third of all school buildings in New York City at the time of trial had sidewalk shedding around their exteriors—simply to ensure minimal safety, not in preparation for remedial measures."[19] In San Francisco's Bryant School, said eleven-year-old Carlos Ramirez, his teacher, Lily Malabed, would spray her students with water when things got too hot. Once, he said, he fainted because the room was too hot. He also said he never ate the school food because "the lunches were green." He was talking not about the salads or the spinach but about the hot dogs.[20] "The roaches and mice are really distracting and discouraging to my students," said Cynthia Artiga-Faupusa, a teacher at San Francisco's Luther Burbank Middle School. "They complain and regularly ask me why they have to go to school in a ghetto."

Poor city kids get the highest doses, but they're not the only ones. Other locations also suffer from such conditions as: student allergic reactions traced to classroom mildew and spores, classrooms "not conducive to learning because students cannot hear over the noise of window air conditioner units," and "labs" where the failed plumbing has long been disconnected and where the wiring was obsolete a half century ago (and, needless to say, where there are no Internet connections for computers, much less decent art or music rooms). In a large Oakland high school, said a teacher, "the only thing that designates a room as a science room is a sink." In rural North Carolina there are high school biology classrooms that, as described by a teacher there, have "only one sink that is clogged, no fume hood and few electrical outlets," and in a large Los Angeles high school the budget for laboratory supplies and equipment for ninety science classes with some twenty-seven hundred students runs between $6,000 and $10,000, an average of less than $3.70 per year per student. In Richmond, California, a junior high school principal testified about roof leaks into classrooms and hallways "almost every time we had a good rain." In Baltimore, a 1992 master facilities plan rated only 16 percent of the city's school buildings as being in good physical condition; 20 percent were deemed to be in poor condition. In the rural South, schools built for blacks in the 1940s and 1950s, in the era of segregation, were barely adequate when they went up.[21]

In 1997, the New York City schools, which then generated thirty-five thousand repair requests annually and which had completed twelve thousand repair projects in the prior year, had an official backlog of nearly twenty thousand repair projects—roofs, walls, windows, furnaces, wiring, plumbing—that had not been completed. "In one of my schools," testified Kathleen Cashin, a New York district superintendent in Brooklyn, "the ceiling in the hallway where kids walk all the time just collapsed." In another, "every time it rained, the children had to be moved out of the classroom. The wall would just get moist and start leaking. The stairways are rippled, I mean it is just rippled. So if I go there wearing anything but sneakers you have to be very careful walking up and down the stairs. I don't know why it is rippled but it is rippled all over the place."[22] In the same year, the State Education Department reported that 420 New York City schools required major modernization; 56 percent needed extensive roof work, 86 percent needed plumbing repairs, 79 percent had problems with their heating/ventilating/air-conditioning systems, and more than half were inaccessible to the disabled:

The situation in New York City is at the breaking point [said a report by the State Board of Regents]. Decades of neglect, deferred maintenance and mismanagement have resulted in overcrowded classrooms, leaking roofs and flooded gymnasiums. Parts of roofs and walls are dangerously falling apart through lack of timely repair. Unhealthful environments exist for many teachers and students. Resources have been wasted by energy-inefficient buildings. Large numbers of students have been denied access to science laboratories, technology or other learning environments necessary to meet the high standards needed for success in today's world. Current spending in New York City is not even able to stabilize existing buildings and prevent further deterioration.[23]

Nor was it just New York City:

In the rest of the state, from small rural school districts to the big cities, the practices of deferring maintenance and minimizing maintenance and capital budgets in favor of competing demands are showing a steady decline toward the catastrophic conditions that exist in our largest city.[24]

With the deferred maintenance came the special problems of overcrowding—thousands of classes where teachers and students scurry around the halls to find enough chairs, or where they double up or sit on desks or on the floor as they did at Balboa, or where closets that have been converted into offices, or where two or three classes are held simultaneously in gyms or cafeterias with each trying to hear over the noise of the others, or the occasional places where students eat lunch under awnings in the rain because there's not enough space to eat inside. In one Paterson, New Jersey, elementary school in the early 1990s, where remedial classes were conducted in a converted rest room, the kids ate lunch in the boiler room; in a school in East Orange, New Jersey, lunch was eaten in shifts in the first-floor corridor; in Irvington, New Jersey, a coal bin had been converted into a classroom.[25]

In some middle and high schools, the remedies include "service classes," periods in which students run errands and do odd jobs for teachers because all the real classes at a given time are too full. Still more common is the experience of Los Angeles high school junior Glauz Diego, who spent three days trying to get a sixth-period class. "I first tried wood shop, but it was too crowded. Next I tried chemistry, but it was too crowded also. I ended up with soccer. . . . It's easy to get a sport because the field is so big." His sister Cindy, trying to find a class, was told to take Advanced Placement Spanish even though she'd already taken it and gotten a top score on the AP test. At Crenshaw High in Los Angeles, D'Andre Lampkin, a tenth grader who, like his twin brother, wanted to enroll in algebra, was told there weren't enough teachers—the classes were full—and was put into a "math investigations" class instead. Leticia Paniagua, who wants to be a brain surgeon and, in addition to her required courses at Los Angeles's Fremont High, sought an elective that she thought would help her chances to get into college, was told there was no room in the journalism course she wanted, so she was put in a cosmetology class. At Fremont, a good proportion of students for whom there's no room in academic courses are dumped into such classes.[26]

Almost inevitably in such schools, even schools in rural districts, teachers like Michael Keim, who teaches social studies at Hoke County (North Carolina) High School, have to become "roamers," the flying Dutchmen of the education system, who go from room to room "with a limited amount of equipment traveling with them" because they have no room of their own. Roamers—in some places they're "rovers" or "travelers"—migrate from class to class, usually pushing a shopping cart or towing a roll-around suitcase stuffed with whatever minimal teaching materials they need: books, charts, videos, lesson plans, all of which have to be unpacked and packed again for the next class. Of course they can't hang anything permanently on classroom walls. And to do any preparation in school, the roamers have to beg space from other teachers because the teachers' lounge isn't big enough for more than two or three people; sometimes they work out of their cars. Given the nearly universal pecking order in schools, sometimes enforced by tradition, sometimes by union contract, it is of course the beginning teachers, people who most need support and stability, who draw the roaming honors.[27] In Los Angeles, there's also a district policy that calculates capacity with "the aim that teachers will travel." (It's probably fortunate that the term *roamer* isn't used there, given the name of the superintendent of the huge system, former Colorado governor Roy Romer.)

And then there are more familiar space stretchers: New York City, which has roughly 60 percent of the state's poor and 73 percent of its ethnic minority students, stuffs five more kids into each elementary school classroom than the state average, seven more into each high school classroom.[28] And in parts of the city, as in many of the high schools in Queens, some of which enroll half again as many students as they were designed for, and in some cases double the number—Cardozo High School, Francis Lewis High School, Newtown High School, Richmond Hill High School, William Cullen Bryant High School, and several others—the solution is double "end-to-end" sessions: from 7:00 A.M. to noon, from noon to 5:00. To do that, one period (of seven) had to be eliminated, which means a lot of students (as in Los Angeles) can't take the courses they want. If they're on the morning shift, they can't participate in sports or other after-school activities unless they have the money to return to school; for many on the afternoon shift, such activities may not be possible at all because their classes run too late.

But the system also creates less obvious difficulties. Ninth- and tenth-grade classes are offered only on the late (less desirable) shift, upper-level courses only on the early shift. As a consequence, as John Lee, the district's superintendent for Queens high schools, pointed out, "the older students cannot take the lower-level remedial courses they may need, while academically gifted younger students cannot take the advanced courses that would challenge and enrich them." It also, of course, inhibits social interaction between younger and older students and makes it still harder to recruit new teachers, who because of the pecking order usually get the afternoon shift but who in many cases have children of their own who get out of school at 3:00.[29] Necessarily, they also get the younger and, in general, the more difficult students. In 1999, only 56 percent of the students who started ninth grade in Lee's district in 1996 were still in school and had reached their senior year.

Still, when it comes to devices to alleviate schoolhouse overcrowding, there's little to match the surrealism of Los Angeles's year-round "Concept 6" multitrack schools. In the City of Angels, a considerable number of schools are now under construction. But for the thirty years after 1970, the city opened no general high school, and very few schools of any kind, despite the district's booming population of children, in part because there was too little money or open land, in part because the people who voted were not the people with children, in part because state school bond allocation formulas had been stacked against the district, and in part because the district was notoriously mismanaged. (In perhaps the most egregious such case on record, Los Angeles was on the way to completing its new $200 million Belmont Learning Center when inspectors belatedly discovered that it was going up on a toxic site—an old oil field oozing with poisonous hydrogen sulfide and methane. There was at least a possibility that the place could blow up.)[30]

Ever since the passage of California's tax-cutting Proposition 13 in 1978, "deferred maintenance" in public facilities has been a mainstay of budget writers and policy analysts. More than 25 percent of the state's students are housed in portable classrooms, which now crowd schoolyards and playgrounds like so many migrant camps. Altogether, 1.3 million California students are on some sort of year-round schedule. But Concept 6 is in a class by itself.[31]

In Los Angeles, some 240 schools with 328,000 students, nearly half the district's enrollment, are on multitrack schedules, most of them following the Concept 6 calendar. Because their schools are the most crowded, nearly all the multitrack students are black or Latino. Among those schools is Fremont High in South Central Los Angeles, a sprawling place, now surrounded by an eight-foot spike-topped steel fence, with 4,800 students, 90 percent of whom are Latino, 10 percent black. (In 2001–2, according to official state figures, the school also had one Asian student and two non-Hispanic whites.) Under the criteria defined by Robert Balfanz of Johns Hopkins University, who studies the problem, any school where the ninth-grade class has shrunk by 50 percent or more by twelfth grade is a "dropout factory." Fremont, whose ninth grade class of 1,573 in 1998–99 had shrunk to 438 seniors in 2001–2, qualified handsomely. When one teacher complained about overcrowding in her classes, said a colleague, "She was told to wait a while and 'attrition will take care of it.' This confirms a sense among many teachers at Fremont, including myself, that the district builds an expectation of a high dropout rate into its planning, creating a self-fulfilling prophecy."[32] Fremont's academic achievement, like Balboa's, is stuck near the bottom among California schools, even those serving similar low-income and minority populations.

To find enough classroom space at Fremont, the system, using Concept 6, assigns its students to one of three tracks.[33] Only two tracks are on campus at any given time, each for a total of 163 days a year rather than the usual 180. The A and C tracks follow a vaguely normal school calendar: the A track begins in late August (the dates are for 2002–3) and runs through Christmas, then, after two months' break, runs again from early March to the end of June. The C track starts around July 1, runs to October 22, and then, after a break in November and December, runs again from early January through April 30. But to make things come out right, the B track is in school from July 1 to August 23, then off for two months, then back from October 23 to Christmas, then back from January 2 to March 5, then off another two months, then back again from May 1 to June 27. These two-month chunks are called "mesters."

Since not all courses can be offered on all tracks, students who are (in more ways than one) on the wrong track may discover that a class they want, or may need for college admission, isn't offered on their track. Students on the B track (who are not in school in March and April) who want to take Advanced Placement exams may also learn too late that they have to take the AP tests in May, well before they finish the courses on which the tests are based. If they want help, they have to come back during their off-track time—provided they can find someone to give it. Sometimes they also have to take critical tests, including the state's exit exam, a day or two after they come back from one of those extended breaks. And because places like Fremont have only one counselor for every six hundred or seven hundred students, there's little chance that students will get much counseling help, especially on exotic matters like college admission. The B track students, meanwhile, can't commit to a vacation job for more than two months at a time. (For working parents of elementary school kids, of course, it's a special headache.) Off-track students who are on athletic teams or in activities like band or chorus have to come back during their break if they want to take part. At Jefferson High, another multitrack Los Angeles school, students who finished first-year French discovered that second-year French wasn't offered on their track the following year, so they took Spanish even though most already knew Spanish and even though the University of California then required two years or more of at least one foreign language.[34]

Teachers such as Steve Bachrach, who teaches at Jefferson High—and some students as well—say the 163-day year doesn't give them nearly enough time for adequate instruction in most courses, especially when "kids come in reading at a third-grade level."[35] That's often true even for good teachers with up-to-date materials, a combination that, in any case, isn't often found in urban schools. Margaret Roland, the principal at Fremont in 2001–2, responds that since the district adds a few minutes to each class period, students on multitrack schedules are getting the same number of minutes of instruction as those in other California schools, who go to school 180 days a year. But the seventeen lost days leave less time for homework, though that may not make much difference if there aren't enough books and materials for the kids to take home. One school administrator said that if the class doesn't cover all the required material in 163 days, it's the teacher's fault.[36]

But the multitrackers were still better off than the students at Fremont and other overcrowded Los Angeles schools who can't be accommodated even with the multitrack system at their home schools and are transported, often for as much as two hours each way, to other schools. The Fremont kids had to show up at school by 6:15 every morning for the bus ride through Los Angeles rush-hour traffic to a school on the other side of the city that had room. In order not to miss the bus back in the afternoon, they couldn't participate in sports or other extracurricular activities. Even so, they didn't get back to Fremont until 4:30. Not surprisingly, Fremont students struggled not to be bused despite Fremont's many problems. When she was asked about it in 2001, Roland, who'd never seen the other school—she didn't even know which school it was or where it was—said she didn't think busing kids affected their learning because "it's the travel time, not the instructional time they are missing."[37]

III

For the most part, the crucial gaps in the schools serving the nation's neediest kids—and, to repeat, many others as well—are hardly exotic or even colorful. They stem from the lack of good teachers, books, or materials, and often all three. Recent data, particularly an analysis of teacher qualifications in New York City schools generated by Hamilton Lankford, an economist at the State University of New York at Albany, puts those generalizations in the starkest terms. In a grim version of those macro images showing the perfect geometric patterns of insect eyes or leaves or flowers, Lankford traced the near-perfect association of weak teachers with low-income schools: the higher the poverty rate, as measured by free or reduced-price lunches, the lower the scores of the teachers on their own preprofessional examinations.[38]

In his massive analysis covering the 1997–8 school year, Lankford divided New York's schools into quintiles, ranking schools from those with the fewest students qualifying for free or reduced-priced lunches (quintile 1) to those with the most (quintile 5). He then calculated average teacher scores on a variety of required state teacher certification tests—the Liberal Arts and Sciences Test, the Elementary Content Specialty Test—and certain national teacher exams. Among the teachers in New York City's highest-poverty schools (quintile 5), 42 percent of elementary teachers had failed the Liberal Arts and Sciences Test at least once. In the schools with the fewest poverty-stricken kids, only 16 percent had ever failed. Among teachers outside New York City, the failure rate was under 7 percent. The same was true of the median scores on those tests: the first time that teachers in the highest-poverty schools took the arts and sciences test they got an average score of 226, barely above the 220 passing mark; for teachers in low-poverty schools, it was 247; for teachers outside New York, it was 257. Between them, going through the intermediate quintiles, there was an almost perfect curve, as if nature itself was at work.

Lankford found the same pattern in the state's test assessments of elementary school teaching skills and in its tests of high school teachers' subject matter knowledge. Among all of New York's high school math teachers, 47 percent failed the state's Math Content Specialty Test at least once. Outside New York, the failure rate was 21 percent.

In the high-poverty schools, moreover, nearly 40 percent of teachers were working with a provisional credential or no teaching credential at all. In low-poverty schools, the number was under 20 percent. Outside New York City, it was 15 percent. Lankford also found that New York City teachers graduated from colleges with weaker academic profiles (in terms of SAT scores and high school grade point averages of entering students, and in ranking in college guides) than teachers outside the city. And some were—and are—truly awful. John Murphy, a former superintendent in two major school systems, called to testify by New York State in its attempt to show that New York City's schools passed constitutional muster, said that after a visit to one school, he changed his whole rating scheme:

> During my five days of observation, I visited 56 classrooms. Normally I rate teachers from below average, to average, to above average, and to excellent when I prepare reports. After this experience, I needed to create a new category—that is "terrible"! I visited a few classrooms where the children would have been better served if they did not come to school on that day.[39]

Making things still more complicated in New York were provisions in the United Federation of Teachers (UFT) contract that, in an effort to protect tenured teachers against capricious negative evaluations from principals who just didn't like them, not only made the evaluation process extremely complicated, as is the case in many other places, but also gave teachers who got unsatisfactory ratings the right to remain in the school for another three years. Combined with the fear that even an innocent transfer would leave a principal with a vacancy he or she couldn't fill, that put a powerful damper on any negative ratings.[40] It's not surprising, therefore, that while dedicated teachers struggle to make things work, some simply blow the job off. A teacher, observing some fisticuffs between two children on an Oakland, California, elementary school playground, called it to the attention of the teacher who was supposed to be supervising the playground, to which she replied, "I don't do fights."

The patterns appear to be similar elsewhere, though the system is not always as byzantine. A recent audit of Chicago's eighty-one worst-performing schools showed that more than one-fifth of their teachers were not certified, that some had no formal training at all, and that many had either failed or never taken the state's basic teacher test in reading and math. In another survey, one-third of the teachers in sixty-six South Chicago schools were found to lack certificates.[41] Teaching jobs in Baltimore are so unattractive that the district hires 62 percent of the people who apply. (In most districts in Maryland, the figure is about 10 percent.) In California, according to the Center for the Future of Teaching and Learning, an independent research organization, of forty-two thousand teachers, some 14 percent (in 2001) didn't have full credentials. Of first- and second-year teachers (in 2001), nearly half didn't have a credential. In 41 percent of the state's schools—mostly white, Asian, and middle-class—there were few or no uncredentialed teachers. But where over 90 percent of students were black and/or Latino, 26 percent of teachers were underqualified. In the lowest-performing schools, one of four teachers was underqualified.[42] (Nationally in 1999–2000, 19 percent of all secondary school classes were taught by people who had neither majored nor minored in college in the subject they were teaching; in high-poverty schools it was 34 percent. In math in high-poverty schools it was 40 percent.)[43]

In some places the numbers, already depressing, concealed even bleaker situations, not merely because a credential is only the crudest indicator of teaching ability (there are, of course, also people without credentials who are great teachers) but because all the turnover and all those subs weren't really measurable at all. Here's twelve-year-old Randell Hasty in 1999, at the time a seventh grader in rural North Carolina, answering a lawyer's questions. Lots of students can tell similar stories:

A. In the sixth grade, I had a substitute that stayed for nine weeks, and this year the substitute stayed for four weeks.

Q. Four weeks this year?

A. Yes, ma'am.

Q. This year in your math and science class, what kind of work did you do when your substitute teacher was there?

A. We read out of the book and answered questions.

Q. And then last year in the sixth grade, you said you had a substitute for nine weeks?

A. Yes, ma'am.

Q. What class was that in?

A. Math and science.

Q. At what point in the year did the substitute teacher come?

A. At the beginning of the year, and we had—we had seven teachers that year that weren't teachers. It was six substitutes and one teacher—two teachers.

Q. Is that in your math and science class?

A. Yes, ma'am.

Q. Had seven teachers in that one class?

A. Yes, ma'am.

Q. And you said you had two permanent teachers?

A. Yes, ma'am.

Q. Did you start with a permanent teacher?

A. Yes, ma'am.

Q. And what happened to her?

A. She left, and we got substitutes.

Q. Okay. And how many substitutes did you have?

A. We had five substitutes.

Q. And at what point in the year did you get another permanent teacher?

A. At the end of the year.

Q. What kind of work were you doing in that sixth grade math and science class when the substitutes were there?

A. We were reading out of the book.[44]

Another student in the same district told about the subs he'd had, including one eighth-grade social studies teacher who never assigned any reading except as punishment for classroom misbehavior. "That was her way of telling us to be quiet; if you don't be quiet, then you got to read two chapters tonight for homework."[45] At the start of the 1999–2000 school year, 27 of the 102 certified staff positions at Hoke County High School, chosen by a court as representative of a large class of North Carolina rural schools, were vacant; of nine mathematics teaching positions, five were vacant; of nine in English, seven were open. There were other vacancies in chemistry, general science, and foreign languages. Those vacancies were filled, sometimes for many months, by strings of substitutes who were not required to be certified, or to be college graduates, or to have any qualifications in the subjects they were teaching. (One math sub had not graduated from high school.) On average, students in such schools spent an average of eighteen days a year—10 percent of all class time—in classes taught by subs. Not surprisingly, a state study also found that teachers who came from the top ranks of their college classes were much more likely to leave the poor rural schools. Those who had the weakest records stayed. In its desperation, according to school administrators, the district "has tried to recruit teachers in unusual locales, including the checkout stand at a Wal-Mart."[46]

All that turnover and all the substitutes marching through those classrooms will never be counted in any set of official statistics. (And what is "a permanent teacher" who leaves at the beginning of the year?) At the same time many districts, and sometimes whole states, fudge the numbers they do report. Under the new federal No Child Left Behind Act (NCLB), which was a keystone of George W. Bush's 2000 election campaign and his first-year domestic agenda, all schools getting Title I funds, money earmarked for schools with high concentrations of students from low-income families, have until 2005–6 to get "highly qualified" teachers into their classrooms. That, for all its good intentions, is a little like King Canute commanding the waves to stop.

The Canute command quickly produced its own fudges. Responding to a U.S. Department of Education survey, the District of Columbia school district, one of the nation's most famously dysfunctional districts, reported that all its teachers were qualified.[47] Similarly, in 2002, New York City, after decades of hiring large proportions of underqualified teachers—and in the face of new federal and state regulations that prohibit the city from putting any uncertified new teacher into its worst schools and requires all New York City teachers to be certified by September 2003—suddenly claimed that because of higher pay and other reforms, 90 percent of its new hires were certified. But as Arthur Levine, the president of Columbia University's Teachers College, gently pointed out, the claim was "disingenuous."

New York had indeed raised beginning salaries. But it had also instituted what many, including Levine, regarded as a watered-down alternative certification program under which the city recruited people in mid-career, plus young college graduates, gave them a month of intensive education courses, and sent them—again—into the neediest schools. That may or may not be as good as the traditional route— in some instances, given the frailty of many traditional ed-school programs, it may even be better—but any celebration was obviously premature. As one measure of how incredible New York City's latter-day claims about its cadre of newly certified teachers really were, in 1998, 56 percent of its new hires were uncredentialed. In that same year, nearly 36 percent of Manhattan high school teachers had two years or less of experience. And so far no one knows how any group of new recruits will do or how long they'll stay. Of all the people who begin in the classroom in this country, more than a third quit before they finish five years. In urban areas, according to Stanford's Linda Darling-Hammond, the founding director of the Commission on Teaching and America's Future, it's half.[48] For Levine, it was yet another betrayal of poor and minority students, who, under one label or another, would still get a disproportionate share of unqualified and inexperienced teachers.[49]

There were similar reports from other cities that, under pressure from NCLB, were in theory to have only "highly qualified" teachers in the core subjects in all schools getting federal Title I funds. The federal deadline was 2005–6, but the law also prohibited districts from hiring new teachers who were not "highly qualified" by 2002–3.

Although the merits of the objective were beyond dispute, the "highly qualified" requirement, like some other parts of the law, was almost certainly beyond reach without massive infusions of money that neither the federal government nor the states were prepared to spend. Districts such as Chicago or Houston, using aggressive recruiting, signing bonuses, housing allowances, and other inducements, and (in Houston) hiring teachers from Puerto Rico, Spain, and even Russia—and sometimes bringing in retired military people or others looking for second careers—claimed to have found good applicants even for inner-city schools. Most have not, and there was doubt even about the claims of many that had. As soon as the law went into effect, both the states and the Department of Education began looking for what one teacher union official called "wiggle room" in the definition of "highly qualified" and a range of other provisions.

Probably the most blatant wiggle was California's, where the State Board of Education, in a sort of miraculous laying-on of hands, submitted data to comply with the new federal law that simply redefined things in such a way that its forty-thousand uncredentialed teachers were suddenly "highly qualified," among them thousands who had no credentials and had barely started in the classroom. That, said Rep. George Miller, one of NCLB's liberal co-sponsors, in a letter to the board, was an "audacious and truth-defying step." It showed, he said, "a lack of regard for students, parents, and taxpayers.... By declaring every teacher 'highly qualified,' the state has essentially abandoned any effort at reform. Instead, the board has in effect voted for inertia."[50] Even California officials acknowledged that the state had a horrendous "distribution" problem for which they had no ready solution. No one has ever tried to measure what such fudges do to the morale of able teachers who have the experience and qualifications that really deserve that distinction.

Nationally, in the mid-1990s, urban schools hired twice as many unqualified new teachers as other schools. In some schools, indeed, it was almost inevitable, since they refused to hire any new people until enrollment had "stabilized" two or three weeks after school started:

> And so [said a California teacher] for a whole month there are classrooms that have way too many children, and then at the end of that month's period, the district would say, okay, you have this many students, we can allocate you this many more teachers to make more classrooms. And then at that point the students who have now been in one classroom for a month... are then pulled out of that class and an overflow class is made for them, which a lot of times is at first run by a sub. Because at the moment the month ends and we're allocated a teacher, then we start the hiring process, so it might be a few more weeks before we have the permanent teacher hired. And a lot of times that sub is someone with an emergency credential or noncredentialed who hasn't been through an education program

of any sort. And the teacher who is generally hired is usually a noncredentialed teacher because by September or October of a school year all credentialed teachers have already been placed in a position in other schools.[51]

In New York State, 31 percent of new hires in urban districts lacked full credentials; in nonurban schools, it was 10 percent. (In one New York City elementary school in 1999, half the teachers were uncertified; in one junior high it was 44 percent, in another it was 39 percent.)[52] In 2001, in the multitrack high-poverty subdistrict in South Central Los Angeles of which Fremont High is a part—altogether, there are fourteen elementary and secondary schools with some fifty-five thousand students—49 percent of the track B teachers were uncredentialed.[53] In California overall, where a class size reduction program in the primary grades put particular stress on the system, and where a lot of qualified urban teachers left for suburbs that offered better pay, better conditions, better support, and fewer troubled kids, 30 percent of new hires in urban schools were uncredentialed; in the state as a whole it was 15 percent. Those numbers are particularly significant because high proportions of inexperienced and under-trained teachers produce a kind of critical mass that strains a whole school. Where more than 20 percent are inexperienced, in the judgment of Margaret Gaston and her colleagues at the Center on the Future of Teaching and Learning, "the school has little or no capacity to improve."[54]

The problem may be even more acute in the ranks of administrators. The high turnover and administrative chaos at Fremont was an outsize illustration of a nationally recognized problem, not an anomaly. According to a survey for the nation's two major principals' associations in 1998, there were shortages of qualified applicants for principals' jobs "among all kinds of schools (rural, urban, suburban) and among all levels" as well as high turnover rates. Fewer and fewer people wanted the job, in large part because of stress and lack of support. Not surprisingly, the toughest schools to staff were also the ones serving the highest percentage of poor and at-risk students. In New York City in November 1999, 212 principals' jobs were open, meaning that roughly one in five of New York's thousand-plus schools didn't have a permanent principal. The following year, 163 New York schools began the year with a substitute principal. Meanwhile, as a Los Angeles teacher said, "it is widely known that incompetent principals are routinely transferred from school to school and not removed from leadership roles."[55] In school administration, if the captain and officers of the *Titanic* can get themselves rescued, they're pretty certain of getting a new ship.

As should be obvious, the schools with the poorest students—and often the least experienced teachers, who need the most help—also tend to be those where books, materials, and other resources are scarcest and where curricula are thinnest. The differences the New Jersey Supreme Court listed in 1990 could apply to countless other states. In Princeton, students began a foreign language in the fifth grade and a second language in ninth grade; Paterson began its foreign language program in the tenth grade. Princeton (in 1989) had one computer for every eight students; East Orange had one for every forty-three and Camden one for every fifty-eight. In Princeton, the high school had seven science labs, "each with built-in equipment. . . . Many poorer districts offer science classes in labs built in the 1920s and 1930s, where sinks do not work, equipment such as microscopes is not available, supplies for chemistry and biology classes are insufficient, and hands-on investigative techniques cannot be taught."[56] In South Brunswick, the industrial arts program offered an automotive shop, a woodworking shop, a metal shop, a graphics shop, and a greenhouse for a course in horticulture; in Camden, "state-of-the-art equipment is not purchased; the old equipment in the classrooms is not maintained or repaired."

In Ohio in the early 1990s, according to Howard Fleeter of the School of Public Policy and Management at Ohio State University, the school districts ranked in the top 25 percent of assessed valuation per pupil offered an average of 399 Advanced Placement courses per district; the districts ranked in the bottom 25 percent offered 40 Advanced Placement courses. Jodi Altier, the valedictorian at Miller High School in Corning, Ohio—she had a 4.0 average—"applied to Notre Dame University, but was not accepted. When she went to be interviewed at Notre Dame, she was asked how many Advanced Placement courses she had taken. Jodi did not even know what Advanced Placement meant. No Advanced Placement courses are offered in the Miller High School."[57]

The many schools where teachers have only one set of books for several classes—if they have that—and where students therefore can't take books home have become almost a cliché. It's also a commonplace that where there are books and other necessary materials, they're often worn, covered with graffiti, and, like many library reference books, outdated. In the mid-1990s, when Alabama ACLU lawyer Adam Cohen traveled around the state, he found a Selma high school student "who told us he was having trouble keeping up in physics because his school could afford only four physics textbooks, and when he wanted to do homework, he had to call around to see if anyone was done with the book." And as have many people in other states, Cohen found ramshackle elementary school libraries with books that "cheerfully predicted that 'one day man will walk on the moon.' "[58] At Rainier Beach High in South Seattle, students walked out of school to protest the lack of textbooks to take home. The district said it was providing enough money; officials at the school said it was not, in part because with the high turnover in enrollment some students who left never returned their books. But that was hardly the fault of the students who remained and who were caught in the bureaucratic cracks. A school running out of textbooks, one student's grandmother told a reporter, was as unthinkable as McDonald's running out of hamburgers.[59]

In his testimony in November 1999 before North Carolina Superior Court Judge Howard W. Manning Jr., social studies teacher Michael Keim, one of the Hoke High School "roamers," showed a school globe—he estimated that it was twenty-five years old—that he uses in his history classes. "It's a little outdated," he said. "Rhodesia is visible on this map. . . . The Soviet Union is still intact. . . . Czechoslovakia is still one country. And I believe there aren't any problems in the Balkans because it's still just one huge Yugoslavia."

"How about Gaul?" asked the judge. "Is Gaul on there?"

"Gaul?"

(A few minutes later, perhaps trying to play off Manning's joke, a lawyer for the state, defending the status quo, asked whether, as a history teacher, Keim wouldn't prefer the old globe so students would know "the countries that used to be in place as opposed to the ones they now call themselves.")[60]

Teachers have come up with all sort of devices—copying pages from books to hand out as substitute homework resources, buying materials out of their own pockets, borrowing sets of books from other classes—to get around the book problem, which sometimes leads to genuinely bizarre results. At Belmont High in Los Angeles, for example, which was to be replaced by the toxin-plagued new Belmont Learning Center, Erika Cabrera and her classmates in tenth-grade U.S. history began the year with no books, either to take home or to use in the classroom. "Therefore, the teacher lectured all the time and put notes on the board," but because the teacher talked very fast and there were no other materials, the students complained they couldn't keep up. It wasn't her fault, the teacher shot back, that there were no books.

By the fifth week, the teacher did borrow some books from another class, though still not enough for students to take home for homework. "Then our teacher needed to return the books to the class where she got them, and we again had no books. Finally, the teacher borrowed books from another class, but again we did not have enough to take home with us. It was a real problem that we were using this second set of borrowed books, because they were really old—maybe ten years old or older. Also, the tests we took were based on material that was not in the second set of borrowed books. Therefore we had open-book tests, but [in another wonderful Catch-22] the textbooks were useless because the subjects of the tests were not in the books we had."[61] In a Rockefeller Foundation–funded survey of teachers in 2002 used by the ACLU in its suit against the state of California, pollster Lou Harris found that nearly a third of teachers said they didn't have enough textbooks for their classes. (One Los Angeles high school puts gift certificates from Kinko's into new teachers' "goody baskets.")[62] From the survey data, Harris also concluded that 1.1 million of the state's 6 million students attended schools in which at least 20 percent of the teachers were undercredentialed, an estimate that jibes with other surveys, and that 1 million were in schools in which the bathrooms were not working or closed.[63]

IV

Nothing in this accumulation of statistics and stories, however, can fully describe the endemic chaos of the worst schools—a combination of high turnover in superintendents of the separate regional districts that big city systems like New York and Los Angeles are divided into and the corresponding turnover of teachers and administrators at the local sites, the endless breakdowns of physical facilities, student emergencies, complicated union work and seniority rules negotiated downtown, and rapidly changing programs and curricula, some dictated by districts, some handed down by legislators and state boards of education, a growing number by federal legislation. The rules imposed by bureaucracy and contract alone were enough to hamstring even the most dedicated principals, who in many districts were unable to hire the best teachers when others, through union seniority rules, had "bumping rights." In many cases, they couldn't hire anyone at all for a vacant spot until all teachers with seniority had gotten their chance at the job first, which sometimes took the process into mid-summer, by which time the best people were gone.[64]

At times the book problem may be merely a problem of money, but as Maureen DiMarco, a senior executive at Houghton Mifflin, one of the country's leading textbook publishers, points out, in some districts there's a reluctance to commit textbook funds until the district is confident that there won't be another decree the next week that will force programs to change again. And when there are books, they often join school walls and toilet stalls as free-fire zones in the battles of the taggers. Because the infatuation in American education with fat, glossy texts crammed with full-color pictures and charts has driven up the cost of many books to $70 apiece, and sometimes more, it's even more understandable that districts shy from any attempt to deal books out too generously. At Fremont High in Los Angeles, when "an unknown sub" replaces a regular teacher for a few days, the regular teacher is asked to lock up the books while she's gone.[65]

Mixed in with all this are the elements of sheer incompetence, mismanagement, and sometimes outright corruption. In New York City in the 1980s and 1990s, well after backward little Kentucky tried to outlaw schoolhouse nepotism and cronyism, five of the decentralized city system's thirty-two "community"-controlled districts were nests of politics, cronyism, and at times outright theft by employees and board members. In certain districts in the Bronx and Brooklyn, where board members were sometimes described as godfathers or godmothers and administrators as the "pieces" they controlled, schools were regarded as personal fiefdoms, and school employees often expected to provide personal services to their godfather—principals working in a community board member's garden or rewiring his house. As described by Edward Stancik, special commissioner of investigation for the New York City School District:

> If you, as a Board member, name a principal at a particular school, you would refer to that principal as your piece. In other words you would say, for example, "I want that piece." Or, "I need more pieces." Or, "I've only got one piece." That would be referring to the principals that you named. Godfather and Godmother would refer to the particular Board member who was the benefactor of that principal. So a principal would say that his Godfather or Godmother was the Board member who appointed—not appointed officially, but who . . . was allowed to name—that principal.
>
> Q. And did those names indicate any particular type of relationship that existed between the Godfather, for example, and the piece?
> A. Well, the Board members had enormous control over the [principals] that they named.[66]

Every time Stancik and his people turned over a rock, there was another bit of slime. There was bribery, there were fancy dinners and parties for board members and their friends, there were "credit pools" where "a large number of bogus expenses are approved so that an amount of money is accumulated that is ready for disbursement on a moment's notice, but the supplies really [don't] exist so the money can go for whatever purposes the person in charge of it wishes and in some cases it was used to pay for trips. . . . [T]he credit pool was this sort of slush fund built up on phony vouchers which were put up for supplies that were never purchased."[67] The creators of the thirty-two semiautonomous community school districts, which have since been gradually stripped of their power and which the state scheduled for final dissolution by mid-2003, "did not intend to establish patronage mills where, every three years, teachers and administrators are forced to become foot soldiers in their bosses' campaigns and educational priorities take a back seat to political imperatives." But that's what some had become, with predictable consequences. In one district, Stancik found that because of the turmoil, there'd been five district superintendents in six and a half years, teacher turnover was "distressingly high," and its schools had "sunk to the very bottom of the citywide scores measuring performance in math and reading."[68] The kids had become an afterthought.

The Stancik investigation also turned up some genuinely creative career-enhancing strategies, particularly one cooked up by principal Marlene Lazar of Brandeis High School on Manhattan's Upper West Side and the school's chief of computer services, Hal Charney. Together they developed an automated system to inflate the school's attendance data by eliminating nearly half the student absences from the reports they sent downtown, thus ballooning her budget and teaching staff and earning special credit for herself for reducing truancy. Worse, says the investigator's report, which was issued in 2000, instead of using the extra teachers to improve instruction, Lazar relieved them of much classroom duty and assigned them to phony jobs with titles such as "cafeteria dean," thereby denying students 154 teaching periods a day. "Brandeis teachers," said Stancik's report, "viewed the comp time positions as perks, and these jobs were in high demand." By failing to report dropouts, or falsely showing they'd reenrolled, Lazar allegedly also created "phantom students" enrolled in phantom classes.[69]

The undercount of dropouts is almost universal, in part because it depends on district self-reporting, which tends to be sloppy anyway. And since districts try to keep their enrollment, and thus their state and federal funding, as high as possible, it makes it sloppier still. Every time a student leaves the rolls, it costs the school and district upward of $4,000 annually, and often a lot more. In district after district and state after state, therefore, official annual high school dropout rates of 1 to 4 percent simply don't make sense when ninth-grade rolls—the 1,573 at Fremont in Los Angeles, for example—are compared to twelfth-grade enrollment (of 438) three years later, much less to the number of graduates at the end of twelfth-grade. Even if one discounts the effects of ninth-grade classes swollen by students who are, in effect, being held back because they failed to master eighth-grade work in middle school, the difference is huge. In 1999, to use one striking example, the Texas Education Agency, trying to put luster on George W. Bush's education record—sometimes called the "Texas miracle"—issued numbers purporting to show that even as the state's test scores had been rising in the previous decade, drop-out rates had been cut from an annual 6.1 percent in 1989–90 to an incredible 1.6 percent in 1998–9. But the state's own numbers also showed that while there were 266,000 seventh graders enrolled in Texas schools in 1992–3, only 197,000 (74 percent) graduated six years later. For Hispanics the attrition in grades seven through twelve was 40 percent. In California, which in 2002 claimed that 11 percent of its students had dropped out between grades nine and twelve in the prior three years, there were just under 366,000 students enrolled in twelfth-grade; there had been 468,000 in ninth grade in 1998–9.[70]

At times the dropout number-fudging becomes truly astounding. In 1996–7 the official seventh-grade enrollment of the class of 2002 in all of Los Angeles was 44,120. By 2001–2, there were 29,206 left. Of every three students, one was gone. Meanwhile, L.A.'s Manual Arts High School, an inner-city school that was 80 percent Latino, 20 percent black, and virtually all poor, claimed that it had a dropout rate approaching zero, that virtually all of its graduates had completed all the courses required for admission to the University of California, and that 80 percent were going on to college. That got the school's principal, Wendell Greer, a press conference with President Bill Clinton in 1999 in recognition of the school's distinguished accomplishment. Those claims, as subsequently disclosed by the rambunctious *LA Weekly*, turned out to be mostly phony. The only wonder was how Greer could have maintained the façade so long.[71]

Perhaps the saddest story of educational deterioration and insult—again, perhaps uniquely, from New York—is almost a footnote to the adequacy drama. But it's revealing nonetheless. From 1903, when the city's Public School Athletic League (PSAL) was founded, until about 1970, the city's schools maintained what was widely regarded as something approaching a model school sports and physical education program, with a wide array of sports and intense community interest in interscholastic competition in the major sports. In the generation between World War II and the early 1970s, games between schools like Brooklyn Tech or Lincoln and Erasmus, sometimes played at Ebbets Field, drew thousands of fans and, of course, intensified community cohesion and school loyalty. Along the way, those programs also produced some singularly gifted athletes. But in the thirty years since, the city's once-proud school sports and physical education programs have been starved and neglected, the PSAL's budget cut again and again. Fields and gyms were allowed to deteriorate to the point where some became unusable, and sports equipment became scarcer and scarcer—by 1999, the district had reduced its five-periods-per-week phys ed program to an average of two and a half periods and quit buying school gym equipment altogether. Teams were getting nothing for uniforms or transportation; sometimes coaches or school administrators would pass the hat among teachers to pay for the bus that would get the team to events.

In the system as a whole, there was one gym teacher for every 730 elementary school students, double the ratio in the rest of the state. At a time when there was more and more talk about the importance of physical fitness, when obesity was becoming an endemic problem among the young, and when it was widely believed that school sports were a major factor in encouraging adolescents to stay in school, New York, in the words of an angry *New York Times* report (1999), "all but walked off the field."[72] Since 1999, largely because of the *Times* story, some fields have been scheduled for restoration, in part with private funds raised through an independent group called Take the Field, but, according to Mary Musca, the organization's executive director, and a survey prepared for the reform group New Visions for Public Schools, New York's basic neglect of sports and phys ed continued. As of 2001, the survey showed, 41 percent of the city's elementary schools and 23 percent of high schools had no regular phys ed classes.[73] While nobody will claim that high school basketball, or maybe even gym class, is a constitutional right, as an indicator of neglect and indifference, this may be among the most telling.

IV

Within schools like Fremont in Los Angeles, it's a never-ending crisis even for the best people, whom, with some wonderful exceptions, those running our toughest schools often are not. Consider Margaret Roland, who'd just become principal at Fremont when her school became a leading exhibit in the suit against the state. Roland was the school's fifth principal in five years. Two years before, the district had sent in a team from downtown to help manage the school after students walked out in protest during the administration of Roland's predecessor's predecessor.[74] The protesting students said they wanted a principal, a subtlety that seems to have escaped some of the adults: Fremont, the adults said, had a principal.

Roland had been passed over several times in her pursuit of a principalship and she was surprised when she got this one, but by the end of her first year she'd barely come to know the place. In her deposition she said she didn't know how many of her 210 teachers lacked full credentials. And although she learned about the court case, with its string of complaints about the lack of books, inaccessible toilets, high-turnover teaching staffs, and overcrowding, soon after she got there, she didn't follow up and never conducted an investigation. Nor did she know her school's ranking on the state's Academic Performance Index—she knew it was low—or what the state expected from Fremont in terms of improvement. If she had more money, she said, she'd hire more counselors and buy more books: "novels, reading for pleasure." She, too, had been asked by students, and almost in the same words as had Patricia Gray in San Francisco, "Ms. Roland, are we going to get a permanent teacher?" The same, of course, could also be asked about administrators, even about principals. At the time Roland testified, the school had four assistant principals. One was a veteran, three were new that year, and one position was unfilled. At that point, even among its "permanent" teachers, between 25 and 30 percent were working on emergency permits.[75]

The sheer bureaucratic magnitude of the system itself was overwhelming, not just for Roland, but for the one assistant principal who had any real experience at the school: the reports, the ever-changing procedures and programs and committees, the negotiations with union representatives about things as mundane as the bell schedule, and of course the endless meetings—leadership council, SHAPO (the senior high assistant principals' organization), the local district meetings. Even labels changed: beginning in 2000, it was no longer permissible to have anything called reading classes in high school because it implied remedial reading for dummies. So in order not to put off students, the classes were renamed "academic literacy." In schools generally, euphemisms sprout like weeds. In Fremont people constantly "dialogue," busing is the "capacity adjustment program," and the box-like portable classrooms that are eating up acres and acres of playgrounds and other open space are called "bungalows." One administrator said she could tell that the most recent set of portables that arrived on her campus were extremely old because they had real wood in them.

At Fremont also, "one of the young ladies did have a problem with a rape situation." Euphemism, as always, functions to conceal conditions that would seem far more ugly—and would require quick intervention—if they were described candidly. No one knows how many rape "situations" and other violent acts aren't reported by school administrators, even in the face of parental demands, either out of fear they will get themselves in trouble or simply because they don't want another mess to deal with. Any number of students say they don't feel safe at school—for parents, safe schools is the highest priority—in part because school employees ignore as much as they can. In a Richmond, California, middle school, a student reported, "My friend was chased by other students who were throwing things and yelling at her. I tried to help my friend get away from the students who were harassing her so that she could get to the office for help. A security guard saw what was happening, but the guard did nothing."[76]

And, of course, there are the constant emergencies, from teachers who suddenly quit (and for whom no sub can immediately be rounded up by Sub Finder, the automated system downtown) to food fights in the cafeteria. "Sometimes we let our operational needs drive us," said Fremont assistant principal Marcia Hines. "We have emergencies with pipes, we have emergencies with floors, we have someone who needs to go home because they did something or other." Every day, the school had roughly five new substitutes, but since it wasn't the school's job to check on the subs' qualifications, no one in the main office was sure whether the algebra sub knew any math or the physics sub had ever heard of Newton or Galileo, and probably no one downtown did either. However, Fremont, trying to avoid damage to the equipment, did make it a practice never to put a computer class sub in a computer lab. That almost assured that the students would learn nothing.[77]

The multitrack schedule itself entailed endless juggling. This was not a September–June calendar with a breather in the summer; on this schedule, teachers and students were, as Hines said, "coming and going, coming and going, and doing a new master schedule every time a new track comes along." Within all this coming and going, a few teachers "rainbow" for extra money, meaning that they teach year-round. Quite a few more fill in, also for extra money, when they're off-track.[78]

Routine stuff: Would there be someone for the Spanish course when the A track returned at the end of August? Would the rooms that had to be converted for computer use be ready? Could a woman PE teacher be found for the girls' gym class? And since all that, and books as well, depended on the great bureaucratic maw downtown, there was no way to be sure. Even after a teacher was hired, it sometimes took four months to get a fingerprint check; until that was done, the hiree couldn't set foot in the classroom.[79] And the same went for almost everything else. Again and again administrators told teachers that they hoped the textbooks would arrive soon, if the order hadn't gotten lost in the long chain between the teacher, the school, the district purchasing department, the publisher, and the book clerk back at the school.[80] Ditto for the countless students who were on the rolls and simply didn't show up at the beginning of each new "mester." Nobody at school really knew what happened to them. Maybe they went to some other school or to some other district. It was supposed to be handled by the attendance office, but until the new person arrived, there'd be nobody to do it.[81] At one point during Hines's long deposition, one of the lawyers asked her to clarify something. Just then, had she been talking about the school year or the calendar year? "School year," she replied. "Is there any other kind? I have no life."

Schools like Fremont and the subdistrict it's located in crawl with consultants and outside experts—ed-school professors, motivational gurus, learning theorists, psychologists—running yet another professional development session or another clinic and pitching yet another jargon-rich program to downtown administrators who think this is the way to be creative or break the monotony. There were always a lot of them, but the new accountability systems and the call (and corresponding boosts in funding) for better in-service training for teachers have increased the pressure still further. And so some new plan is always just getting off the ground—training yet to come, details still to be explained. At the time Hines testified, Fremont had several, among them something called Academic Literacy Across the Curriculum for Achieving the Standards (the acronym, ALACASA, means "at home" in Spanish), run by a San Francisco State University teacher named Kate Kinsella, that appears to be focused primarily on Latino students whose primary language is Spanish. "Reading & Writing to Learn," says its Web site, "is the goal of ALACASA's ambitious professional development component for teachers [who] cycle through a series of seminars on topics related to developing academic literacy skills in all content areas." Fremont also was beginning something called Co-nect, which promised to show "schools and districts to use project-based learning and technology to support teachers, enhance the quality of student work, and integrate real-world projects into today's standards-based curriculum." But that, Hines said, was "just getting off the ground, too."

There are hundreds of such programs, few of them with much of a research base, if any, and who knows how many thousands of consultants ministering to desperate school district patients. But their real problem, aside from diverting money, time, and energy from other uses, is that they contribute to the school-site confusion created by endless change. In the past decade, school administrators have complained loudly about all the stuff that's foisted on them by politicians and state officials, but they're not shy about doing a lot of foisting themselves.

There is no foolproof gauge of the cumulative effects that dismal schools, with their filth, their lack of competent staffs, and their constant turmoil, have on the students who are stuck in them. Nor is there any measure of the demoralizing effects on the teachers and administrators who are trying to do conscientious jobs. But as countless students have testified, the insult is inescapable. Michelle Fine, a City University of New York social psychologist who runs structured focus groups with students, believes the impact is enormous, transforming "yearning for quality education into anger, pride into shame, and civic engagement into public alienation." Fine, who has done scores of such studies, was hired by the lawyers in the pending California suit to give her analysis:

> The California schools in question [she reported] are educating poor and working-class youth, and youth of color, away from academic mastery and democracy and toward academic ignorance and civic alienation. Despite the fact that the youth are asking for clean and safe school environments, quality educators, and rigorous instruction, the evidence suggests that the more years they spend in their schools, the more shame, anger, and mistrust they develop; the more academic engagement declines; and the more our diverse democratic fabric frays. We can ill afford to have youth—particularly poor and working-class youth and youth of color, so in need of higher education—continue to decide early in their academic careers that schools are not designed for them.[82]

It takes no expert analyst to know that thousands of students survive those schools and go on to productive and happy lives, and sometimes careers of great distinction. American lore is crammed with their stories. But neither does it take much imagination to understand the depressing, alienating impact of our schools of disregard. Americans who can afford it do not choose high schools such as Fremont or Newtown or Hoke for their children; they run from them as hard as they can. "The conditions at Burbank," said teacher Mei-Ling Wiedmeyer, "make [the children] feel as if no one cares about their education. I can see them internalize the belief that if no one cares about their education, then they won't either." The only surprise about the Fine report is that anyone found it necessary to try to "prove" such things at all.

V

If all American schools were falling down around their teachers and students, if they all had rats in the halls and ratty books in the classrooms, if they all had squadrons of untrained teachers, and "if absolute equality were the constitutional mandate, and 'basic skills' sufficient to achieve that mandate," as the New Jersey Supreme Court said in 1990, "there would be little short of a revolution in the suburban districts when parents learned that basic skills is what their children were entitled to, limited to, and no more."[83] But of course that's not the case. In most, the roofs don't leak, the ceiling tiles aren't falling down, there's no coal dust on the desks, the playing fields don't flood with backed-up sewage, and most seventh graders graduate six years later and go on to college.

Yet even in the average school, the average teacher who majored in education as an undergraduate—and many still do—is likely to have scored lower in college admission tests than students in most other majors and intended professions, to make less money, and to work under conditions unpleasant enough to strain many people's dedication and idealism. (In 2001, SAT scores for entering college freshmen intending to be education majors were third from the bottom on a list of twenty-three majors, above only home economics and two grab-bag categories.)[84] In many states, the school isn't likely to have a full-time librarian, especially if it's an elementary school, or even a library at all. In many, the counselors barely have time to make certain that students take the courses required to meet the district (and increasingly the state) graduation requirements. Intelligent college and/or career planning is a relative luxury. First-class music and art programs are a rarity.

But with the exception of growing complaints about the lack of well-trained teachers—and with the questions about what is good training the subject of another controversy—probably the most pervasive belief about schools through much of the past generation, at least the schools attended by other people's children, was that they were too flabby. The most vocal critics, both in the business community and among think-tank conservatives, thought them too dominated by old progressive theory favoring such things as whole language and constructivist math, and suffused with bleeding-heart tenderness about self-esteem, at the expense of phonics, systematic learning of "math facts," direct instruction, and real achievement measured by honest, objective assessment. Along the way they were believed to have shunned, even demeaned, cultural literacy, as defined most prominently by E. D. Hirsch Jr., the University of Virginia professor of English and author of *Cultural Literacy*, the bestseller with the five-thousand-item list of what everybody should know.[85] (The kids have no idea even in what century the Civil War took place, can't tell Robert Frost from Jack, and think a soprano is a member of a mob family on television.) Meanwhile, Chester ("Checker") Finn and Diane Ravitch, both former federal education officials from the Reagan-Bush years and probably the country's most articulate educational conservatives, argued all through the 1980s and 1990s that, compared to that of students in other countries, American students' academic prowess was pretty dismal. We were suffering, they said, "from the tyranny of dogma."

Those conclusions were backed by the comparative scores on TIMSS, the Third International Math and Science Study, showing American students not testing as well (in eighth-grade math, for example) as students in Singapore, Korea, Taiwan, or even Bulgaria, Malaysia, and Hungary.[86] At the same time, American school districts claimed their students were doing fine and parents (for the most part) were smugly satisfied. Everybody thought they knew about the rotten schools attended by the black and Hispanic children across town, where many started kindergarten two or more years behind, got further behind every year they were in school, and often dropped out by the time they were sixteen (though in fact most of us knew far less than we thought). Although nobody much uses the phrase "the blackboard jungle" anymore—in the 1950s it was both a best-selling book and a movie—the image still lingers. But the schools on this side of the tracks were not like that; they were safe and the kids succeeded.

We were thus, in the view of people like Finn and Ravitch, all being hoodwinked by the spin called the Lake Wobegon effect—the reports from local schools, sometimes based on their own tests, that all their kids were above average even as standardized tests showed that they were not.[87] In one frequently cited report, Harold W. Stevenson and James W. Stigler also found that in Japan and China, where students outperformed their U.S. peers, parents and children rated effort as much more important in school success than U.S. parents. Conversely, in the United States, mothers believed natural ability more important than did mothers in China.[88] The parents of American students who were scoring below their overseas peers on those international comparisons thought their kids were doing much better than the parents of the kids in Japan who were getting higher scores. It was this observation that, more than anything else, set Checker Finn and a critical mass of American politicians on the pursuit of statewide testing systems that might inform parents how poorly their children were really doing.[89]

All those generalizations have set off huge battles about the validity of the international comparisons in light of major cultural differences, not to mention the average age difference between U.S. high school seniors and those abroad, and about the trade-offs between rote learning, known affectionately as drill-and-kill, and the relative pedagogical freedom in many U.S. schools that's said to foster creativity and critical thinking. In any society—Japan, say, or Taiwan—where few get to go to selective academic secondary schools and even fewer are admitted to good universities and get financial aid or low tuition, the academic competition may be far more intense than it is in this country, where almost any student can find a place in a college somewhere.[90] But the international tests have helped drive the accountability and testing movements and the push for higher standards, and in a totally unintended side effect, they have reinforced the adequacy argument. If the average school isn't good enough in Mason City, Boise, or Oswego, how could the average school in Harlem or South Central Los Angeles make the grade?

The conservative diagnosis—and often the diagnosis generally of legislatures and businesspeople—is that the problem lies primarily in curricula, teaching methods, and establishment turf protection, and in many cases that's at least partly correct. Curricula and teaching techniques do matter, and often they're no better than uninspiring; sometimes they're awful. But when a school has a string of subs, no books to give the kids for homework, and constant shifting of classes and bodies, when it's bereft of functioning labs and counselors to deal with student crises, and when for one of many reasons the leaky roof doesn't get fixed, the chances of teaching anything well go down fast. Hamilton Lankford's perfect curve in New York showing that as the poverty level of a school goes up the training and measured ability of teachers goes down almost certainly has corollaries in most other school resources as well, had we only statistics to measure them— from rich curricula to the availability and quality of books and labs to the condition of the windows and the paint on the walls. In North Carolina, where high school students are expected to use graphing calculators on state tests (they cost about $100 each), teachers in poor schools had to borrow them on test days from other schools "and let students try to use the calculators on the tests without enough practice."[91] In some districts, parents are required to buy them for their children out of their own pockets. (The same is often true for team, band, and cheerleader uniforms, but those, at least, are not required for academic success.)

The Lankford curve also corresponds almost exactly to the similar curve that Marguerite Roza and Karen Hawley Miles, two researchers at the Center on Reinventing Public Education at the University of Washington, found when they looked at the disparities in intradistrict school funding in three U.S. cities: Seattle, Cincinnati, and Houston. While the districts claimed they were funding each of their schools at roughly the same level, they were doing it with a budgeting fiction that, because of wide discrepancies in the cost of teachers' salaries, subsidizes schools serving affluent kids at the expense of the schools serving the poorer kids. Seattle's Martin Luther King School, for example, where most students are poor enough to get free lunches, was budgeted to get $3,926 per student, but because of its inexperienced (and thus low-paid) teachers it got only $2,928. Meanwhile, the Wedgwood School, located in an affluent neighborhood, was budgeted at $3,731 per student but got $4,019.

> How is this possible? [Roza wrote.] While the district is careful to report its school-by-school budget figures, what you can't see from the reports is that these figures represent a sort of "play money"—schools are required to use the budgeted money to buy back artificially priced goods from the district.
>
> So in reality, the budgeted money is not the same as what it actually costs to operate the school. For example, the district charges schools a fixed false rate for all teachers, principals and other administrative staff, regardless of what these staff are actually paid by the district. The district then pays out the real salaries—salaries that are not fixed but vary substantially with experience and other qualifications.
>
> Schools such as Wedgewood, which can attract the best teachers (typically the most expensive teachers) can really benefit from this scheme. They don't use any extra play money to hire an expensive teacher than they do an inexpensive one. The district's budget reports don't even reflect that Wedgewood teachers are some of the most expensive in the district.[92]

Roza says the districts seemed not even to understand the discrepancies. They have since moved gradually, each in a different way, to adopt a modified form of student-based budgeting and thus reduce the discrepancies in some classes of funding. Houston, which has gone the farthest, appears even to be contemplating a cap where schools with high proportions of experienced teachers would be required eventually to hire only low-paid rookies. But that hasn't yet happened. In view of the likely uproar from the wealthy neighborhoods, no district is likely to eliminate the gaps in pay, and thus teacher quality, anytime soon.[93]

Of course there are exceptions, statistical outliers; they're clear both on Lankford's scatter diagrams and in the communities around us—

middle-class schools that don't teach well, high-poverty schools that do and where students do well. The conservative Heritage Foundation, for one, is crazy about principals and teachers at schools full of minority kids whose test scores are high. It gives the school people awards and shows them off at its meetings and in its literature. Their achievement, often only grudgingly recognized by the establishment, not only seems to show that the right cares about black and Latino kids—and believes in their potential—as fervently as the left but also appears to demonstrate that some schools can raise test scores significantly, and that poor children can learn, without more money. And it seems to show that the main reason most public schools are failing (and thus that vouchers are necessary) is that the public system is stuck in its costly, self-serving, and politically correct futility: the tyranny of dogma.

In a lot of communities, test and accountability programs seem to be having an odd effect. Of course there are the well-known cram programs to which schools in states such as Texas devote nearly all their time in the two months before the test is given. There is fudging of numbers, either by hiding students who are not likely to test well, by putting them in classes for the handicapped, by temporarily re-designating high-achieving Anglos as Hispanic to bring up that group's scores, or simply by outright fraud. But for parents with kids with high scores (which, needless to say, may tell little about either school quality or real achievement), testing has probably reinforced the Lake Wobegon effect. It strengthens the prior conviction that the kids are doing okay and the schools are fine. It also drives up real estate values handsomely. In Texas, and probably elsewhere, when local schools get exemplary ratings from the state education agency—and quite a few of them do—Realtors and developers post the ratings on billboards, brochures, and Web sites.[94]

But Lankford's curve is still there. And so while students like Randell Hasty are taught math and science by a string of subs and Alondra Jones and Erika Cabrera aren't getting anything close to what the kids get in the fancy suburbs or at selective public high schools like Lowell (much less what they get at Marin Academy), there is no quantum break—the poor kids on this side of the resource line, the rest on the other—which was the moral basis of the equity suits of the 1970s. As long as everybody is in some kind of school with some adult in the room, somebody could argue—as the U.S. Supreme Court indeed did—that kids in underfunded schools were not suffering anything dire enough to constitute denial of equal protection under the Fourteenth Amendment. Conversely, all through the 1990s there were—and probably still are—schools in the comfortable California suburbs, and elsewhere as well, where the roofs also leaked, where there were too few counselors, no art program, no school nurse, no Internet-connected computers, and where the books in the library also eagerly awaited the day man would walk on the moon. At Ensign Intermediate School in Newport Beach (among the state's plushest suburbs), "when it rains, the library is off-limits because the roof and windows leak. At Costa Mesa High, the gymnasium floor is riddled with holes. . . . Jagged metal snags locker-room users. In the new state-funded computer lab, ceiling tiles fall on students' heads."[95]

Once you make the adequacy argument, however, you may be able to ride up the Lankford curve as easily as the system had ridden it down. Maybe your local school is safe and well maintained, and maybe all the kids in the neighborhood will eventually get into college. But maybe it could also be better (and the value of your home could rise). If Alondra Jones wasn't being served well, it's possible that some middle-class children weren't being served adequately either. The trouble was that in most states, nobody had ever bothered to find out, much less structure governance and finance systems consistent with what it took to provide decent schooling for the contemporary world. Until somebody began to measure what was really needed, there was no way to know.

CHAPTER TWO

Kentucky Landmark

Nobody ever said that as Kentucky goes, so goes the nation. Kentucky, to those who thought about it all, was where they bred racehorses, strip-mined coal, made baseball bats, distilled great (and some not-so-great) bourbon, and, for those who remembered their history, where Lincoln was born. It was also one of the poorest states in the country, beautiful in many places, horribly ravaged by those mines in others.

But beginning in 1990, after the Kentucky legislature completely revamped the state's famously decrepit education system, a lot of people—educators, businesspeople, school reformers, lawyers, politicians—started to pay attention, and for them, at least, Kentucky began to mean something else.

The new law, the Kentucky Education Reform Act (KERA), touched every aspect of public education, linking a fundamental change in the state's famously inequitable school finance structure and hefty increases in school funding to tougher academic standards and a statewide testing and accountability system. Those reforms might never have happened, certainly not to the same extent, without *Rose v. Council for Better Education*, the sweeping Kentucky Supreme Court decision handed down the previous June (1989).[1] In *Rose* the court ruled that the entire state education system—"every part and parcel"—violated the state constitution. Because of its sweep and what followed, the decision became a powerful precedent for judges and reformers in countless other states.

There could have been no better model than Kentucky. The state had been at or near the bottom in virtually every national measure of education: adult literacy, graduation rates, test scores, spending, teacher salaries, facilities. In the little county school districts of Appalachia, moreover, where nearly half the adult population was functionally illiterate and half the ninth graders never made it to graduation, the schools suffered from a level of political corruption and nepotism uniquely their own. Since most school funding still depended on the local property tax, and since the tax base in the impoverished Appalachian hills and hollows was low to begin with and was further depleted by the favoritism of local assessors—people such as Reo Johns in Pike County, where, in the words of the *Lexington Herald-Leader*, "property taxes depend on how much the assessor likes you"—schools were starving even by Kentucky standards.[2]

In ingrown places such as Perry County or Morgan County or Letcher County, where only one of every six adults was a high school graduate, it was hard even for the well-intentioned to hire teachers, clerks, janitors, and school bus drivers who weren't somehow related to the superintendent or to school board members. But in most places people had long ago stopped trying. It was simply part of the system: the schools were far and away the biggest and best employer in the region. They were jobs, contracts, and bank deposits first and education a distant second—and thus, of course, campaign money and political power for the superintendents and board members who controlled them. Although many teachers, especially those in the remote hollows, had never finished college, their prime concern wasn't math or reading; it was finding enough shoes and old clothes for the children in their classes. Sons succeeded fathers, wives worked for husbands. Combses worked for other Combses in schools named Combs. Outsiders were rarely hired. "They want people who will be docile," a clergyman told me when I visited the region in 1964. "Even if an outsider wanted a job here he couldn't get it. The way to get hired is for someone to go to a board member and say 'poor old so-and-so needs work.' When they're hired that way they'll cooperate. Those that don't get sent up a hollow."[3] At the Dennis C. Wooton School in Hazard, where Dennis C. Wooton was the superintendent, Wooton's son-in-law was the principal. In Floyd County as late as 1989, Gary Newman was the principal of the Stumbo Elementary School, where his wife and "three or four cousins" were teachers.[4] In

Appalachia, these arrangements were not exceptions; they were the system.

But by 1988, when the case that led to the state supreme court's *Rose* decision went to trial, things had begun to change. The suit, sparked in part by a former long-term state education official named Arnold Guess, who'd been fired after he supported the loser in the race for state school superintendent, was filed by a coalition of sixty-six county and city school districts that had organized themselves as the Council for Better Education (CBE). It also included some individual school districts and nineteen students and parents complaining about low-paid teachers, rundown buildings, high dropout rates, truncated curricula, and unfair disadvantages in the struggle to get into college.

When they first brought the suit, their primary demand was equity in resources among districts and thus more reliance on state funding and less on the capricious and inadequate local property tax. But as Jack Moreland, then the superintendent in Dayton, Kentucky, and one of the original members of CBE, said recently, "The stars were lined up."[5] In state after state, there was growing concern for what was widely regarded as the flabbiness of American schools. In 1983, the Reagan administration had issued *A Nation at Risk*, the endlessly quoted report that warned that if American schools didn't shape up, the Germans and the Japanese would beat our economic brains out. "If an unfriendly foreign power had attempted to impose on America the mediocre educational performance that exists today," said the report, "we might well have viewed it as an act of war. As it stands, we have allowed this to happen to ourselves. . . . We have, in effect, been committing an act of unthinking, unilateral educational disarmament."[6] In state after state, governors and legislatures were trying to upgrade academic standards, raise high school graduation requirements, and keep undereducated teachers out of the classroom.

Meanwhile, Kentucky was generating its own internal pressures, both from academics and from a business community that had begun to realize that the state could no longer depend solely on coal and the extraction of other minerals to sustain its economy. Contrary to the years when low-wage unskilled labor was an attraction, the Chamber of Commerce now had trouble selling the state, with its poor education system, in its effort to attract new businesses. As a result, in 1983 a group of high-profile business and civic leaders organized the Committee for Academic Excellence—now known just as the Prichard Committee—to get word out on the condition of the state's schools and on the relationship between schools and better jobs. Among other things, the committee sponsored a televised statewide forum on the plight of Kentucky's schools, connecting 140 local sites in which some twenty thousand people participated. Ultimately, it would file an amicus brief in the CBE lawsuit against the state, an extraordinary measure for an establishment organization. And when companies such as Toyota, which in 1987 built a major new manufacturing plant in Georgetown, let it be known that they would hire only high school graduates, the message was driven home even more emphatically.[7]

But there was also an element of good fortune in the two major figures that drove Kentucky's reforms. One was Edward Prichard, for whom the committee is still known. A Kentucky original, Prichard was the brilliant son of a bluegrass wheeler-dealer and Democratic Party pol, who'd graduated from Princeton and Harvard Law, where he'd been a student and friend of Felix Frankfurter. When Franklin Roosevelt named Frankfurter to the Supreme Court, Prichard became his law clerk. During World War II he worked for Fred Vinson and Robert Jackson, who were to become Supreme Court justices themselves, and came to be regarded as one of Washington's most promising young men.[8]

After the war, Prichard returned to Kentucky to practice law and get into politics, where he was regarded as a comer, a future governor, maybe even president. But in 1949 Prichard was charged with stuffing ballot boxes in the 1948 election in Bourbon County, convicted on federal charges, disbarred, and sent to prison, where he served the first six months of a two-year sentence before Harry Truman commuted it. By Kentucky standards, forging 254 ballots was no big deal, especially in an election whose outcome was a foregone conclusion. But when FBI director J. Edgar Hoover learned that Prichard was the same man who'd been quietly investigated and wiretapped as a possibly subversive left-winger when he worked in the U.S. attorney general's office in 1941, he issued orders to "press vigorously and thoroughly."[9] At least two others were involved, among them one of

Prichard's friends, county attorney Bill Baldwin, but Prichard was the only one who was convicted.

Although it took the better part of two decades, Prichard's smarts and charm—and his many political connections—enabled him to rehabilitate himself, both as a lawyer and as a man of influence (whose reputation might in some ironic way have ultimately been enhanced and legitimized by his earlier troubles). Thereafter, he lobbied for civil rights, for mine safety, and for better education at all levels, and he became an unofficial advisor to governors and other politicians. "I'd rather have my pecker cut off," Lyndon Johnson supposedly said, "than deny Ed Prichard."[10]

The other major figure in the case—and one of Prichard's many connections—was Bert T. Combs, Prichard's friend, a former governor, and a former federal appellate court judge, who became the lead attorney in the school case. Combs left much of the legal work to his associate Debra Dawahare, but he was a shrewd enough politician to understand that however his case came out, getting real results would eventually require the political support of the legislature and governor and so planned his strategy accordingly. Combs's refrain, Dawahare later told an interviewer, was "Keep it simple, keep it quotable and don't get bogged down on the technicalities." So what Moreland and his associates at CBE had originally regarded as an equity case—a search for roughly equal school funding for each child, regardless of the wealth or poverty of the district he or she lived in—turned into an adequacy case, based on the contention that few of the state's children were getting the resources, teachers, books, facilities, equipment, and courses they needed in the modern world. Unlike the outcomes in equity suits in other states, Combs told his associates, this was not going to be a Robin Hood case, where in the effort to redistribute resources there were likely to be losing school districts as well as winners. To neutralize the opposition and to convince the court, everybody had to be winner.[11]

In Kentucky, with its dismal funding, its wretched schoolhouses, its underqualified teachers, and its political corruption, it was an easy case to make. "We were at the bottom of the barrel," said Bill McCann, a Combs law partner and now a member of the Prichard Committee.[12] In 1985, the year the suit was filed, the state spent

$3,759 per pupil, just 66 percent of the national average, putting it forty-seventh in the nation (forty-eighth counting the District of Columbia) on that measure and fortieth in the country in teacher salaries. It was at the very bottom in adult literacy and adults with high school diplomas—in Appalachia 48 percent of the population was functionally illiterate, and statewide fewer than 70 percent of ninth graders were graduating from high school four years later. Five years later, when the National Assessment of Educational Progress published its first state-by-state breakdowns of student test data (for math in the eighth grade), Kentucky was eighth from the bottom.[13]

As elsewhere, the state contended that while the Kentucky constitution required the legislature to "provide for an efficient system of common schools throughout the state,"[14] inequities and other school failures were the "result of mismanagement, waste and poor tax collection practices" on the part of the local districts.[15]

But as Combs and Dawahare argued before the court, the legislature itself had consistently blocked effective local attempts to increase school support and end local corruption. Not surprisingly, given the clout of the coal companies, it continued to exempt unmined minerals—the coal in the ground—from general property taxes. And after the state supreme court held (in 1965) that property had to be assessed at fair market value, "the General Assembly immediately aborted the effect (of the decision) by . . . reducing the tax rates on real property to offset the increase in assessments. Thus the inequities created by random and faulty tax assessments practices . . . were officially frozen into the system."[16] Shortly after passing this "Rollback Law," the legislature also capped all local property taxes. Any increase of over 4 percent was subject to a voter referendum. As property values increased in the intervening years, rates declined. Thus almost none of the increment was available to the schools, or indeed to any other local public service. "The Rollback Law," wrote Franklin County circuit judge Ray Corns in the trial court's decision, "continues to cast a long shadow over common school revenues." Because of such restrictions, "the system of financing Common Schools bears no rational relationship to the state's duty to provide an efficient system throughout the Commonwealth."[17]

Corns's ruling, handed down on Memorial Day in 1988, was itself pretty damning. Kentucky's school finance system, he wrote, is "unconstitutional and discriminatory.... It violates the Plaintiffs' right to equal protection of the laws and their fundamental right to an education under the Constitution." In the state constitution, he said, the term *efficient* "means the system must be adequate, uniform and unitary."[18] Thus this was not just an equity ruling; it included, as a major element, the adequacy standard Combs and Dawahare sought. But instead of telling the legislature what to do, Corns named a commission to draft a master plan that "with no intention to intrude on the prerogatives of the executive and legislative branches ... but rather as an aid, will serve as a guide in establishing the parameters" of the state constitution's requirements.[19] The whole trial had lasted just six days.

As expected, the Corns decision was just a way station to the state supreme court, which, because of its importance, took it directly after the leaders of the legislature—John Rose, then president pro tem of the state senate, and state house speaker Donald Blandford—appealed (though Governor Wallace Wilkinson, announcing his support for the decision, did not). And the court acted with surprising speed, rendering its decision barely a year after the Corns ruling. More striking still, the court's 5–2 ruling, written by Chief Justice Robert Stephens, went far beyond the narrow menu of fiscal reforms that the plaintiffs had hoped for:

> Lest there be any doubt, the result of our decision is that Kentucky's entire system of common schools is unconstitutional. There is no allegation that only part of the common school system is invalid, and we find no such circumstance. This decision applies to the entire sweep of the system—all its parts and parcels. This decision applies to the statutes creating, implementing and financing the system and to all regulations, etc., pertaining thereto. This decision covers the creation of local school districts, school boards ... school construction and maintenance, teacher certification—the whole gamut of the common school system in Kentucky.[20]

A child's right to an adequate education, Stephens wrote, "is a fundamental one under our Constitution. The General Assembly must protect and advance that right." Notwithstanding the state's argument, the schools were a state responsibility, not a local one. Then Stephens, borrowing from a similar case in West Virginia, held that in order to satisfy the Kentucky constitution, the state's education system had to include as its goals the duty to "provide every child" at least seven "capacities":

> Sufficient oral and written communication skills to enable students to function in a complex and rapidly changing civilization; sufficient knowledge of economic, social, and political systems to enable the student to make informed choices; sufficient understanding of governmental processes to enable the student to understand the issues that affect his or her community, state, and nation; sufficient self-knowledge and knowledge of his or her mental and physical wellness; sufficient grounding in the arts to enable each student to appreciate his or her cultural and historical heritage; sufficient training or preparation for advanced training in either academic or vocational fields so as to enable each child to choose and pursue life work intelligently, and sufficient levels of academic or vocational skills to enable public school students to compete favorably with their counterparts in surrounding states, in academics or in the job market.[21]

What had begun as a case about fiscal equity had grown into a precedent-setting decision about adequacy, which, in short, meant everything. "We wanted a thimbleful," Bert Combs said, "and we got a bucketful."[22]

The decision left any number of questions unanswered. What did "sufficient" mean and how could anyone be sure when "sufficient" was achieved? Did every child have to achieve those goals before the system was adequate (and, in Kentucky's case, in constitutional compliance), and if not, what resources would be adequate to give every child the opportunity to achieve them? Did money matter at all, and if it did, where could it be spent most effectively? Such questions had been haunting the nation's education debates at least since the nineteenth century. Justice Charles Leibson, one of the dissenters in the case (again like many other judges), agreed with the state defendants that the courts had no business wading into this swamp. The decision, he said, is "a Pandora's box [which] may well create havoc in the educational process. It adds to the General Assembly's burden in seeking to improve our educational system rather than lightening the load.... Local school districts who are the members of the Council for Better Education, the moving force behind this lawsuit, may be eaten up by the monster they created when they invited the courts into the dialogue."[23]

But in this case at least, the legislative outcome was brighter than the prophecy. The court itself had characterized its decision as "an opportunity for the General Assembly to launch the Commonwealth into a new era of educational opportunity which will ensure a strong economic, cultural and political future." *Rose*, said McCann, "made it impossible not to take some action." And here, too, there was an element of political good fortune: some 90 percent of the 600,000 children in Kentucky schools were (and are) white. The state's greatest poverty was concentrated in the hills and hollows, where the names— the Napiers, Brashears, Caudills, and Combses—and family roots were often the same as they were in Lexington and Louisville. They were the cousins, uncles, grandparents, and sometimes brothers and sisters of the voters in the rest of the state.

In any case, the politicians, shielded by the cover that *Rose* provided, seized the opportunity. As soon the decision came down, Governor Wilkinson, a defendant at the trial level, jumped on board. "The [court] has given us a great opportunity," he declared, "and an even greater responsibility."[24] There was opposition from the beginning from the fundamentalist Family Foundation of Kentucky, an educational and lobbying organization which feared that the state was about to take over local schools and control local school curricula.[25] At the same time, the legislature, jealous of its prerogatives, was fuming after the Corns decision. Nonetheless, it had started working on both the education and revenue issues even before *Rose*. It could fix things without some damn judge telling it what to do.

The ground had been prepared well before. Prichard, nearly blind and suffering from kidney failure caused by diabetes, died in 1984. But in the years immediately preceding his death, Prichard, an inveterate talker and storyteller, continued to use his charisma and considerable manipulative powers lobbying and raising money for the committee—sometimes, it's said, even when he was connected to his dialysis machine—talking up the cause that, in his roller-coaster career, would become his legacy.[26] (The daily work of Prichard's committee—then as now—was directed by Robert Sexton, a former university administrator who'd been instrumental in picking Prichard in the first place. Prichard was chosen for his stature and clout). There was, in addition, increasing help from the Chamber of Commerce, from executives at Ashland Oil, from people at some of the big banks, and from other major business figures, most of whom had been rallied by (and were often members of) Prichard's committee.

Less than a year after *Rose* was handed down, KERA, the Kentucky Education Reform Act, became law. Together, the two politicians, Combs and Prichard—now with the active support of Governor Wilkinson, who in his 1987 election campaign promised "systemic reform"—had turned the general reformist mood, strongly backed by the state's major newspapers, into a political coalition of business and education interest groups that was nearly irresistible. Where the Kentucky Education Association (KEA), the state's big teachers' union, fearing that job security and professional prerogatives might be jeopardized, had previously squelched attempts to impose effective accountability measures, the promise of more money—lots of it—now brought the KEA on board. Conversely, the business community now got the testing and accountability, including a system of rewards and sanctions for teachers and principals, that had been its condition for accepting the higher taxes—ultimately in the form of a one-cent sales tax increase—that better school funding demanded. There had never been a better example of the "dialogue" among judges, elected politicians, and the general public that school reform lawyers dream about.

KERA, which Wilkinson signed in April 1990, was an alphabet soup of interlinked school reforms in every area of K–12 schooling, from governance to child care. There was Support Education Excellence in Kentucky (SEEK), a new fiscal formula, bolstered by a 20 percent sales tax increase, to allocate more state funds to local schools and partially uncap the locals' authority to raise their own property taxes. There was a new primary school structure that, in the belief that age mattered less than academic and social readiness, put six- and seven-year-olds in the same ungraded primary classrooms. There were funds for greatly expanded preschool programs and for the Family Resource and Youth Service Centers (FRYSC), a network of programs at schools serving low-income children. There were higher academic standards. There was new money for professional development, textbooks, technology, and school safety. There was a controversial system of financial rewards for successful schools, and sanctions, including probation for the entire staff, in schools deemed as failing.

To evaluate performance there was the new statewide testing program, Kentucky Instructional Results Information System (KIRIS), which turned out to be famously unreliable. After a series of major scoring errors, it was replaced in 1998 by the Commonwealth Accountability Testing System (CATS). Legislation implementing CATS was passed only after an extended battle between conservatives, spurred by the Family Foundation, pushing for a standardized national test with multiple-choice questions and progressives demanding portfolios of essays, open-ended test questions, and other "authentic assessments."[27] CATS is a compromise, but considering its heavy dose of open-response questions requiring student-constructed answers in all major fields (as well as multiple-choice questions), its writing portfolios, and the fact that it required testing on a nationally standardized test only after grades 3, 6, and 9—federal law now requires testing in grades 3–8 every year—KERA was a lot more than comprehensive reform. At a time when a lot of states were going back to the drill-and-kill "basics," this was radical reform, especially for a state like Kentucky, with a hefty dose of progressive, nontraditional theory.[28] No wonder the Family Foundation was fuming.

Perhaps the most unusual feature of the law, and one that, in addressing a problem unknown in most other jurisdictions, has rarely been noticed in the national context, was its detailed prohibition of nepotism. With certain exceptions, relatives of a superintendent could no longer work in the same district; principals could no longer hire spouses or other relatives; those who were grandfathered (or grandmothered) in had to be evaluated by another administrator; school board members were required to have a high school diploma or a GED; contributions to school board candidates were capped at $100 for individuals; and candidates could no longer solicit school employees for contributions or services.[29] What was common to all those reforms, however—and almost certainly necessary in a state like Kentucky—was that they sought to make certain that the new money would not just be spent the old way, or, worse, merely disappear into a maw of inefficiency and corruption.

The very fact that a poor state like Kentucky had accomplished such a broad sweep of reforms in such a short time helped get attention. President George H. W. Bush called it a model for the country; the *New York Times* lauded it as "the most sweeping education package ever conceived by a state legislature"; the increasingly reform-minded business community embraced it; and in state after state education reformers began to speak of Kentucky as the beacon.[30] (KERA, said the Family Foundation, no doubt with unintended irony, "is a religion.") Other states had previously embarked on reforms. In 1979, the supreme court of neighboring West Virginia, a state as poor as Kentucky, had produced a list of items seeking to define an adequate education. But it came before the education standards movement had gotten fully under way and it was much less sweeping in the reforms that ensued, so few people paid much attention to it. *Rose,* as a pair of education law experts recently observed, "sparked what many scholars have called the 'adequacy movement' in courts, state houses, and education policy circles around the country."[31] In the years since, courts in Massachusetts, Alabama, New Hampshire, and other states have pointed to *Rose* as a model as they hammer out the reforms that the judges seem to have in mind.[32]

II

Even before *Brown,* much of the history of the nation's public schools revolved around the battles for, and the uncertainty about, equal opportunity for religious minorities (i.e., non-Protestants) and for poor (and in many cases working-class) children generally. Those struggles were rooted in the belief, first articulated by Jefferson and Horace

Mann and echoed ever since in state constitutions, in the crucial role of schooling in a democracy and the importance of the common school as a provider of opportunity and an equalizer among classes. Education, "the balance wheel of the social machinery," Mann had written, "does better than to disarm the poor of their hostility toward the rich. It prevents being poor."[33] "Common schools make patriots and men who are willing to stand upon a common land," said a delegate to the Kentucky constitutional convention of 1890. "The boys of the humble mountain home stand equally high with those from the mansions of the city. There are no distinctions in the common schools, but all stand upon one level."[34]

At the heart of *Brown* was the declaration, repudiating the Court's 1896 ruling in *Plessy v. Ferguson,* that separate schools were inherently unequal. But the limits of the *Brown* decision soon became apparent, even in the courts. In the ensuing years, federal judges ruled that *Brown* did not apply to districts that were segregated because of de facto housing patterns, held that white suburbs could not be legally required to take part in metropolitan desegregation plans, and in general "relaxed the standard that applied to school districts that had previously discriminated."[35] In the same period, states enacted laws blocking busing programs and, perhaps most telling, a great many black parents began to question the wisdom (and maybe the implicit racism) of policies founded on the belief that only if black children were bused into white schools across town could they get a decent education.

The result is that in many places the nation now has what are, in effect, two school systems, making schools perhaps the clearest embodiment of the warning in 1968 of the National Advisory Commission on Civil Disorders that America was drifting toward two societies, "one black and one white, separate and unequal."[36] Although racial segregation of black children was nearly absolute before *Brown,* not only in the South but in many other parts of the nation, a larger percentage of African Americans are now attending predominantly minority schools than was the case thirty years ago. Schools attended by Latinos, now a larger minority than blacks, appear to be more segregated than ever.[37]

As Harvard's Gary Orfield points out, that hardly means, as some critics claim, that there's been no progress since *Brown* and the passage of the U.S. Civil Rights Act in 1964; on the contrary, they've had great impact in all sectors of American life. Nor does it mean that poor and minority students can't succeed in the schools they attend. But the end of desegregation and the beginning of resegregation made the need to find other means to ensure the effectiveness of those schools ever more crucial. And so the search for better schooling for poor and minority children began an odyssey of overlapping stages: from desegregation to compensatory education, which reached its peak with the enactment of Head Start and Title I in Lyndon Johnson's Elementary and Secondary Education Act of 1965, designed to provide extra help to schools with large numbers of disadvantaged children, to the legislative and legal campaigns for equity in school funding between rich and poor districts. Along the way a long list of other elements was added to the mix: migrant and bilingual education, and court decisions requiring appropriate education for handicapped children, children with limited English proficiency, and countless others.

For most of the twentieth century, the states had provided some funding—generally called foundation programs—to make certain that even the poorest communities could provide minimal schooling. In some places that funding was pinned to local matching formulas and therefore was itself regressive, creating what some experts have called an "equalization myth...a hoax."[38] (In New Jersey, for example, the state supreme court found the minimum aid formula to be "counterequalizing." It provided money only to districts whose tax base exceeded a state minimum—"in other words, only to relatively richer districts.")[39] But for the most part school funding rested primarily on the local tax base, as it often still does, and that tax base was also inherently unequal: people in poor districts could tax themselves to death without being able to generate as much per-pupil funding as affluent districts could with ease. (In 1817, after the Virginia legislature defeated his proposal to levy a tax to support the state's education system, Jefferson said that depending for funding on local revenues wouldn't work "because the rich will not pay for the education of the poor.")[40] In 1997, a General Accounting Office analysis found that in six states, people living in the poorest districts spent more than twice as large a share of their income in property taxes as residents in the wealthiest districts.[41]

In the past decade the funding gaps have closed somewhat; in California and a number of other states they've nearly vanished. In Kentucky, as a consequence of *Rose* and KERA, the gaps have actually been reversed. Similarly in New Jersey, a series of court decisions has produced higher school spending in high-poverty districts than in middle-class districts. In some states, the gap closing has been abetted by property tax revolts that have necessarily shifted a greater share of school support to the state. But in much of the country funding gaps persist to this day. In Illinois (in 1999–2000) per-pupil spending in the quarter of districts with the lowest child poverty was $7,460, while in the quarter of Illinois districts with the highest rates of child poverty it was $5,400; in New York the comparable figures were $8,598 as against $6,445; in Pennsylvania, $7,285 as against $6,037. In Pennsylvania, the top 20 percent of school districts spent an average of over $10,000 per child; none of the districts in the bottom half spent over $8,000.[42] In a class of twenty-five students, those differences will buy a lot.

It was such fundamental inequities that prompted John E. (Jack) Coons, then a young law professor at Northwestern University, to collaborate with two students, William H. Clune and Stephen D. Sugarman, in developing the legal theory that led to the influential California lawsuit that eventually became *Serrano v. Priest*.[43] The California constitution, like most others, included an expansive equal protection clause. Unlike the U.S. Constitution, it also defined public education as a duty of the state, requiring the legislature to "provide for a system of common schools by which a free school shall be kept up and supported in each district."[44] In the fall of 1967, after Coons, followed by Sugarman, joined the Boalt Hall law faculty at Berkeley, he was introduced to John Serrano, a middle-class social worker whose own children attended school in a low-wealth southern California district. Serrano's children appeared to be doing fine, but the tax and funding inequities angered him.[45] And so he became the lead plaintiff in a case—ultimately it went to the state supreme court twice, once in 1971, then again in 1976—in which the court ruled that the state's school funding violated both the state constitution and, in the first decision, the U.S. Constitution as well.

The court found that with a tax rate of $4.78 per $100 of assessed value, a low-wealth community such as Baldwin Park, some twenty-five miles east of Los Angeles, could only generate less than half the per-pupil revenue that Beverly Hills raised with barely half that tax rate. In 1976, a rate of $1.00 per $100 in Baldwin Park would have produced $170 per child in school revenues; in Beverly Hills it would have raised $1,340. "Affluent districts can have their cake and eat it too," the court said. "They can provide a high quality education while paying lower taxes. . . . Poor districts, by contrast, have no cake at all."[46] The inequities between rich and poor districts, the court held, violated the state's equal protection clause; in 1976 in *Serrano II*, it upheld a trial court ruling that the legislature equalize the funding.

Long before the courts were done with *Serrano*, Coons had hoped that the U.S. Supreme Court would eventually find that the kind of wildly unequal tax bases that were at the heart of *Serrano* violated the U.S. Constitution's equal protection clause as well. But in its crucial 1973 ruling in *San Antonio v. Rodriguez*, a case brought by Mexican American parents in the Edgewood School District in San Antonio, the court overturned lower federal courts that, in finding impermissible disparities in funding, had ruled for the parents.

The circumstances in Edgewood were almost identical to those in California. The district's tax base was so low that even a high local tax rate generated only $356 per student. In neighboring (and mostly Anglo) Alamo Heights, a lower tax rate yielded $600 per student. But in its 5–4 decision, the Supreme Court ruled that education was not a right guaranteed by the Constitution.[47] "Texas virtually concedes," wrote Justice Lewis Powell for the majority, "that its historically rooted dual system of financing education could not withstand the strict judicial scrutiny that this Court has found appropriate in reviewing legislative judgments that interfere with fundamental constitutional rights or that involve suspect classifications."

Powell, echoing *Brown*, acknowledged the "importance of education to our democratic society. It is required in the performance of our most basic public responsibilities, even service in the armed forces. It is the very foundation of good citizenship."[48] But then, paradoxically, he contended that the court had "no indication that the present levels of educational expenditures in Texas provide an education that falls short. . . . The Equal Protection Clause does not require absolute equality or precisely equal advantages." Given the huge differences between the opportunities offered affluent children and those tendered to the children of the Edgewood parents, that phrase "absolute equality" was the euphemism of the year.

That threw the struggle back into the states, as Justice Thurgood Marshall predicted in his angry dissent, which is where it's remained ever since. In California, where the state supreme court had decided *Serrano I* on both state and federal equal protection rights, it now reaffirmed the decision solely on state grounds. "I wish we'd been more involved in *Rodriguez*," Coons said later. If he and his colleagues had been allowed to handle the Supreme Court case, he believed, they might have won. All he would have needed was one more justice. But, judging from Powell's opinion, it's also apparent that the Court was extremely reluctant to wade into the state and local school finance morass that a judgment favoring the Edgewood parents would have entailed. "This case," Powell had written, "involves the most persistent and difficult questions of educational policy, [an] area in which this Court's lack of specialized knowledge and experience counsels against premature interference with the informed judgment made at the state and local levels."[49] The court, despite the hopes that it raised with *Brown*, had no wish to get into this thicket.

Even at the time of *Serrano I,* there were questions about the assumption that most poor children necessarily lived in low-wealth districts (and conversely, of course, that high-wealth districts provided great schools for their poor students). More generally, there were warnings that meddling with the local property tax and thus local control could create as many problems as it solved. In 1977, following *Serrano II,* the California legislature, seeking to comply by equalizing per-pupil spending, passed a bill that effectively discouraged property-tax-based revenue increases in high-wealth districts and that sought gradually to raise state aid to poor districts. But in 1978, before the process could get fully under way—and in part perhaps because of the *Serrano* reforms—California voters overwhelmingly approved Proposition 13, which rolled back local tax assessments, allowing them to increase only when property was sold, and capped the tax rate at

1 percent of that reduced value. Overnight, therefore, the state became the major source of school funding—depending on how one views it, the only source—and thus an increasingly dominant power in all school policy decisions.[50]

That made it fairly easy to equalize California's school spending, as *Serrano* required, but instead of leveling it up, it was effectively leveled down, and dramatically so, sinking from the top ten among the states in the 1960s to the bottom ten thirty years later, well below the national average and pathetically low against the other major states. In the late 1990s, when California was spending under $6,000 a child, New York and New Jersey were spending upward of $9,000. The results were the largest class sizes in the country; deep cuts in counseling staffs, nurses, and music and arts programs; and in many districts, including the suburbs, rotting buildings and overcrowded classrooms graced by little except emergency maintenance.[51]

Nonetheless, equity became the dominant theme of school reform in the 1970s and early 1980s. In 1984, a decade after their loss in the Supreme Court, the Edgewood parents, backed by the Mexican American Legal Defense and Education Fund and the San Antonio–based Intercultural Development Research Association, returned to court. Using the state constitution's education clause to attack the blatant inequities in school funding, they waged an eleven-year battle in the state courts that one observer called "judicial purgatory." Along the way, however, they won a series of decisions, including four state supreme court rulings, which slowly forced a reluctant and notoriously parsimonious Texas legislature to adopt a reform plan that includes, among other things, the recapture of local property tax revenues from Texas's eighty-four most affluent districts for redistribution in poor districts.[52]

Although the court ruled that Texas violated constitutional provisions that it maintain an "efficient system" of public schools—what Texas had, the court said, "can only charitably be called a 'system' "—the justices were primarily addressing the inequities in local tax wealth and unequal access of poor districts to revenues. (One commentator called it "equity plus.") Similar suits, generally based on state equal protection grounds, were successfully brought in Connecticut, Kansas, Montana, New Mexico, Tennessee, and a number of other states. But according to New York's Campaign for Fiscal Equity, in about two-thirds of the cases the states rebuffed those attacks.[53] In at least one, Minnesota, plaintiffs lost in the state supreme court (in 1993) after they were forced to concede that the state's funding was equally distributed and provided enough for an adequate education.[54]

But the shortcomings of Texas-type shifts of school funds from rich to poor districts slowly became apparent. In the affluent suburban high schools of Dallas, for example, rising costs, property tax caps, and state-mandated redistribution of revenues to poor districts have forced major program cuts and heavier teaching loads (and thus less opportunity for teachers to read and discuss student work). The students will probably survive, but the strategy invites political backlash from those with the clout to be heard. In 2001, the high-property-wealth districts filed suit challenging the cap on local tax rates. The trial court dismissed the case, but it's hard to imagine that the pressure will diminish. Worse, it's an awful symbol: Does the system really have to deny the best to some students in order to be adequate for others?[55]

Because such problems began to demonstrate the problems of equity, the emphasis has shifted from equity to adequacy—that vague and stultifying label whose origins no one knows and which survives only because no one has managed to think of any other. Instead of trying to equalize spending and leaving school resources to the political sausage machine in the annual budget fight and to the vicissitudes of state revenues, one must determine what resources are required to educate each child—teachers, books, buildings, labs, class size, social services—and calculate funding requirements accordingly. Since the question of what resources are required is hardly an easy one to answer, since higher funding is in no way a guarantee of good schools, and since the needs vary according to the circumstances of different children—poor children, gifted children, children who speak little English, disabled children, children with learning handicaps—the calculations become more complicated still.

But it was precisely those questions that the fiscal neutrality mandated by equity decisions had left unadressed. As the Campaign for Fiscal Equity's Michael Rebell said, equity "finessed the critical issue of educational need. [It] provided a judicially manageable standard only because it avoided dealing with the complexities at the core of the issue—how to assure an adequate level of education for all students and especially those with distinctive educational needs."[56] Urban districts faced higher costs, not only because they were expensive places to live but because they tended to have more at-risk children and had to provide social services that more affluent places didn't need or provided from other sources. In some places, moreover, the failure to educate children depended less on inequities in the tax base than on local policy choices, or on the kind of mismanagement and corruption that afflicted parts of the New York City school system in the 1980s and 1990s and afflicts a great many others still. In most districts, the least experienced and least qualified teachers (and thus the lowest paid) were disproportionately concentrated in the schools serving the poorest children with the most severe social and educational problems.

Thus the intradistrict disparities, as University of Washington researchers Roza and Miles concluded, could be as great as those between districts. In their studies (cited earlier) in Seattle, Cincinnati, and Houston, they found that because of the differences in teacher qualifications and pay, per-pupil expenditures in different schools ranged from $4,000 to $10,000, with the gap almost always favoring the schools with the more affluent students.[57] Although there's a nascent movement to focus on student-level or school-level equity, there's yet far too little data to follow it through.[58] And since the largest inequities were among states, not within the states—even between neighboring states such as New Hampshire and Vermont, or Colorado and Utah—real inequities can never be resolved by state-level campaigns to reduce the effects of different assessed property values in different districts.

But where lawyers (representing children and parents, or school districts) have succeeded in getting judges to follow Kentucky down the adequacy road, as they now have in more than a dozen states, equity assumes a different meaning, becoming at most a test of how well various groups of children are served and not an end in itself.[59] In some states, judges are requiring more than dollar equality for disadvantaged children. In some, the courts, while rejecting equity claims, have all but invited adequacy suits in their place. In 2000, for example, the Wisconsin supreme court (in *Vincent v. Voight*) agreed that, in an extensive litany of other problems, there were enormous disparities in school resources. Low revenues in poor districts

> resulted in increased class size with classes sometimes taught in partially condemned buildings, basements, storage rooms, hallways, auditorium stages, unused shower facilities elevator shafts and janitorial closets.... Maintenance of facilities is often delayed, resulting in leaking roofs, antiquated heating and cooling systems, inadequate lighting and water running through the walls. Furthermore, the circuit court found that in some districts textbooks are outdated and a lack of options in advanced math, science, electives, computer technology and extracurricular activities exists.[60]

Nonetheless, in a decision reflecting a sharply divided and troubled court, the justices held that the evidence presented by lawyers for the long list of students, parents, taxpayers, school boards, and others who were named as plaintiffs in the case, "however meticulously gathered, fails to demonstrate that any children lack a basic education in any school district. Merely showing disparity of the financial resources among school districts is not enough in this state to prove a lack of equal opportunity for a sound basic education." But Justice N. Patrick Crooks, writing for the majority, also launched into an extensive discussion of adequacy "as an alternative way to analyze school finance systems because previous decisions centered on equality have not lessened the disparity between school districts ... that will equaliz[e] outcomes, not merely inputs."[61]

He then went on to spell out an ambitious list of skills and attributes for which the state was supposed to provide learning opportunities: proficiency in mathematics, science, reading and writing, geography and history; instruction in music and the arts, health, physical education, and foreign languages. In doing so, moreover, it needed to take into account the special needs of disabled students, economically disadvantaged students, and students with limited English-language skills.[62] Amazingly, the court concluded that the legislature provided all that and that the state system thus "passed constitutional

muster." But in its lengthy discussion of adequacy, its passing reference to the apparent failure of equity decisions to improve the lot of
many students in other states, and that list of state responsibilities,
the court seemed to lay down a marker for the future.

But far and away the most important driver of the adequacy strategy in the past decade has been the states' own aggressive policies in
setting higher academic standards, defining the general outlines of
curricula, restricting so-called social promotion, and mandating high-
stakes tests on which a lot rides for both teachers and students, including high school exit exams that students have to pass in order to
graduate.[65] New York now requires all students to pass the Regents
exams in the major academic subjects that had once been taken only
by those intending to go to four-year colleges. In many other states,
tests also became a standard, and often the only standard, for accountability systems to rate schools; teachers and principals in high-
performing schools are rewarded with salary bonuses, and schools that
fail to make the state standard are sanctioned. And since, in an effort
to make sure minorities weren't neglected, schools in states such as
Texas and California were rated not just on annual improvements for
the school population as a whole but for individual subgroups—African Americans, Latinos, poor children, children with limited English
proficiency, handicapped children—the pressure was even greater. In
Florida, Governor Jeb Bush and the legislature created a voucher
system (overturned by a state trial court in August 2002 as a violation
of the Florida constitution's ban on tax support for religious institutions, and now on appeal) that permitted students in the state's lowest-
performing schools to attend any other school, public or private, at
public expense.

In his presidential campaign in 2000, Jeb's brother George W. Bush
proposed a similar plan for the nation as a whole. Because of stiff
opposition from Democrats, his education bill, the No Child Left Behind Act (NCLB), passed by Congress in December 2001 and signed
by the president in January 2002, has no voucher provisions for private school. But it does require local school authorities to allow children in the worst-performing schools—again measured by test scores,
now mandatory under NCLB—to transfer to any other public school
and to pay for the necessary transportation. The huge problems of

defining and implementing that mandate became clear almost from the moment the bill was signed. What about students who want to attend good schools that are already full? What about the costs of transportation and the conflicting requirements of long-standing legal desegregation agreements? What about the principle that neighborhood children should have priority? But the pressure it creates is real enough.[64]

Among the most effective figures articulating the test-resources link has been Kati Haycock, director of the Education Trust in Washington, D.C., who, unlike many other liberal school reformers, understood the connection and its political importance. The tests, as much as anything, have brought attention to the need for better teachers and resources, especially in our worst schools, and helped in "dispelling the myth"—the phrase is an Education Trust refrain—that poor and minority children can't learn and that their schools are doomed to fail.[65] Accountability programs such as the one in Texas, in basing rewards and sanctions not merely on average performance in every school but on the progress of every major subgroup, ethnic and economic, have at last brought the system's attention to the education of the Latinos and blacks that the schools had so long neglected. While many people in the civil rights movement attacked TAAS (TEXAS ASSESSMENT of ACADEMIC SKILLS), which until its replacement in 2002 had been Texas's testing system—The Mexican American Legal Defense and Education Fund (MALDEF) had unsuccessfully challenged it in federal court—Haycock cheered it. A lot of things about TAAS were dubious—critics charged that some schools encouraged low-performing students to skip the tests or drop out altogether—but all through the 1990s, Texas reported significantly improved scores, especially for Latinos and blacks, both on its own tests and on the generally respected National Assessment of Educational Progress (NAEP). Haycock thought she knew not only why the scores were up but also how such data could be used to get more for the children who needed it most.[66]

The joining of conservative educational practice to liberal objectives is almost entirely new and still widely misunderstood. Haycock's col-

league Russlynn Ali, who worked both for Marian Wright Edelman
at the Children's Defense Fund and with a firm of civil rights lawyers
in Los Angeles and who now runs the Education Trust's West Coast
programs, says the frontier of civil rights is now education—it's the
real arena in the battle to secure equal rights. Ali says she's distressed
that the groups she feels closest to still don't get it. Some, acting in
the belief that higher standards and tougher tests are at best mis-
guided, at worst yet another trick to discriminate, and at an extreme
a plot to justify the breakup of public education altogether, vehemently resist them.

The two sides—the conservatives of objective testing, phonics,
tough demands, and direct instruction; the liberals of "authentic assessment," whole language, and exploratory learning—are not likely
to end the fight. It's been going on for a century, often in the same
terms, and, in reflecting the ambivalence in America's own values
between uncompromising requirements and perennial opportunity, is
probably part of our psyche. But at least at the edges, they've drifted
together. It was more than political cynicism that led George W. Bush
to purloin Marian Wright Edelman's lovely phrase, "Leave no child
behind," now transposed to "No child left behind," for his own campaign and, later, for NCLB, his big education bill. He had wanted
some limited vouchers, but his own proclamation of success (without
vouchers) in Texas, exaggerated though it was, and the stout resistance of congressional Democrats frustrated that effort.

But stripped of vouchers, NCLB had two highly visible liberals as
co-sponsors, Senator Edward Kennedy of Massachusetts and Representative George Miller, a labor Democrat from Martinez, California,
and was supported by countless other Democrats. Its many parts included not only the requirement, cited earlier, that any low-
performing school that did not improve in meeting its state's standards
had to allow its students to transfer to a better school and to pay for
their transportation and that by 2005–6 every teacher in a district
getting federal Title I money be "highly qualified." It also required
all states to test every child between grades 3 and 8, and provided
$1.5 billion in additional Title I funding for high-poverty schools, as
well as additional funds to train (and retrain) teachers in the teaching
of reading. More important, it targeted the Title I money more di-

rectly toward poor children, thus reducing the widespread tendency among districts to use it as a form of general aid, and it required that the scores of all major groups of minority students be included in school performance reports. Under the NCLB rules, a school could not succeed without attention to blacks, Latinos, and the poor. The administration, much to its liberal supporters' subsequent frustration, didn't appropriate nearly as much money as necessary to meet the standards it was setting. But it is on such a combination of testing, standards, and resources—the fusion of conservative tactic with liberal purpose—that the future of the adequacy movement is likely to rest. "No other developed country," said the liberal Education Trust in its subsequent defense of the act, "allows family wealth to be more predictive of educational achievement than America. By the end of high school, African American and Latino students have the same reading and math skills as white students at the end of middle school. But these achievement gaps are not inevitable."[67]

The link between accountability and adequacy should have been clear from the start—if the states are making schools and students accountable, why isn't it equally imperative that states also provide the resources to enable them to meet the standards?—but only in the past few years has it started to come clear. Accountability, said a legislative committee in California in a remarkably candid (but so far largely unimplemented) declaration, should be a two-way street, not just imposed from the top down but placing concomitant requirements on the people who impose them. Although the language varies, virtually all states, with their historic faith in public education, have constitutional provisions requiring the legislature, in the most common phrase, to maintain a "thorough and efficient" system of public schools, or "a system of free common schools" or an "ample education."[68] Those mandates have become the constitutional foundations on which the legal cases rest.

Adding force to the specific state constitutional provisions is the long-standing principle of "opportunity to learn," which goes back at least to 1979, when a federal appellate court, in *Debra P. v. Turlington*, ruled that the state of Florida had to give students enough notice and time to learn the material on which its high-stakes graduation tests were based. In 1979, when the decision was handed down, 20 percent of black students failed. (Less than 2 percent of whites failed.) Many had begun in segregated schools that, the court said, "were inferior in their physical facilities, course offerings, instructional materials, and equipment.... [They] created an atmosphere which was not as conducive to learning as that found in white schools [and] constituted a serious impairment to Plaintiffs' ability to learn, especially in the early grades which most educators view as a formative stage in intellectual development."[69]

More important, the state had given teachers and schools only a few months' notice of the standards on which the test was based. Before that, the court noted, the state had no testing program and no systematic way to determine who needed remediation in what way. A state task force had found that:

> at the eleventh hour and with virtually no warning, these students were told that the requirements for graduation had been changed. They were suddenly required to pass a test constructed under the pressure of time and covering content that was presumed to be elementary but that their schools may or may not have taught them recently, well, or perhaps at all.

Thus, said the court, they "were informed of a requirement concerning skills which, if taught, should have been taught in grades they had long since completed." The court gave the state four years to get its act together. It could use the test to focus remedial programs but not as a basis for denying diplomas.[70]

The *Debra P.* decision did not make public education into a right under the U.S. Constitution any more than *Rodriguez* did. A subsequent attempt to overturn Texas's state testing program failed when a federal judge ruled that, notwithstanding differences in school resources, the state had provided ample opportunities for students to learn the material on which they were tested.[71] But the decision did give opportunity-to-learn principles a visibility and legal prominence they never had before. Because of them, states are now under constraints to make certain that the standards and curricula necessary to pass their tests are in place and that all concerned know about them well before the test is given—and, of course, to make sure that the tests test only the things children have had the opportunity to learn.

Susan Phillips, who, as both a lawyer and a testing expert, is a widely recognized authority in the field, says that it's doubtful that the federal courts will regard unqualified teachers or shortages of textbooks as sufficiently egregious to constitute denial of equal protection to students in inferior schools who fail to pass some high-stakes test.[72] With the exception of the opportunity-to-learn challenge to Texas's TAAS test (in which Phillips testified for the state, and which the trial court rejected), the *Debra P.* standard hasn't been seriously raised in the adequacy context and, given the increasing conservatism of the Supreme Court, isn't likely to be for many years. Nonetheless, Phillips also says that where a state, for example, doesn't have enough teachers to provide all students the instruction in the algebra that they're to be tested on, or where the schools don't provide opportunities for remediation, there's likely to be a legal problem.[73] Opportunity to learn, both as legal principle and moral imperative, hangs over the adequacy cases like a "brooding omnipresence in the sky."[74]

For now, however, it's the gap between those state constitutional mandates and the educational requirements imposed by state law—and to a considerable extent by the demands of the modern world—that the adequacy strategists, legal, pedagogical, and ethical, are using. In some states, the resources provided poor children—and in a number of places middle-class children as well—are so meager, school conditions so marginal, and outcomes so dismal that the courts hardly require any elaborate standard. At the same time, as Rebell put it, "the extensive educational reform initiatives most states adopted [to meet the challenges of the global economy] provided the courts workable criteria for developing the judicially manageable standards that were necessary to craft practical remedies."[75] Justice Powell in *Rodriguez* had argued that since Texas was providing some minimal level of schooling even for the poorest children, it was not violating their federal equal protection rights. Now, with their new tougher academic demands, the states themselves were repudiating Powell's minimalism.

Still, as Rebell well knew, and as he was to learn again in a crucial New York case where he was the lead co-counsel, some courts could label what the states were formally demanding in their academic prescriptions as "aspirational" standards that, in the view of the judges, were far beyond what the state constitution required.[76] Was adequacy measured by inputs or outcomes? Did it mean a high school diploma and readiness for postsecondary education, or was the equivalent of an eighth-grade education enough? Did everybody have to pass the test? Should every student be prepared for a high-tech job or can the courts be satisfied with something much more modest? Can a person be a thoughtful juror and voter without sophisticated analytical and literary skills?

Coons, for one, thinks that in most places, "adequacy" in the constitutional sense has been reached, and some judges obviously agree with him. And more troubling still, given the general agreement that a student's social and economic circumstances are a major determinant of academic achievement, to what extent should additional money be spent to change those circumstances—through generous housing subsidies, better social services, counseling, health care, recreational opportunities, and all the rest? In Wyoming in 1995, the state supreme court, ruling on adequacy, ordered the legislature to determine what constitutes "a proper educational package" for Wyoming students, determine its cost and then fund it, regardless of political considerations or budgetary problems. In effect, it put school funding first in line in claims for state resources.[77]

Not surprisingly, such questions and the hugely different costs that their varying answers entail have spawned a whole new cottage industry of fiscal experts and consultants: university professors, academic researchers, and former state education officials, as well as countless individual academics, many of them collecting hefty fees doing adequacy studies and testifying as witnesses. In some cases state officials or advocacy groups commission the studies on their own initiative; more often it's governors and legislatures trying to rebuff adequacy lawsuits or attempting to comply with the court judgments they produce.

The experts have contrived different measures of adequacy. One is "econometric," trying to calculate costs according to the presumed (and controversial) relationship between spending and pupil performance; another, developed by James Guthrie of Vanderbilt University and Richard Rothstein of the Economic Policy Institute (and for a time education columnist at the *New York Times*), assembles professional panels of teachers, administrators, and finance experts to look at the requirements set down by courts or legislatures to calculate what every element of an adequate school would cost, from band uniforms and Bunsen burners to teacher salaries—which are themselves subject to almost infinite policy considerations.[78] There's research, for example, that shows that teachers who went to selective colleges requiring relatively high SAT scores make a substantial difference in raising the performance of their own students. But they also earn higher salaries; thus a policy choice to attract such teachers is itself fraught with major budgetary consequences.[79] Another method of calculation is simply using "successful" schools—generally defined as some stratum of schools with high test scores—as models. "The assumption," said John Augenblick of the Denver-based consulting firm of Augenblick and Myers, in a quick summary of the entire adequacy dream, "is that any district should be able to accomplish what some districts do accomplish."[80]

In many cases, the numbers are adjusted for the regional cost of living, even for the climate. What, for example, is the trade-off between the difficulty and dangers of busing children over long distances on icy winter roads in rural Wyoming as against the cost of the smaller classes required if schools are located closer to home? (In the expensive upscale resort town of Jackson, Wyoming, the courts have also awarded the schools, seeking to attract more teachers, a housing cost adjustment. In the Silicon Valley, where even two bedroom bungalows sell for over $700,000, teaching slots go unfilled because there's no place to live.) And of course there are the varying educational and social characteristics of the students to be served. If an average student is weighted as a 1.00, for example, a student from a poor family (generally defined, as in most schoolhouse poverty measures, as a student who qualifies for a free or reduced-price lunch) might be an additional 1.2, meaning that spending for his or her education would be calculated at 2.2 times that of an ordinary student. The courts have carefully avoided using school outcomes as an ultimate measure; the fact that a high percentage of low-income children fail isn't—and can't be—considered conclusive proof that the resources are inadequate. But outcomes are certainly part of the evidence.[81]

Such calculations tend to have relatively large dollar signs attached to them—larger, certainly, than what's currently being spent in most of the affected schools.. In one hypothetical study, two respected scholars in public finance at Syracuse University's Maxwell School calculated that districts with high concentrations of low-income children in New York State would need two or three times as much to educate each child as the affluent suburbs of New York City.[82] And while such numbers have rarely been proposed in practice, the calculations of expert consultants have sometimes been large enough that legislatures haven't been reluctant simply to change the consultants' assumptions.

In 1998, for example, the Ohio legislature, responding to a court decision declaring the state's school financing system unconstitutional, commissioned Augenblick to develop a model based on average spending in the schools that, on the basis of a cluster of measures, fell in the top 5 percent in achievement. On that basis he recommended that the state set a "foundation" of $4,269 per pupil per year— essentially the sum of what would be raised by a minimum local tax rate plus the state's contribution. (If a district wanted to tax itself at a higher rate, it could do so). The legislature then determined how much it wanted to spend—$3,851 a year, barely above the state's commitment at the time, and a figure that happened to be precisely 90 percent of Augenblick's number, which some regarded as already too low—and simply changed the formula to make things come out right. "Although we recognize that deciding what methodology to adopt is a policy determination," said the Ohio supreme court, "we are perplexed by the General Assembly's actions of enlisting an expert in the area of school financing and then, with no adequate explanation, altering his method." The answer, as the justices surely knew, is that that's the way political budget making has always been done.[83]

At the same time, judges are often frustrated that the experts themselves are unsure. James Guthrie of Vanderbilt, who testifies frequently in school funding suits, says he's often asked how much decent schools would cost. When he starts to talk about the complexities, he says, judges jump in: "You mean you don't know?" "Applying the adequacy standard to school finance," said a National Research Council Commission report, "is at present an art, not a science." To minimize misuse, there has to be "appropriate recognition of the need for policy judgments and of the incomplete knowledge about the costs of

an adequate education."[84] Making such judgments still more complicated is that much depends not merely on the amount but on the
way that amount is spent. An increment of a few hundred dollars is
not likely to make any difference if it's distributed in the same proportions as the rest of a district's funds, as indeed it often is. "You
have to triage," said David Gordon, regarded as one of the most
successful superintendents in California—meaning that it's necessary
to concentrate new money where it will be most effective. Just pouring it into the general pot brings minimal results at best. Further
complicating things is the fact that constitutional adequacy can't be
a static number, or one frozen in a nineteenth century three-R's concept, but one that has to be adjusted constantly as needs and demands
change.

Given the complexities of determining adequacy standards, both
advocates and courts sometimes use equity and adequacy as reciprocal
measures, the one a surrogate for the other. Even as a focus on adequacy has replaced equity, and as constitutional mandates that states
support "thorough and efficient" systems of common schools have
replaced equal protection as the underlying legal justification, courts
have used equity in funding as a partial standard. In New Jersey, the
court explicitly required the state to fund poor urban districts at the
level at which wealthy suburbs were spending. Even in Ohio, where
the legislature commissioned Augenblick's adequacy study, the court
had focused on equity of inputs rather than on questions about what
it would take to give each student a decent education.[85] Still, as some
legal scholars have pointed out, "the meaning of 'equity' in 'adequacy'
cases is very different—that all children have equitable access to adequate education opportunities." But increasingly the courts have also
begun to accept the proposition that to be truly equitable, spending
for poor and educationally handicapped children may have to be
higher than spending for the average student. More fundamentally,
said Augenblick, with perhaps more optimism than the situation deserves, "the environment has changed. The legislatures don't have to
be prodded anymore." What's more probable is that "despite their
amorphousness," state constitutional provisions on education, as legal
scholars Paul Minorini and Stephen Sugarman said, "could become
truly powerful sources of children's rights."[86]

III

Because they've been in place for more than a decade, and because they became such pervasive national examples, *Rose* and KERA are far and away the best indicators of the difference that fundamental school reform can make. And on some measures, the results are stunning. In 1985–86, just before the suit was filed, Kentucky spent $3,759 per child, forty-eighth among the states and shamefully below the national average ($5,679). A decade later, with its $600 million annual tax increase, it was spending $5,906, thirtieth in the nation, and still below the national average ($6,546) but with a far narrower gap. Measured in constant dollars, American school spending had increased 15 percent during that decade, Kentucky's by 57 percent. Teacher pay increased dramatically, and the huge spending gaps between the richest and the poorest districts were closed—indeed, as noted earlier, on average, the poorer districts now spend slightly more than the richest.[87]

What have those changes bought? KIRIS scores consistently rose from 1993 to 1996, but because KIRIS, the state's original testing system, was replaced after a series of scoring errors and because so much of it came from uncertain measures, there is no reliable set of state test statistics covering the whole period. On the nationally normed CTBS test that's part of the CATS system that replaced KIRIS in 1997, there were significant gains in the primary grades) from the 49th percentile to the 58th percentile in both reading and math between 1997 and 2001, but little notable improvement in the tests given at the end of grades 6 and 9, which hovered around the 50th percentile. Discounting normal year-to-year gains that can be expected as teachers and students become familiar with a test, particularly when schools, looking for the goodies in the accountability system, begin teaching to the test, the numbers are even more modest. The Kentucky Family Foundation, which has been a thorn in the side of the Kentucky reformers ever since KERA was enacted, says even those scores are inflated.[88]

Secondary school dropout rates are similarly inconclusive, declining from 29 percent for the class of 1998, which was in the fourth grade when KERA was enacted, to 27 percent in the KERA era class of

2001.[89] Prichard Committee head Sexton lists some high-poverty Eastern Kentucky schools where scores are extraordinarly high. In 2000, a decade after the passage of KERA, the Millard Hensley School in Magoffin County, where 89 percent of the students qualify for free or reduced-price lunches, was fourth on the state's list of the highest-scoring schools in both fourth-grade reading and fourth-grade science. Frakes School in Bell County, where 92 percent of the students are classified as poor, was eighteenth on the reading list. But the overall pattern makes clear, as Susan Perkins Weston of the Kentucky Association of School Councils put it, that "wealth still matters." Of the twenty elementary schools with the highest overall performance, only one, Bowen in Powell County, had a large proportion of poor children (55 percent). Meanwhile, the lists of the state's worst-performing schools were dominated by high-poverty schools. At the high school level, the association between wealth and high performance was even more pronounced.[90]

On the widely respected NAEP, however, the numbers, as many people in other states have noticed, are much more encouraging. In 1998, Kentucky was tenth in the nation (among forty-four states and territories participating) and among the three or four states that made the highest gains in fourth-grade reading since 1992, the earliest and latest years for which there are state breakdowns, and sixteenth in eighth-grade reading. There were even larger gains in fourth- and eighth-grade math between 1990 and 2000.[91] In an analysis of all seven NAEP tests in math and reading given between 1990 and 1996, David Grissmer and a group of his colleagues at the Rand Corporation listed Kentucky ninth among the states making the greatest gains—not anywhere as large as Texas or North Carolina, but better than 27 other states covered by the study.[92] In fourth- and eighth-grade reading, Kentucky students scored above the national average, itself a remarkable record.

There can't be many people who doubt that the Kentucky school climate has changed and that in most respects things have gotten perceptibly better. "Whatever conclusion one draws about the improved learning that children in Kentucky have experienced as a result of reforms," said Minorini and Sugarman, "it seems clear that opportunities to achieve learning at higher levels are being offered in

areas of the state and to schoolchildren who prior to the reforms were
not receiving such opportunities."[93] Most of the rotting school buildings
of the 1960s—the little Scuddy Schools at the end of the hollows—
have been replaced, and even the better ones have been renovated.
There is more professional development money for teachers and, more
important, every elementary school in which more than 20 percent of
the children are eligible for free or reduced-priced lunches has a Family
Resource Center offering before- and after-school child care, counseling, and health care. Every secondary school with a similar proportion
of poor students has a Youth Service Center offering employment and
mental health counseling, referrals to health services, and after-school
and summer job development programs. Sexton says he no longer
hears complaints about nepotism.[94]

There continues to be widespread criticism of the inability, or
maybe the unwillingness, of the teacher training institutions to adapt,
as there is in many other parts of the country, but Sexton is certain
that the values and attitudes of teachers have changed dramatically—
the accountability system, he says, "makes them focus on results every
day"—and so has classroom practice. But he also acknowledges that
a dozen years after passage he "would have expected things to be
further along. Progress has been slower than we'd hoped."

Worse, the backsliding had begun. The increased school funding
that started so hopefully in the early 1990s was being choked off. In
1995, the legislature cut state taxes by (for Kentucky) a hefty $150
million annually, eliminating 25 percent of the increase approved only
a few years before. And with the recession that began in 2000, cuts
in state funding left the schools in what one paper called "a financial
stranglehold." Teacher salaries, which had been rising toward the
national average, began to slip again, and measures (in the year 2000)
to pay bonuses to teachers willing to work in hard-to-staff schools, to
compensate teacher mentors, and to create an independent standards
commission to oversee the state's recalcitrant schools of education were
voted down. To make things worse, while the legislature mandated
teacher compensation increases in 2002, it appropriated no money to
pay for them. In a telling acknowledgment, Governor Paul Patton
told a group of educators that while "we've achieved relative eco-

nomic equity... we have not yet achieved adequacy."[95] Even landmarks don't last forever.

The group Patton addressed was the same Council for Better Education, the coalition of school districts—now numbering about 140 of the state's 176 districts—that had filed the original Kentucky suit. In 2002, Moreland, who had been with CBE from the beginning and later became its executive director, reactivated it. In the years following the passage of KERA, he said, the group had "no real mission." But by 2002 it clearly did. "The idea of adequacy is woven throughout the 1989 Supreme Court decision," he said, "but until now, no one has defined adequacy as it relates to the funding mechanism."[96] Although there was no serious talk about another suit, CBE hired Deborah Versteggen, a school finance expert at the University of Virginia, to do an adequacy study in Kentucky to determine how much an adequate education would cost, and what it would take to meet a set of proficiency targets the state has set for itself. That, they hoped, would give them new ammunition when the legislature took up its next biennial budget in 2004. The state, meanwhile, hired its own experts to do a parallel study, also aimed at the 2004 session.

CBE's precipitating complaint may have been as much about the schools' recently shrinking share of the state pie as it was about adequacy. In 1995 the schools got 44.3 percent of the state's budget; by 2001, that had declined to 39.6 percent. "We've seen our market share erode over the years," Moreland told a Kentucky reporter.[97] And so in some respects, it appears as if the Kentucky struggle has come full circle. Still, no one claims that anything is remotely like what it was in the 1980s—for the moment, at least, the basic principle is settled. The growth in funding has tapered off, as Sexton says, but at a much higher plane, and services are being offered to children who never had them before. And by most measures outcomes have improved along with it. The argument is about how much, not about whether. Schools are the priority that the legislature, even in the worst of times, is trying to protect. "I feel blessed," Moreland said. "I'm so proud of my role in this."

CHAPTER THREE

"A Right to the Privilege of Education"

I. California: "To Shock the Conscience"

When Mark Rosenbaum, the general counsel of the American Civil Liberties Union of Southern California, joined with a half-dozen other civil rights organizations to sue the state of California, he hoped— and maybe halfway expected—that the state would negotiate and try to settle out of court. The case, *Williams v. California*, filed on May 17, 2000, the anniversary of the *Brown* decision, focused on the long and familiar recital of educational negligence that by then had become as banal as it was offensive. It asked the court to order relief that was as sweeping as it was brief: provide all necessary books and materials to all students; repair and maintain facilities "and keep them habitable for use at all times public schools are in session; provide sufficient numbers of qualified credentialed teachers who can deliver instruction capable of enabling students to achieve State standards [and] provide equal educational opportunity to all California public school children."[1]

Subsequently, Rosenbaum and his colleagues also asked the court to order the state to "establish baseline standards to constitute a floor of minimal constitutional conditions and tools essential for education; establish a system of statewide accountability whereby the state (1) regularly informs itself of the absence of essential learning tools and conditions and (2) ensures the repair or improvement of those conditions and supplies those tools in a timely manner; and provide basic educational necessities to all California public school children." As it was, the state didn't even have data on whether students had books.[2]

Under the specifics of the complaint, there lay a broader, though unstated, set of circumstances. For the prior two decades, California had been well below average in the nation in its per-pupil spending and dead last among the major industrial states. That made the stress particularly acute in a state with a large percentage of disadvantaged students, including the 25 percent of all students whose native language was something other than English. Ever since the early 1990s, when state-by-state comparisons first became available, its academic achievement in math and reading, as measured by the National Assessment of Educational Progress (NAEP), was near the bottom among the states, even in interstate comparisons of the same ethnic groups. Latinos in California scored significantly lower than Latinos in Texas; African Americans in California scored lower than those in Texas. A major Rand Corporation study concluded that those differences were largely attributable to California's larger classes, lower preschool and kindergarten participation, higher teacher turnover, and inferior classroom materials and other resources for teaching.[3]

Rosenbaum and Jack Londen, his co-counsel from the San Francisco law firm of Morrison & Foerster, knew well enough that the filthy toilets and leaky roofs, sweltering classrooms (sometimes said to exceed 100 degrees), falling ceiling tiles, and schoolhouse vermin that led the list of particulars in the ACLU's press releases (along with photos of same) were not the heart of the state's mistreatment of its students, particularly the long array of poor and minority students who were named as the primary plaintiffs. But the rats and the putrid facilities were bold attention getters for both judges and the media—"appalling conditions" so repulsive or acts so egregious that they anger the public and, in the courts' common phrase, "shock the conscience." ("Dumbing things down for judges," someone said.) Rosenbaum would put it another way: this, he said, "is the Mississippification of California schools, a separate but unequal system for the have-nots that would make Linda Brown shudder."[4] The state, he would say, had more rigorous standards for barber colleges, restaurants, and traffic schools. In the public schools, "the buck is stopping nowhere."[5]

Among the defendants were Delaine Eastin, then the state's independently elected superintendent of public instruction; the State Department of Education, and the State Board of Education, whose members are appointed by the governor. Significantly, the suit didn't name Governor Gray Davis in the hope that if California's famously controlling chief executive wasn't named as a defendant, he might be more willing to negotiate rather than litigate. (In 1999, a few months after he was elected, Davis, chafing at some minor act of legislative noncooperation, had called on the lawmakers to get out of his way because it was the job of the legislature "to implement my vision.") Rosenbaum and Londen also understood that ultimately the remedies would have to come primarily from the political system; the courts could not conjure up the resources, raise taxes, police the schools, or restructure the system to make it serve children as they deserved to be.

Rosenbaum had attacked the schools' failure to provide adequate educational resources for poor and minority students before, most recently in a suit on behalf of a group of minority students charging that in offering only a small selection of Advanced Placement courses, their schools put them at serious disadvantage vis-à-vis students from more favored schools. AP courses, as the name implied, had been designed to allow college students to satisfy some freshman-year course requirements and thus get a leg up in their university careers. In the high schools that offered them in abundance, they usually brought a whole lot of other resources: better teachers, better labs and textbooks, better school libraries. More specifically, the University of California (UC) and other colleges also added a premium to grades earned in AP courses, a grade of 4.0 (an A) would become a grade of 4.5 or even 5.0 in an AP course. Because of that system, thousands of UC applicants had grade point averages of over 4.0. Since 1995, when the UC Regents prohibited race preferences in UC admissions, and 1996, when the voters passed Proposition 209 banning affirmative action in all state operations, California, in effect, had an officially race-blind policy. Everybody was to compete on a level playing field, but the field of course wasn't entirely level. Catch-22.

The AP suit, which never went to trial, turned out to be just a tune-up for *Williams*. Nonetheless, it prompted the state to act. In his next state-of-the state address, Governor Davis promised (but never delivered) funding to make certain that every California high school would offer at least four AP courses. As a solution, it was likely to be as ineffective as it was inelegant, but it indicated that the governor was listening and thus reinforced Rosenbaum's hope that Davis would be at least minimally flexible.

A significant number of senior people inside the California State Department of Education who understood that ultimately the issue would have to be negotiated, not litigated, privately shared Rosenbaum's hope. Eastin's own speeches were riddled with calls for better teachers, for more computers, for relief of overcrowding, for billions in new facilities. More important, the legislature was responsive: in the years just before the suit was filed, it had begun to appropriate substantial chunks of new money for both textbooks and school libraries. The voters, for their part, had shown a growing willingness to pass state school construction bonds to deal with California's decrepit and overcrowded school facilities. There was also a fair chance that in November 2000 they would approve a constitutional amendment lowering the margin required to pass local school bonds from two-thirds to 55 percent. (They eventually did.) The governor, therefore, could easily have responded that the state was already doing a great deal and with time might mitigate, if not eliminate, the inadequacies.

Davis himself had staked his governorship on reforming and improving the schools; education, he'd said when he ran in 1998, was to be his "number one, number two, and number three priority." And once in office he quickly pushed through an array of school reform measures: an elaborate plan to hold schools accountable for test scores, rewarding those that did well and assisting (and, if necessary, punishing) those that did not; new money for teacher training; plus a number of other measures. Meanwhile, the University of California, acting on its own initiative, had begun to change admission requirements to make it more accessible to poor and minority students after Proposition 209 passed. It was now admitting the top 4 percent of the graduates of every California public high school, regardless of SAT

scores, which had always been a major barrier to poor and minority
students. Just a few months before, UC president Richard Atkinson
had also gotten front-page attention when he attacked the SAT itself
as an unfair distortion of the educational process, making it ever more
likely that there would be still more fundamental changes in UC
admission and thus more access for minority students.[6] Surely all that
could, at the very least, be brought to the negotiating table as evidence
of good faith. "The governor," said Rosenbaum, "could have been a
hero."

But that's not what Davis did. Instead of negotiating, he chose to
fight the kids with the biggest weapons he could find. Under normal
circumstances, the state attorney general would have handled such a
case—Attorney General Bill Lockyer estimated it would cost about
$105 an hour for his office to do it, cheap by any standards for such
litigation—assuming the state chose to fight at all. Under normal
circumstances, Eastin would at least have been consulted. But rather
than coming to the table or engaging in a holding action, Davis hired
O'Melveny & Myers, an old and very tough Los Angeles law firm
with strong political links to the Democrats through former Secretary
of State Warren Christopher, who is a senior partner, and others. And
to head the O'Melveny legal team, Davis got John Daum, generally
regarded as one of the most combative litigators around—a "legal
attack dog," somebody called him—at $325 an hour for Daum and
each of the eight other lawyers who worked on the case. That was a
lot less than the firm's regular fee, but three times what it would
have cost the state if the attorney general's office had handled it.
Lockyer himself sent a letter to the governor pointedly disagreeing
"that the breadth and complexity of this matter require retention of
a private law firm with expertise in education law, but we will accede
to the governor's wishes."[7]

Expertise in education law wasn't what Davis was after. But if
Davis wanted to beat down the plaintiffs, O'Melveny & Myers were
probably worth every penny the state was paying. Daum, who had
represented—indeed, still represented—Exxon in the multibillion-
dollar *Exxon Valdez* oil spill case, was among other things a master
of legal delay, a common tactic when lawyers for deep-pockets corporations face underfunded adversaries. And with the state treasury

paying the bills, O'Melveny had very deep pockets behind it: it could afford to try to drag things out. In 2000–2, the first two years of the contract, the state paid the O'Melveny & Myers lawyers $10 million. For 2002–3 it had budgeted another $3 million.[8] On the other side, Morrison & Foerster, a firm with a long association with liberal causes, was working *pro bono* on the school suit—indeed, it was financing most of the plaintiffs' case.

The governor's basic position was simple: Rosenbaum and his colleagues were suing the wrong people. The long list of problems alleged in the case was not the state's responsibility. The state was handing out the money to the locals, and so if there were no books or lab equipment or if buildings were shabby, that was the responsibility of the districts. What was the state supposed to do, asked John Mockler, who was the governor's education secretary when the suit was filed, inspect every toilet in every one of the state's eight thousand schools?[9] Given Davis's push for a centralized accountability system, it was a strange argument for his people to make. "We've had local control of schools for 50 years," the governor had told *Washington Post* columnist David Broder soon after he took office in 1999, "and it's been an abject failure. When you have an earthquake or a natural disaster, people expect the state to intervene. Well, we have a disaster in our schools."[10] But that was now forgotten. And just to make sure that the districts didn't get too cozy with the *Williams* lawyers, Davis and Daum filed a cross complaint, a suit against the districts that had been named in the ACLU complaint that reiterated the same list of failures that the ACLU had charged the state with. San Francisco Superior Court judge Peter J. Busch, himself a new Davis appointee—this was his first big case—quickly put the cross complaint on hold, but it effectively neutralized the districts. Anything they said or did that could help the *Williams* plaintiffs might eventually be turned against them. "The districts," Rosenbaum said, "are freaked out."[11]

Daum, pressing the state's position in pretrial motions, argued that Rosenbaum and colleagues, rather than pursuing the ample administrative remedies professedly available to them in the districts, wanted "to proceed with a massive lawsuit whose apparent objective is to overturn the existing system of public education in California

and replace it with a system administered by platoons of lawyers."
More centrally, he contended that under the California constitution
and *Butt v. California*, the governing case, the state was not accountable for the mismanagement of local districts unless it was so severe
that "the actual quality of the educational program of a given district,
'viewed as a whole,' fell 'fundamentally' below prevailing standards,
after giving effect to the deference constitutionally required for 'local
programs, philosophies, and conditions.' "[12]

Butt arose in 1991 after the school district in the East Bay industrial
city of Richmond, having mismanaged itself into penury, was on the
verge of shutting down all its schools six weeks before the end of the
spring term. The state contended that while that was unfortunate, it
had no responsibility to keep them open: it had provided equal funding, and if the Richmond schools misappropriated the money, that
was their fault. Parents sued, won a temporary order to keep the
schools running, and, in a decision handed down in 1992, a very
conservative California Supreme Court unanimously agreed with
them. "The legislative decision to emphasize local administration,"
wrote Justice Marvin Baxter for the court, "does not end the State's
constitutional responsibility for basic equality in the operation of its
common school system. Nor does disagreement with the fiscal practices of a local district outweigh the rights of its blameless students
to basic educational equality."[13]

Judge Busch soon rejected Daum's arguments. *Williams*, he ruled,
was about "the State's system of oversight and that system's alleged
deficiencies and failures." "That the state has chosen to carry out
certain of its obligations through local school districts," he said, citing
Butt, "does not absolve the State of its ultimate responsibility."[14] (How
do you seek administrative remedies from a dysfunctional district,
Rosenbaum asked, much less sue it?) Busch also agreed that *Williams*
should be a class-action case, which meant that the original sixty-
some student plaintiffs had now grown to over a million.

But that, of course, was just the start of a case that may not be
finally resolved for years, and Daum immediately set to work to de-
construct it. He attacked the validity of the particulars in the students'
affidavits, first in his legal motions and then in a string of depositions.

The statement of Olivia Saunders, a seventh grader, that "we can only use our social studies textbooks in class [because] there are only enough books for one class set, which is why we cannot take any books home," was "factually unsupported and conclusory." And seventh grader Silas Moultrie's statement that his books were "raggedy" and "real old" was "vague and ambiguous"—and how did he know that it was because of the lack of books that his class didn't get any homework? Seventh grader Elly Rodrigues's worry that because she never had homework in the classes without books to take home—"I will not be able to keep up with my school work," she'd said in her affidavit—was irrelevant and immaterial to the case. Her statement that "part of learning is being able to work at home and to understand on your own what is taught in class" was "unqualified expert opinion."[15]

Once the discovery phase of the case started and depositions began to be taken, the questioning became more surreal. There was an attempt at the circular rationale—yet another Catch-22—that often students didn't need to take textbooks home since teachers weren't assigning homework anyway (which in many cases was the result of the teachers not having books in the first place). If there weren't any books to take home, how did Watsonville High School senior Manuel Ortiz do homework? (Answer: by reviewing what he'd already done in class. Often, in fact, homework and class work were identical.)[16] Since Alondra Jones had been admitted to all those colleges, how was she hurt by the subs, the lack of books, and all the other alleged failures of Balboa High School? Did eleven-year-old Carlos Ramirez, a fifth grader at San Francisco's Bryant School, know anything about his role in the *Williams* suit or what the case was about?

Well, yes, he knew it was to make the schools better: "They can give us more books."

And who, asked O'Melveny lawyer Michael T. Rosenthal, are "they"? And what else did Carlos think might make the schools better?

A. They can fix the bathrooms and the yard, more balls.
Q. Do you know who the "they" you're referring to is?

A. No. . . .

Q. Are you aware that this action was filed as a class action?

A. No.

Q. Do you know what a class action is?

A. No.

Q. Do you know what the definition of the proposed class in this action is?

A. No.

Q. Do you know what a class representative is?

A. No.

Q. Do you know if you are a class representative in this action?

A. No.

Q. Do you know what your responsibilities are as a class representative?

A. No.

Q. Do you know if you have any duties to members of the proposed class?

A. No. . . .

Q. Are you being paid to be a class representative in this action?

A. I don't know.

Q. Do you know that you may be held liable for costs in connection with this action? Do you know you may have to pay costs in connection with this action?

A. I don't know.

Q. Do you know if you have any duty to supervise your attorneys in this action? Can you tell me if you've been supervising your attorneys in any way in connection with this case?

A. No.

Q. You have not been?

A. No.

Q. Approximately how often do you speak with your attorneys about this case?

A. Not a lot.[17]

Again and again, the questions from the governor's lawyers suggested that the students had been manipulated into this suit and had no real idea why they were doing it: why are you involved, who approached you, what do you really know about this case? But the kids knew enough. When O'Melveny attorney Steven LaCombe asked Watsonville High School senior Manuel Ortiz about an ACLU press conference he'd attended when the suit was filed—who was there, whom had he talked to, what had he said—he threw it back in his face. "I remember very clearly what one of the kids was complaining about, because that's what really gets me upset about school conditions. Because that little kid he said he wanted to be a math teacher but he didn't even have a math book. So how can they be teachers if they don't even get math books for them?"

Ortiz had talked to the reporters at the press conference about school conditions, "and I told them, 'Doesn't the State of California care about us?' ... I really want that kid to go and be a math teacher, if that's his dream. If there's kids that want to be astronauts, why should the State of California shatter their dreams? They should help them out with their dreams."[18] The governor's lawyers also appeared to be in pursuit of acknowledgments from students, and sometimes teachers, that despite the lack of books, or the heat or the rats, students were learning. How was Ortiz's education affected by the dirty bathrooms? Didn't Cindy Diego learn anything in those service classes at Fremont, any worthwhile skills? Did she help manage the class, orient new students, operate copying machines, work with computers, use any math skills? (Answer: no, no, no, no, and no. "I don't think it helped me gain any skills at all.")[19] Did the mouse droppings affect Alondra Jones's ability to learn? And how, asked O'Melveny lawyer Michael Rosenthal, did she account for the A's she got in U.S. history, "even though there were a number of unfair conditions in that class?"

"Just because the state failed," she answered, "doesn't mean I have to. The state failed my Spanish class, and I almost failed my Spanish class, too. That's why I got out of my Spanish class. I wasn't about to allow that to happen in my other classes. I simply refused. That's why I'm in the lawsuit."[20] And in ironic tribute to Shane Safir, who had helped stir Alondra Jones's anger and who Alondra described as a person "very qualified to teach anything," she said she'd also learned a lot in Safir's prelaw class, despite what Rosenthal called "these unfair conditions that you told me about." Again and again, Rosenthal and his colleagues elicited descriptions of makeshift arrangements—teachers who bought their own supplies, copied books or swapped texts with other teachers, or traded textbooks for chairs; copies of the *Iliad* and *Hamlet* that suddenly appeared after an unfavorable story about a shortage of books in a local weekly—and of extraordinary teachers who, like Safir, or Mr. Brady, who "is qualified to teach every subject in every class in that school," enabled them to learn. Obviously, she said at another time, "anything is possible if I can get into Berkeley despite going to Balboa."[21]

What might have been most touching about those student-witnesses was how, despite the conditions in their schools, those who had low grades usually believed those grades had been deserved: they blamed themselves. They hadn't worked hard enough, had been absent too often, lacked the needed discipline. The students obviously knew about those conditions—understood, as did Alondra Jones or Manuel Ortiz, that the schools they were forced to attend were sometimes insulting and maybe even abusive, and their testimony left no doubt about their feelings. But with a few exceptions, they could hardly have comprehended the collective impact of those conditions in dampening the spirit of a school. Their very ability to articulate their circumstances and their success, when they had it, in transcending them tended to soften the case their lawyers were trying to make. If things were so bad, why were they so good? Here was a network of forensic veins that Gray Davis's lawyers would mine again and again.

If the state had a team of powerhouse lawyers, so did the plaintiffs—Rosenbaum, Catherine E. Lhamon, and others at the ACLU, who were working for modest cause-attorney wages; Londen, Michael Jacobs, and Leecia Welch at Morrison & Foerster—all of them bankrolled out of the law firm's deep pro bono pockets. By the summer of 2002, the firm had spent $6 million on the case, roughly half of what the state had spent at O'Melveny, but nothing to sneeze at, and there was every sign that it would have to spend a great deal more. If they won, at some point it might get its money back in a settlement or in court-awarded legal fees, but there was no certainty of that. This was no ordinary traffic-accident contingency-fee tort case. Nonetheless, they had no doubt about what they were doing, and were proud of it. "If we don't do this," Londen said, "what *do* we do?" It was in the schools that much of the future of the nation would be determined.

Although the parties, under pressure from Busch, had started meeting with a court-appointed mediator to negotiate some of the issues, which meant that discovery was suspended, neither side expected the talks to resolve the tougher issues, if indeed they resolved any. Thereafter, they would very likely be back in court—not at trial, which almost certainly would not occur until well into 2003, if then, but on discovery, and particularly on the "couple of hundred" depositions that Londen estimated still had to be taken. (Each of those depositions had to be staffed by at least three lawyers, and often several more—one for the plaintiffs, one for the defendants, and one for the nervous local district, sued by Davis in his cross complaint, from which the witness came.) Daum, living up to his reputation as a master of delay, had already suggested in court that the case might require six years of trial preparation and discovery, a schedule that would have elevated *Williams* to the status of a major antitrust case and that would almost certainly be rejected, but a useful negotiating ploy nonetheless. Rosenbaum wanted to have an impact when the present generation of students was still in school, not when their children were being enrolled.[22]

By the end of October 2002, negotiations had broken down, as expected, and they were back in court. Yet now that the clock had started to run again, it would take at least a year to get to trial even under the best of circumstances. There was every chance that the plaintiffs would eventually prevail: Londen, plainly angry at the schoolhouse disparities and inadequacies inflicted on poor kids, expected the judge to be as offended as he was. "It will be difficult for the court," he said, "to go along with this historically honored hypocrisy." But in the summer of 2002, as the lawyers sat around a large conference table at UCLA with a team of economists and education researchers assembled by Jeannie Oakes, director of UCLA's Institute for Democracy, Education, and Access—some forty people in all—there was also a growing appreciation of the difficulties they were facing.

The team, which was developing a set of papers on the myriad aspects of the adequacy issue, included some of the stars of the field. Even though some of them were insistent critics of the state's accountability system, which rested on the results of one set of tests just then being aligned with the state's academic standards, most of them were confident of what the data showed. But on the broader issue of legal and political strategy, the academics were hardly as sure. Does inequity generate outrage? And if, as seemed probable (to quote one of them), "people don't care, how do we transfer the outrage in this room?" Conversely, if they did succeed in persuading parents and voters about how troubled some schools were, would they turn to vouchers? To what extent "can we trust parents to make decisions?" To what extent would a case like this give "the monster in Sacramento" still more power to dominate local schools? There were schools in California that were nothing but portable classrooms, and most of those at the UCLA meeting hated them. But could you even make them an issue when parents would kill to get their kids into a high-achieving school even if it was all portables?

As they met that summer, the negotiations had already lasted longer than they'd expected. Among other things, Daum was demanding that any settlement include a commitment by the plaintiffs to keep students from pursuing this kind of case again for many years. "In return for that," said Londen, "we need something very, very good." Conversely, what remedies could the court impose? There was a good chance that the first remedy from the court would be nothing but an order telling the state "to please do better." In many other states, he knew, the first decision was merely the start of a sort of "judicial dialogue," an "iterative process" with the legislature that, in combination with the appeals that were sure to follow, could take more years.

What, then, were the trade-offs between more flexibility in the negotiations, which got you less but got it faster, and litigation that might get you nothing for years? *Williams* had already had tangible results in many of the named schools. "They're going to dozens of places to fix things," Londen said, which was both good and bad— good for the students where they'd improved things, bad because such ad-hoc fixes, many of them temporary, were like sticking fingers in a dike that was leaking in a thousand places and needed systemic reform, not just patches. (In the fall of 2002, Fremont High in Los Angeles, one of the dark stars of their case, suddenly reported that 87 percent of its teachers were fully qualified.) And, of course, it tended to undercut the specifics of their case, requiring them to find new schools.[23]

And that was only the beginning of the list. "After counsel wins," said economist Stephen Levy, director of the Center for Continuing Study of the California Economy in Palo Alto, "the real struggle begins." Any effective solution will require either "a mind-boggling transfer of money from wealthy schools to poor schools" or new taxes. It also had to be done without taking money from crucial health and welfare programs, which in fact was exactly what Davis, trying to deal with a $24 billion budget deficit, was then doing. Health and welfare programs, to which the voters are relatively indifferent, were being particularly hard hit so that Davis, then in a tough reelection campaign, could say he wasn't cutting education, which was popular.[24] That, said Levy, meant reaching the "hearts and mind of citizens" to persuade them of "the connectiveness of society." It would require showing, as had been done in Kentucky and elsewhere, that earnings and education go up linearly, that substantial benefits accrue from the acquisition of specific skills, and that while disadvantaged kids are likely to benefit more immediately from better education re-sources, even the performance of nondisadvantaged people depends on the skills of their co-workers. It thus required public investment "beyond the tax system we have now."

It meant, in short, a political campaign that necessarily would be as intense and complicated as the litigation, and maybe more so. It also meant, as Londen said (as gently as he could), not getting caught up in the minutiae of ed-research theory. The defense would focus on the question of causality, as indeed it already was doing; if the plaintiffs got "carried away with the separate effects" of the issue, they'd get sliced up so badly that the state would avoid responsibility again. More important, it meant laying aside the whole litany of progressive-educator complaints about the flaws of the existing ac-countability and testing systems. There certainly were reasons for concern, many of them familiar enough: that instead of teaching kids to think and encouraging them to be creative, the accountability sys-tem fostered questionable drill-and-kill teaching practices and cram courses designed mainly to bolster scores, caused schools to neglect things like art and music and higher-order skills that were not tested, and drove more students to drop out. But to pursue those issues was to divert attention and undercut the case they were trying to make.

Londen also pointedly reminded them that they couldn't start arguing with California's Proposition 227, passed by voters in 1998, which sharply restricted bilingual education, much as some of them wanted to. The same was even more emphatically true of the tests, which were a key element in the suit. "If we start impeaching the one tool we have," he said, "we lose the best part of our case"—a remark whose brevity belied its importance, not just in California but as a major element in the politics of equity and adequacy in state after state. It was not simply that the new standards and accountability programs had helped spark the adequacy movement, but that there was a growing understanding among moderate liberals that the best weapon they had for bringing better teachers and schools to low-income children and—in general—for upgrading the schools was those tests. The idea, as Stanford law professor William Koski put it at the UCLA meeting, "is to leverage the standards for more resources." A large part of California's standards, he said, "imply the use of computers." Where were they? The standards also called for major emphasis in sixth-grade social studies on the Ming Dynasty. That meant well-stocked elementary school libraries: where were those?[25] The high school exit exam that students were already taking included algebra. Where were the algebra teachers? In the best of circumstances, it would be a long road.

II. New Jersey: Abbottizing the Schools

When Jack Londen talked about the iterative process, and when Steve Levy said that when counsel wins, the real battle begins, they could have been drawing on the record in any of a number of states—Ohio, Maryland, Alabama, Texas. But probably the best candidate was New Jersey, where in 1981 the Newark-based Education Law Center (ELC) sued the state, charging (in *Abbott v. Burke*) that the Public School Education Act, New Jersey's response to judicial orders issued in a series of prior decisions, was still inadequate and violated the state constitution. In those decisions, dating back to 1973 with *Robinson v. Cahill*, which were very much modeled on California's *Serrano* case, the state supreme court had found that New Jersey's dependence on local property taxes discriminated against children in poor cities and ordered the state to create a more equitable school funding formula.[26]

Even implementation of *Robinson* had been difficult. The Public School Education Act, which began to move the state off the local property tax, was passed in 1975 despite warnings from the Education Law Center that the new system still wouldn't end funding inequities. But in 1976, after the legislature failed to appropriate money for it, thus leaving poor districts still badly underfunded, the state supreme court, showing that it too could play political hardball, ordered all the state's schools shut down. They stayed closed for eight days. It was then that New Jersey enacted its first income tax.

Abbott relied primarily on the state's constitutional provision charging the legislature with the obligation to maintain a "thorough and efficient" system of public schools, thus giving it the form and rationale of an adequacy case from the start. But its principal thrust, rooted in a generation of civil rights battles, continued to be equity in funding for the urban districts serving the state's poorest children. That was hardly surprising, since Marilyn J. Morheuser, ELC's lead attorney, was a dogged and demanding litigator—a larger-than-life figure—who'd spent some fifteen years as a Sister of Loretto, teaching in church schools in a half-dozen different states and demonstrating for civil rights whenever her order allowed it.

In 1963, deciding that things had become too confining—she described the order as a "box" that had windows to see out, but wouldn't let you out—she quit and spent the next seven years protesting school segregation, suburban racism, and police brutality. In 1970 she enrolled at Rutgers Law School, where one of her teachers was Paul Tractenberg, who would eventually hire her as executive director of ELC, which Tractenberg started in 1973. ELC was going to be the legal advocate, he said, the voice, for New Jersey's poor and disadvantaged children.[27] In Kentucky, it had been the school districts and superintendents who sued. Here, as in California twenty years later, the (at least nominal) complainants were children and their parents.

Among the plaintiffs, all students in urban school districts, was

Raymond Arthur Abbott, then a twelve-year-old seventh grader in a run-down junior high school in Camden, then as now one of the poorest cities in the nation. It was his mother, Frances, a teacher in another Camden school, who had signed him up for the suit. According to Nancy Phillips, a *Philadelphia Inquirer* reporter who interviewed him in 1990, Abbott, who was already having serious difficulties in school, was never very much interested in the suit that would eventually attach his name not just to a string of court decisions but to governmental departments and committees, to the state's biggest school districts, and to a variety of other things in New Jersey education.

Tractenberg told colleagues from the beginning that any serious campaign to end disparate school funding and to provide adequate resources to students in the state's major urban districts would be a long haul. Those districts, now thirty altogether—Newark, Jersey City, Trenton, East Orange, Hoboken, Camden, and some two dozen others that enroll 300,000 of New Jersey's 1.3 million students—would soon be officially designated as Abbott districts. But it's doubtful that either Tractenberg or Morheuser, who became ELC's executive director in 1979, understood how long a haul it was to be. Two decades after the suit was first filed, *Abbott* was still in the courts. When the state supreme court handed down yet another decision in 2002, it was *Abbott VIII*, almost like a member of a dynastic house. In between, the issue bounced among an administrative law judge, the supreme court, several state education commissioners, the legislature and governor—actually four governors—and back again, not once but several times.

For most of those two decades, New Jersey politics has been dominated by the *Abbott* cases, the reforms they've generated, and the fiscal battles that accompanied them. One of the four governors, Democrat Jim Florio, died a premature political death, succumbing to the backlash of the early 1990s against the $2.8 billion tax increase he'd pushed to close an inherited deficit and pay for the school reforms ordered by the court in *Abbott II*. His Republican successor, Christie Whitman, who had beaten him in 1993, and the Republican legislators that were swept into office with her compounded the problem by approving a set of tax cuts whose costs were temporarily concealed

by borrowing and deferrals but would severely erode the state's finances. Whitman, facing a disastrous budget crisis caused in part by
the tax cuts and in part by the cost of complying with the five *Abbott*
decisions handed down while she was governor, may have breathed
a deep sigh of relief when George W. Bush brought her to Washington in 2001 to run the Environmental Protection Agency.[28]

The seminal decision in what the court was to call "this genera-
tional struggle" was *Abbott II* (1990), which, though limited to what
would become the Abbott districts, held that the state's funding system was "neither thorough nor efficient." The decision grew out of
the findings of Steven LeFelt, an administrative law judge named by
the court in the hope—vain, as it turned out—that the issues could
be settled without the exercise of a lot of judicial muscle. LeFelt found
a strong relationship between the tax wealth of a school district and
per-pupil school expenditures. He also found that inequality of educational opportunity was itself a violation of the thorough and efficient mandate, and that the Public Education Act that was passed to
satisfy *Robinson* therefore was unconstitutional. But state education
commissioner Saul Cooperman rejected those findings. If there were
any problems, he said, they weren't systemic and could be remedied
at the district level.

The court's unanimous response, written by Chief Justice Robert
Wilentz, couldn't have been more unequivocal: "The inadequacy of
poorer urban students' education as measured against their needs is
glaring," he said. "Whatever the cause, these school districts are failing abysmally, dramatically and tragically." The constitution did not
require funding equality—different students had different needs—
although funding clearly was a measure of whether the state was
providing the "specific substantive level of education" that was required. Indeed, until recently there had been no other gauge. (In
1984–5, the richest districts raised $4,755 per pupil, 77 percent more
than what poor districts could.)

The court did not directly address the question of whether low
property values caused lower spending, though it obviously believed
that they did. What seemed to offend the judges more was the apparent belief of education officials that for poor kids, second best was
good enough—that districts serving poor children "should not be dis-

couraged by their students' failure to perform at the level of [districts with little poverty], or should not expect them to." Wilentz also denounced the state's blithe contention that if low-wealth districts wanted to spend more, all they had to do was raise tax rates. "The social and economic pressures on municipalities, school districts and citizens of these disaster areas . . . are so severe that tax increases in any substantial amount are almost unthinkable. To pejoratively label . . . resistance to increased taxes as 'political' fails to recognize the situation that some school boards face."[29]

But in the end, the judges, having cited a long list of specific disparities in facilities, equipment, and other resources between rich and poor schools, recognized that they lacked any better alternatives, and again turned to financial indicators. Research had shown that "money alone has not worked. . . . But it does not show that money makes no difference. What it strongly suggests is that money can be used more effectively." They also noted that while the state had been generous in what it spent for education, "there is absolutely no question that we are failing to provide the students in the poorer urban districts with the kind of education that anyone would call thorough and efficient." Accordingly, the court ordered the state to spend enough to "assure [that per-pupil expenditures] are substantially equivalent to those of the more affluent suburban districts, and that, in addition, their special disadvantages be addressed." That was a whopper.

If the claim is that these students simply cannot make it, the constitutional answer is, give them a chance. The Constitution does not tell them that since more money will not help, we will give them less; that because their needs cannot be fully met, they will not be met at all. It does not tell them they will get the minimum, because that is all they can benefit from. Like other states, we undoubtedly have some "uneducable" students, but in New Jersey there is no such thing as an uneducable district, not under our Constitution.[30]

The court's words, moving as they were, resonated with an unexpected meaning. On June 5, 1990, the day that the decision was handed down, Raymond Abbott, whose name would be permanently institutionalized in New Jersey education, was in the Camden County jail. Abbott, who was then twenty-one, had dropped out of school in the middle of his senior year, got hooked on cocaine, and been in and out of jail on a series of minor felonies—burglary, attempted burglary, receiving stolen property, and various parole violations—ever since. He told reporters who found him there that he was happy: "I feel as though I've done some good for the kids—getting more money for their schools." He didn't blame the Camden schools for his own troubles, although he said that they'd failed to diagnose a learning disability that forced him to struggle and that eventually led to his dropping out. "I'm just hoping the money will help schools and help kids, and hopefully they'll realize that [jail] isn't the place to be." He himself was working on his GED, he said; "I don't think it's all over for me."[31] But by 2002, nobody seemed to know where he was.

In New Jersey, the process that some lawyers envision as a dialogue between the courts and the rest of the state, and particularly with the other branches of government, turned into a sort of monologue, a one-way exchange between the court's orders and a legislature that was only marginally responsive and, through much of the 1990s, frequently hostile. The rhetoric of *Abbott II* (and some of its successors as well) thus was intended to be as much a message to the public and its elected representatives as it was a legal opinion. If the legislature, and often other state officials, were adept at delaying and averting full compliance, the court would be no less persistent not only in holding their feet to the fire but in increasingly demanding more.

Despite strong Republican resistance, both in the administration and in the conservative antitax legislature that replaced the Florio Democrats in 1993, a decade of judicial pressure in the 1990s not only began to equalize per-pupil spending between the thirty Abbott districts and the rest of the state but slowly reversed the gap, so that by 2002 the Abbott districts were spending more in state and local money per student than the state average, in some cases well over $15,000 per child.[32] Overall, according to a survey by the Education Trust, the 25 percent of New Jersey school districts with the highest concentrations of poor students were getting an average of $324 more per child each year—that was before federal funds were calculated in—than the 25 percent of New Jersey districts with the lowest concentrations of poor students. And in contrast to California, where *Serrano* and Proposition 13 leveled spending down—and by a lot—New Jersey, which had been among the highest-spending states in the nation even before *Abbott*, spent more than any other state. In 1998–99, when the national average was $7,000, New Jersey was spending an average of $10,700 per year per student.[33]

But that was only part of the change. The state had continued to insist that students in wealthier districts "who [in the court's words] receive more educational resources are receiving superfluous and un-needed educational benefits, and those students who receive less ed-ucational resources nevertheless will receive that which is needed to provide a thorough and efficient education." As the state failed to develop adequacy standards, such rationales seemed make the court even more determined and perhaps angrier.[34] The judicial mandates became broader—a sequence of incremental decisions not just to force the other branches of government to stop their foot-dragging and take unpleasant measures such as raising taxes but also perhaps to ulti-mately require things like redistributing taxpayer money from rich to poor districts, a process that would win the politicians a lot more enemies than friends.

In raising the ante, the judges also expanded the scope of their court-ordered reforms. By 1998, with *Abbott V*, what had begun as primarily a funding equity case eight years earlier had broadened to include requirements that the state fund full-day kindergarten and preschool for all Abbott district three- and four-year-olds; a sweeping state-managed school construction and renovation program to elimi-nate overcrowding and provide adequate space for all urban school-children; suitable art, music, and science programs based on student need and parity with suburban schools; additional health and social services; after-school and summer programs; and "whole school reform (WSR)."[35]

WSR was well intended: to try to effectively use the generous amounts of money the courts had ordered the state to spend in the Abbott districts.[36] The issue, said Allan R. Odden, co-director of the Consortium for Policy Research in Education at the University of

Wisconsin, who had been named a special master by New Jersey trial judge Patrick Michael King, was not sufficiency but educational strategy and management: to make sure that the money didn't dribble away and that there would be a real impact in the classroom.[37] But WSR soon became an example of the dangers that arise when a court ventures too deep into the thickets of education practice. It had been sold to King and then to the state supreme court not by the Education Law Center, which opposed it, but by Christie Whitman's education commissioner, and blessed by Odden. As the high court saw it, WSR was

> a comprehensive approach to education that fundamentally alters the way in which decisions about education are made. A school implements whole-school reform by integrating reform throughout the school as a total institution rather than by simply adding reforms piecemeal. If carried out successfully, whole school reform affects the culture of the entire school, including instruction, curriculum, and assessment. The reform covers education from the earliest levels, including pre-school, and can be particularly effective in enabling the disadvantaged children in urban communities to reach higher standards.[38]

But what the commissioner proposed, and what the court called for, was not progress in outcomes but a very specific prescription: Success for All (SFA), a system developed in the late 1970s and 1980s by Robert Slavin and his wife, Nancy Madden, at Johns Hopkins University that the court, echoing the commissioner, called "a nationally proven program that addresses the reading deficits of low-income, at-risk public school children."[39] (Slavin had also been one of the commissioner's experts.) By the time of *Abbott V*, SFA had evolved from its beginnings as an intense, rapidly paced, and highly scripted drill-based instructional technique for teach reading and math into a program to restructure whole schools. SFA, with its old-fashioned phonics exercises, had gained wide respect over a decade and a half for its apparent success in raising disadvantaged children's command of the basics of reading and math, had gotten considerable backing from the U.S. Department of Education as well as many state education agencies, and was being used in some fifteen hundred schools in all parts of the country and in some schools abroad. "Under the Commissioner's recommendations," said the court, "SFA could be fully operative in all Abbott schools within five years." Particularly in schools where many teachers themselves had trouble with language, the scripted call-and-response formula had considerable appeal.

SFA, however, might not have been quite as shiny as the judges thought—in education almost nothing ever is. By the late 1990s it had become increasingly controversial, the subject of serious questions and criticism for its allegedly exaggerated claims, its failure to bring its students up to grade level, and more broadly for the way that government agencies had been pushing what critics regarded as Slavin's cookie-cutter approach. It was also anathema to educational progressives, who detested its lockstep methods, the children chanting their answers in unison, the lack of room for creativity on the part of both teachers and students: Some people called it a teacher-proof method. In an evaluation of SFA in Baltimore, where the program started and where it should have done well, a University of Delaware researcher named Richard Venezky found that "after the early primary grades, SFA students begin to fall behind the average students nationally and by the end of fifth grade are almost 2.4 years behind. In addition, increasing time in SFA schools does not lead to increasing advantage in reading performance."[40] Since then other researchers have joined the hunt. "There never was scientific evidence of the success of SFA," wrote University of Arizona professor Stanley Pogrow in one of a series of broad attacks:

All the advocacy by Slavin and Madden is simply that—advocacy, not science. The work is not that of researchers but of marketers with a lot at stake. They provide no new insight into the nature of learning or testing, nor do they even recognize alternative perspectives on reform and student progress. Rather then ushering in a "revolution," SFA is another in a long line of programs that have failed to accelerate student learning after the third grade. In terms of results, it is the same old, same old—with lots of bucks and political influence behind it.[41]

Early evaluations in New Jersey of the local schools' post-*Abbott* implementation of whole school reform and Success for All were generally positive but hardly ecstatic. (Because of resistance, a couple of other whole school reform plans had been added as alternatives.) SFA had elicited less than rousing enthusiasm from teachers and other school people offended at its top-down regimen, a finding that was especially telling since Slavin himself demanded strong teacher buy-in before a school could adopt his program. Thus, the researchers' finding that more than three-fourths of the teachers who were brought into the Slavin program by the *Abbott* ruling felt they hadn't been consulted in the selection of their school's reform plan and that they "expressed a tremendous amount of frustration over the limited amount of empowerment that accompanied the introduction of site-based management" were hardly signs of great promise.[42]

And while the criticisms of people such as Pogrow and Venezky were hardly conclusive, even Slavin conceded that although his students "were substantially ahead" of their peers in the control groups, most didn't reach grade level. Success for All, he said "is not magic." Judge King had gathered extensive material on the various options before him and had visited some of the SFA schools that were already operating in New Jersey, and he had been impressed. But what worked in one place with one group of enthusiastic teachers might not work in another. The mixed early results were a cautionary signal about the danger of any judicial romance with across-the-board programmatic remedies imposed by even the most thorough judges— and even when they were advised by the most knowledgeable and best-intentioned people.

With the election of Democrat James E. McGreevey as governor in 2001, the state entered into a "partnership" with the Education Law Center that sought to minimize further litigation and, in the words of Steven Block, ELC's longtime research director, "fix the prior administration's screwups," including, not least among them, the state's embrace of Success for All. The partnership was institutionalized in an Abbott Implementation and Compliance Coordinating Council, an advisory group that included representatives of major state agencies as well the ELC. The council soon created five Abbott Work Groups on, among other matters, early childhood education, measuring school achievement and school facilities. It was, said ELC, an attempt to "ensure ongoing state compliance with the Abbott rulings through cooperation and collaboration, and to eliminate or at least minimize court intervention."[43] At the same time, the Department of Education, reflecting what one spokesperson called a "different tone and mood," created a Division of Abbott Implementation. There was no certainty that it would in fact end the litigation. But in the face of the budget crisis in 2001–2, ELC, which believed that there were still major areas in which the state hadn't complied with prior Abbott rulings, gave the state a year to get its act together.

Even if the fight returned to court, it seemed likely that it would be about implementation of the *Abbott* orders, not about their substance. "The principles," said Tractenberg, "have been established." But there still remained countless devils in hundreds of major details: a State Department of Education whose performance, in Tractenberg's words, had been "incredibly irresponsible"; a state data system that was such a "disaster" that it was hard to track very much of anything about school performance; nagging questions about the quality of the preschool programs, especially the private groups that ran the preschools attended by 70 percent of the forty thousand Abbott district kids who participated.

Most perplexing of all, despite all its investment in urban schools and its high per-pupil spending generally, New Jersey still had no effective mechanism for evaluating the academic achievement of its children. The state had embarked on a massive school construction program—a total of $10 to $12 billion, of which more than half would be spent in the Abbott districts. It had numbers showing encouraging increases on such things as participation in preschool programs. It reported some vague progress on the ever-mutable tests in reading, math, science, and social studies that it developed for itself and which it gave students in the fourth, eighth, and eleventh grades, all known by acronyms that made them sound a little like the weird sisters in a sci-fi gothic: GEPA, HSPA, and ESPA.[44] (Under President Bush's No Child Left Behind education law, that testing program will soon have to be augmented with annual tests for all students in grades 3–8.)

But New Jersey's tests measured only self-defined proficiency levels. Since the tests seemed to change every few years, since the state used no test that allowed comparisons with students in other states (although some districts did), and since it hadn't participated in the NAEP since 1994, there were no reliable comparative criteria of any sort. Even the state's own tests, based on state academic standards, were vulnerable. In 2002, soon after he took office, William Librera, McGreevey's new state education commissioner, announced that students wouldn't have to take the science and social studies tests in 2002 and that local schools, not the state, would score the fourth-grade tests. Although both were economy moves, there was enough of an uproar that Librera quickly reversed himself, but it was nonetheless an indication of the frailty of the state's assessment system.[45] In late 2002, McGreevey and Librera announced plans to establish yet another new testing program, based on a plan developed by the Business Coalition for Educational Excellence of the New Jersey Chamber of Commerce, that was to be part short-answer test and part "authentic assessment"— student projects, problem-solving exercises and other work. But it wasn't scheduled for full implementation until 2008.[46]

Ever since the late 1980s, community and political leaders in most other states had demanded, and usually gotten, assessment programs and accountability systems that included nationally normed testing, sometimes as the quid pro quo for support of increased funding, sometimes in their own right. Why hadn't New Jersey, which had been immersed in school reform for over two decades, become part of that many years earlier?[47] Block, who joined ELC in 1980 and watched the *Abbott* process from the beginning, thinks some of it may be due to the fact that until recently, the New Jersey business community failed to involve itself vigorously enough in school policy issues— itself unusual, if not extraordinary, at a time when, for better or worse, businesspeople have been drivers of school reform across much of the country. In part it may also be due to the dogged opposition of New Jersey Republicans to any part of the adequacy reforms and thus their estrangement from the kind of debates that took place in other states.

Whatever the cause, it leaves people such as Tractenberg with a long-term problem: how to demonstrate to the voters and taxpayers that they were getting something for that Abbott money. Since most of the major Abbott reforms weren't in place until after 1998, and sometimes much later, it was far too early to look for significant results. But the questions were beginning to emerge. In the summer of 2002, as the recession and Whitman's tax cuts and pension fund borrowing began to take their toll in the form of a $2.9 billion state budget deficit, and middle-class mid-level districts took their proportionate hits, the state supreme court ordered the legislature to appropriate an additional $240 million in state aid to protect the Abbott districts. It wasn't surprising, therefore, that voucher proponents and conservatives began to see the hefty spending of the Abbott districts as ever more tempting targets.

"The state pays for 85% of the cost of Newark schools and 95% of the costs of Camden schools," said the Web site of a pro-voucher organization called Excellent Education for Everyone. "Do we get what we pay for? New Jersey spends more per pupil than any other state, almost $12,000 on average per child each and every year. And, frighteningly, the cost is even higher in the very school districts where the results are poorest, a staggering $17,000 per child in many of the state's Abbott districts."[48] Bret Schundler, the maverick former mayor of Jersey City and the GOP gubernatorial candidate who lost to McGreevey in 2001, was even more explicit:

Newark's public schools now spend $16,000 per child, yet less than 20% of Newark Central High School's ninth graders graduate. Meanwhile, nearby parochial schools are graduating over 90% of their students at a small fraction of the cost.

Jim McGreevey says that $16,000 is not enough to educate a child in Newark. He wants to cut state funding for suburban public schools so that he can spend even more money in Newark and other cities.

The problem in Newark is that McGreevey refuses to make its public schools accountable, and is instead using their failure to justify trying to get more tax money out of New Jerseyans' pockets.

I have proposed an Abbott District School Voucher Program that would fund vouchers at about 50% of what the public schools in our urban school districts are spending per child, so that we can increase accountability in these urban school districts and make their schools better, even as we immediately increase educational opportunity for the children who are being so terribly disserved today.

As a side benefit, my proposal would save so much money in these state-funded Abbott School Districts that the State could reverse its cuts in funding for New Jersey's suburban school districts.[49]

New Jersey had never shown much support for vouchers, despite Schundler's consistent efforts to talk the issue up. But those big spending numbers in places like Newark (and, of course, in Schundler's own Jersey City, where the dysfunctional district had been taken over by the state) were hard to ignore. That became particularly apparent in the reaction in the many districts that were getting socked by state budget cuts—places that were neither poor enough to be an Abbott district nor wealthy enough to compensate for the state's sharply reduced funding with their own resources.

The longer it takes to get reliable test and accountability measures in place, the more likely that someday there would be a backlash that could sweep much of the *Abbott* edifice away. In light of the endemic civic decay and corruption in Camden and some of the other Abbott cities—in Camden three of the five mayors since 1970 have been convicted and sent to prison on fraud, bribery, or other federal political corruption charges—the chances of any quick turnaround in the schools were even more tenuous. Every week, it seemed, some other New Jersey official was being charged or tried.[50] Even beyond the complaints of voucher supporters, there were serious questions about whether the Abbott districts had the capacity—in governance, in leadership, in community engagement—to spend their new money well. In the summer of 2002, McGreevey approved a bill appropriating an additional $175 million for the Camden schools and giving him control over the schools in an effort to keep the money out of the wrong pockets. But a trial judge quickly rejected the takeover as a violation of New Jersey's constitution.[51] There were all sorts of ways in which accountability could get complicated.

• • •

Tractenberg, who began it all back in 1973, has been frustrated that the country has tended to see the *Abbott* story more for its length and apparent lack of closure than for what he regards as its very real achievements. He talks about court decisions in other states that, in rejecting adequacy arguments, cited *Abbott* as a horrible example of the morass the courts can get into if they venture down the adequacy path. If anyone thirty years ago had told him that New Jersey's public education system would ever be where it now was, "I would have said, you got to be kidding." He wasn't sure how much things had changed in the classroom—it *was* too early for that; outcomes were "still up for grabs"—but they were light-years beyond where they were when they started. The attention that was now being paid to poor kids, and the resources that were going to them, were quite special. It had taken longer than even he had expected, but they were now well beyond what they'd hoped for. It had been "an enormous success."[52]

III. Ohio: The Crocodile in the Bathtub

Among the things that kept *Abbott* on course—probably the indispensable thing—was a group of state supreme court justices committed and secure enough not to yield to the politicians and bureaucrats whom the judges were trying to coax and sometimes compel, among them the governors who named them. Just to say that raises horrendously tough questions about the role of courts in a democracy. To what extent should judges ever stray into the prerogatives of the other branches, and at what risk? To what extent are the constitutional safeguards that depend on the separation of powers inevitably endangered when the judges wander into the realm of the other two? "John Marshall has made his ruling," Andrew Jackson supposedly said when the U.S. Supreme Court ruled (in 1832) that Georgia had no jurisdiction over Indian lands. "Now let him enforce it."[53] As in thousands of issues, different judges in different courts, and often on the same court, reading the same words, have come to radically different conclusions. But it may be particularly difficult with respect to educational policy, with its endless string of famously fuzzy issues.

What's certain is that the court's strength in New Jersey depended in considerable part on a constitutional structure that, unlike those in most states, never requires a justice to go before the voters. New Jersey justices are appointed by the governor, confirmed by the state senate, and, six years later, subject once more to senate confirmation. Thereafter they serve until the mandatory retirement age of seventy. In that respect, said Tractenberg, it's almost like academic tenure. It gives the judiciary great independence—and thus probably also draws men and women more focused on the law than on staying in the good graces of the electorate and the various interest groups that have the means to make life difficult at the ballot box. That allows them to be noblesse oblige aristocrats who, if they choose, can protect minorities and the poor against the power of the majority. In the thirty-eight states where they periodically face the voters, either in periodic yes-or-no reconfirmation elections or in contested elections (or, worse yet, in contested partisan elections), judges, for better or worse, are likely to be far more attuned to the politics of the street and the marketplace and far more beholden to their political contributors.[54] Former California Supreme Court justice Otto Kaus, asked about the problems of deciding controversial issues in the face of the state's periodic reconfirmation elections, said it was like "finding a crocodile in your bathtub when you go in to shave in the morning. You know it's there and you try not to think about it, but it's hard to think about much else."[55]

In Ohio, where a group of 550 school districts organized as the Ohio Coalition for Equity and Adequacy in School Funding (E&A Coalition) had been in court with the state since 1991, the judges were in the room with the tub with the crocodile. The litigation, which began with the familiar challenge to the state's property-tax-based school funding system, has since been up to the state supreme court four times (*DeRolph v. State*, 1997, 2000, 2001, 2002).[56] Like other adequacy cases, *DeRolph* rested not on an equal protection rationale but on the contention that the tax system violated the state's "thorough and efficient" schools requirement. But as the case shuttled between the courts and a stubborn governor and legislature devoted to the baby-splitting doctrine of governance, the judges, who issued ringing declarations ordering sweeping reforms in the first two *DeRolph* rulings, both decided by 4–3 majorities, began to experience a notable loss of passion.

There never was much dispute about the facts, even among the judges who felt that the state's funding system passed constitutional muster. In Ohio, as in other states, the gap in per-pupil funding between high- and low-wealth districts varied enormously. In 1993, the Cleveland suburb of Cuyahoga Heights, with a 22-mill (2.2 percent) property tax levy, could spend nearly $12,000 per pupil; East Cleveland, taxing itself at triple that rate, could spend just over $5,500.[57] Those inequities—in funding, teachers, equipment, and facilities— were so glaring that, it appears, they truly shocked the judges' conscience.

"The defendants, the State of Ohio, the State Board of Education, the Superintendent of Public Instruction, and the Ohio Department of Education . . . indicated that there are few facts in dispute," a lower court justice had written. "Of course, there aren't—they agreed with almost everything the [plaintiffs] stated. In fact, an examination of testimony by defense witnesses in this case would indicate that these witnesses stated that the system of funding was immoral and inequitable. If there was ever a case where the parties acted more in concert than this one, I haven't seen it."[58] In 1987, after voters had passed a constitutional amendment requiring that all profits from the state lottery go to the public schools, the legislature quickly reduced education funding from other sources, leaving the schools with less state money than they had before. In 1988, the share of local funding that came from the state declined from 35 to 31 percent. In the 1990s, the state pledged $100 million toward the construction of new professional football stadiums for the owners of the Cleveland Browns and the Cincinnati Bengals but avoided the state's $16 billion school construction and repair backlog.[59]

In the face of those facts and the attendant failure of the legislature and governor to enact the major reforms that the schools appeared to require, the court lashed out at the politicians in language that no one could misunderstand. Because of the suit, said Justice Francis E. Sweeney in the first *DeRolph* decision (1997), the legislature had "scrambled to enact new laws to soften the blow of a failing system." But while some desperately needed funds had been appropriated (for things like new technology), "they are simply insufficient to get the job done and do not rectify the serious problems inherent in Ohio's financing scheme." Neither the General Assembly nor the court, said Justice Paul E. Pfeifer in a concurrence, could require "parents to love their children . . . challenge and nurture their children, to read to their children. . . . [But] we can require the General Assembly to comply with the Constitution of this state. . . . Neither the plain language of the Ohio Constitution nor our collective consciences allow us to do otherwise."[60]

Then the court directed "a clear message to lawmakers":

The time has come to fix the system. Let there be no misunderstanding. Ohio's public school financing scheme must undergo a complete systematic overhaul. The factors which contribute to the unworkability of the system and which must be eliminated are . . . the emphasis of Ohio's school funding system on local property tax; . . . the lack of sufficient funding in the General Assembly's biennium budget for the construction and maintenance of public school buildings. The funding laws reviewed today are inherently incapable of achieving their constitutional purpose.

We admonish the General Assembly that it must create an entirely new school financing system. . . . A thorough and efficient system of common schools includes facilities in good repair and the supplies, materials, and funds necessary to maintain these facilities in a safe manner, in compliance with all local, state, and federal mandates.[61]

In a concurring opinion, Justice Alice Robie Resnick stressed that the aim wasn't equality but "a threshold amount of funding provided by the state which affords each district in Ohio the ability to meet certain standardized requirements." She castigated a dissenting colleague who maintained that the legislature had in fact discharged its duty to fund the schools adequately.

The question to be answered after reviewing all of the evidence is whether a thorough and efficient system exists in a school district where some students are taught in a former coal bin, or where there are not enough books for each child, or where the science lab has no gas valves or running water, or where handicapped children are carried up and down stairs because the buildings are not accessible to wheelchairs, or where the buildings are structurally unsafe, have inadequate plumbing, or are without sanitary or indoor restrooms, or where the school buildings cannot be rewired for computers until an asbestos hazard has been eliminated. This is not a close question.[62]

But if the condition of Ohio's have-not schools was not a close question, then surely the matter of what the constitution required and who was responsible for fixing it was. As Chief Justice Moyer wrote in a dissent in a subsequent decision, the legislature "had in fact established a statewide school system in which the schools were open, teachers were teaching, buses were running and all Ohio children had available to them an opportunity to learn." And, Moyer said, questions about levels and method of funding and about educational quality— qualitative judgments—belonged to the people as expressed by the legislature and local school boards. They were the province of "legitimate policy makers—not the courts."[63]

DeRolph, which handed the Democratic minority in the Ohio legislature a major campaign issue, infuriated Republicans, and they wasted no time before they began firing back. On March 25, 1997, the day after the decision was announced, Ohio governor George Voinovich and the two senior legislative leaders, all Republicans, held a press conference to excoriate its authors. The court's majority opinion, said the governor, "is a thinly veiled call for a massive, multi-billion-dollar tax increase ... a meat axe approach ... [by judicial activists who] decided they wanted to act in place of the General Assembly and in place of the administration. They have created the basis for litigation for years to come." This could only lead to the evisceration of local school districts, he said, and turn the General Assembly into the state's school superintendent.

As Voinovich spoke, listing the measures the legislature had taken to close the funding gap between rich and poor districts, he became so angry, shouting and banging the lectern, that at one point House Speaker Jo Ann Davidson quietly stopped him before he could finish issuing a threat to amend the Ohio constitution to cut the courts out of school adequacy matters altogether. And then—incongruously, in light of his statements about judicial meddling—he complained that the court "admonishes the General Assembly that it must create an entirely new school financing system, yet it provides the General Assembly with minimal guidance to develop such a system."[64] "No one in power believed," said E&A Coalition executive director William Phillis, "that the court would ever rule against them." Whatever they expected, however, the press conference blast was not a propitious way to begin serious reform. In Phillis's advocate's eyes, "It set the stage for the state to do nothing."[65]

The legislature had, in fact, taken some steps in the previous year, raising the state's share of school spending and narrowing the gaps between the have and have-not districts and, after the much more diplomatic and amiable Bob Taft succeeded fellow Republican Voinovich as governor in 1998, it would take many more. Taft, someone said, "went to meetings, he went on trips into the field, he listened." Phillis himself called Taft "a fine human being [who] really has empathy for public education." Most important, Ohio began a major school construction program, to be funded in part by the state's share of the national multibillion-dollar tobacco settlement, to begin meeting the facilities backlog that by 1997 had stuck Ohio in the lowest ranks in national surveys of school conditions. At the same time, the state hired Denver consultant John Augenblick to conduct the study and generate the formula for what it would take to provide each child a presumably adequate education (and which the legislature ultimately sliced to conform to its own budgetary objectives).

Even the angry Voinovich implicitly acknowledged that the per-pupil funding gap was still huge. In 1996, 73 percent of districts spent between $4,000 and $5,550 a year, itself a fairly wide range, especially considering the varying needs of different students. That meant that among one-fourth of the state's districts the gaps were greater, ranging from a low of $4,000 to a high of $12,000. Under the pressure of the court decision, the Republican-dominated legislature put up more money. But there was no systemic overhaul, as Phillis said, leaving the possibility that in bad times "they will drag it down to what it had been."[66] He saw the money as an unsuccessful attempt to bribe the districts—his constituency—to abandon the suit.

The political anger generated by the DeRolph decision would extend well beyond press conferences. In 1998, when Justice Paul Pfeifer, a Republican who'd voted with the 4–3 *DeRolph* majority, ran for another six-year term in the state's nominally nonpartisan elections, some leading GOP legislators turned on him. Most prominent among them was Bill Batchelder, the speaker pro tem of the Ohio House, who'd urged Pfeifer's opponent, a conservative Democrat named Ron Suster, to run and now strongly endorsed him. Pfeifer was known for his frequent departures from the preferences of his party—judges, after all, were supposed to be independent—but the clincher for Batchelder was *DeRolph*. Suster, Batchelder said, would offer "a nice choice for the voters between an activist and a judge who is pretty much bound by the plain language of the law."[67]

Batchelder had plenty of company from conservatives and from a business community eager to strike a blow against judges, including Pfeifer, whom it thought too cozy with trial lawyers in their legal opinions, and especially in overturning parts of a ten-year-old Ohio tort reform law that had limited damage awards in personal injury and malpractice cases. But it was his vote in *DeRolph* that, as much as anything else, triggered their opposition. The result was an almost total reversal of political forces, with labor unions and trial lawyers funding the Republican's campaign, insurance companies and other business interests backing the Democrat.

In the end, Pfeifer, who outspent his opponents by a margin of roughly two to one, got 71 percent of the votes and beat Suster easily.[68] But the election didn't dampen the GOP's attacks on the justices or put the spirit of *DeRolph* into the hearts of the legislature and governor. Even before the 1998 election, Common Pleas Court judge Linton D. Lewis Jr., who had originally heard the case at the trial level and to whom the case was remanded after *DeRolph I*, was conducting new hearings on the state's compliance with the decision— Karl Marx himself, state solicitor Jeff Sutton told the judge, couldn't have devised a fairer way to fund the schools—and in May 2000, the supreme court ruled 4–3 that the state's funding formula was still inadequate and unconstitutional and, in the kindliest terms possible, ordered the legislators to shape up.[69]

Justice Alice Robie Resnick, writing for the court's narrow majority, was effusive in her praise for the efforts that Governor Bob Taft was making to improve the schools, citing a long list of measures the state had enacted to increase funding in low-wealth districts, as well as its substantial school construction program. She quoted at length from a report done by Achieve, Inc., a respected national organization founded by a bipartisan group of governors and business leaders to promote high academic standards in American schools, and paraphrased a good deal more. Voinovich, in his last days in office, had commissioned the report for Taft.

> Ohio [said the Achieve report] can be proud of a substantial set of policy initiatives it has launched in the 1990s, and of the deepening investments it has made in educational improvement. Since Fiscal Year 1991, state education funding has increased by approximately 50 percent, twice the rate of inflation. The increase has been greatest for low-wealth districts. Legislation already enacted guarantees an additional 40 percent increase in state aid over the next five years.
>
> Over and above these increases in general state aid for education, there have been substantial new investments in early childhood education, technology, facilities, and urban education, and major policy initiatives to overhaul teacher education and strengthen public accountability for results.

Nonetheless, the court found that the state was still relying too heavily on the local property tax and still played accounting games with "phantom revenues"—paper increases in local tax receipts based on increases in local valuations that the state then deducted from its own support of a district's schools. Under a rollback law, in essence a cap on individual property taxes, whenever assessments went up, property tax rates had to be lowered proportionately so that the total tax remained the same, which meant, of course, that those paper increases were in fact never collected.[70]

Even the construction program had problems—not only, in the words of the report Voinovich had commissioned for Taft, because "too many Ohio children, especially in poor rural and urban districts, [still] attend classes in dreadfully sub-standard facilities," but because the state, while tripling its investments in capital improvements, had no idea of what it had accomplished or what it still needed to do. "Without a reliable inventory of the state's facilities and a solid cost estimate for bringing all Ohio school[s] up to standard," the report said, "it is impossible to know just how much progress has been made."[71] The program, Resnick said, was riddled with "inefficiencies, bureaucratic red tape, and politics."

Resnick acknowledged that Ohio had joined dozens of other states in establishing an academic accountability system that was to keep fourth graders who couldn't read from being promoted, increased the number of academic courses required for high school graduation, and established a system of report cards for schools and school districts to annually grade performance on a variety of indicators. But, she added, while justices "agree that accountability is an important component of a system that provides funds, [what was] problematic [was] a system that increases academic requirements and accountability, yet fails to provide adequate funding." What was even more problematic was that while the one-cent sales tax increase that the legislature had placed on the ballot in 1998 had been rejected by voters, the new accountability mandates, now unfunded, remained in place. The court declined to tell the legislature how to do its job and refused to appoint the special master that the plaintiffs had asked for. Instead it specified seven areas that required reforms, told the politicians to get their act together, and, like a parent chastising an uncooperative child, gave them a year to show progress. "We hope that partisan views will be put aside and that everyone will work cooperatively for Ohio's children, as they are our future," Resnick wrote. "The General Assembly, in particular, must look beyond the political considerations involved, and must provide Ohio's school children with a thorough and efficient system of common schools as the Ohio Constitution requires."[72]

The most visible response to the decision, however, which was already gathering steam when *DeRolph II* was handed down, had nothing directly to do with school reform. It was an ugly campaign to dump Resnick in her bid for reelection in November 2000. Robert T. Bennett, chairman of the Ohio Republican Party, created an operation called Defeat Alice Resnick's Tax Hike (DARTH), based on the Republicans' claim that the tax hike would be necessary to pay for the fiscal restructuring that the court ordered. Meanwhile, the Chamber of Commerce and its affiliate Citizens for a Strong Ohio, whose vice president was also the political director of the Ohio Chamber, launched what was to become a $4 million television issue ad campaign, with the refrain "Is Justice for Sale?" accusing Resnick of trading judicial favors for campaign contributions from trial lawyers and other supporters.[73] The campaign, for which Taft, despite his charm offensive, quietly raised money, was so widely denounced both for its inaccurate charges—the *Dayton Daily News* called it "the most disgusting, debasing election seen in these parts in a long time"— and for the refusal of Citizens for a Strong Ohio to disclose its contributors that Chamber president Andrew E. Doehrel promised that in 2002 Citizens for a Strong Ohio would mend its ways. It would identify contributors and run a campaign "that is positive and informative but avoids the errors that raised questions two years ago."[74] It would not, however, be the end of such campaigns.

Resnick, bolstered in part by the backlash to the ad campaign, won reelection by a comfortable 57–43 percent margin; if anything, her experience with the crocodile in the tub seemed to make her even tougher. But after the legislature failed yet again to enact the fiscal reforms that the previous decisions seemed to require and the case returned once again to the high court, the justices had been worn down. In September 2001, a new majority in effect declared that it was tired of the battle and, it appeared, was ready to make a separate peace with the politicians.

"A climate of legal, financial, and political uncertainty concerning Ohio's school-funding system has prevailed at least since this court accepted jurisdiction of the case," said Chief Justice Thomas Moyer, who had dissented in the previous decisions and was now writing for the new majority. "We have concluded that no one is served by continued uncertainty and fractious debate. In that spirit, we have created the consensus that should terminate the role of this court in the dispute." The essence of that consensus, while acknowledging that the legislature had not overhauled the financial structure to get the state off its property tax dependency, was to accept the legislature's many fiddles as the beginning of compliance. In any case, it was time to end the fight. Justice Andrew Douglas, one of the two judges who switched sides, mentioned messages he'd gotten telling the court, "Don't give in to the General Assembly. Hold them in contempt and put them in jail." He'd also heard the talk about impeaching judges. Both made him shudder.[75]

"None of us is completely comfortable with the decision we announce in this opinion," Moyer said, but "we are convinced that the defendants are committed to improving primary and secondary education. That commitment has operated, and can be expected to further operate, to ameliorate the undesirable educational conditions shown in *DeRolph I*."[76] That spring, the legislature had made some changes in the fiscal structure and appropriated an additional $1.4 billion in school funding over a two-year period, which, state officials claimed, would mean an average of $400 more per pupil.

The evidence, Moyer said, showed that the state's schools were already improving. Sixty percent (compared to 49 percent previously) of fourth graders had passed the state's mathematics test, with 56 percent (compared to 48 percent) passing the science test, and 61 percent (compared to 55 percent) of sixth graders had passed the mathematics and science tests. The state's new $2.7 billion construction program, though still leaving a lot of old and run-down schools, was under way, and the politicians, beginning with Governor Taft, were showing good faith: the court's new majority trusted them. Even without the restructuring, once the legislature fully implemented the changes it intended to adopt, Ohio would have a thorough and efficient system of public schools.

Resnick was furious. After the "clear message to lawmakers" that had been sent barely four years earlier requiring the state's school financing scheme to "undergo a complete systematic overhaul," this was surrender. "In its Machiavellian maneuver to halt this litigation," she wrote in her dissent, "the majority gives its seal of approval to a system of public education that, even with the judicially legislated adjustments of the majority, falls well short of the system required by the Ohio Constitution."[77] She criticized her colleagues both for what she regarded as their surrender and for the detailed fiscal and policy prescriptions they wanted the state to follow in order to achieve full compliance with the constitution. Then she recited the long list of horribles that the case had started with and that in her view persisted, though sometimes in altered form.

"The type of 'residual budgeting' identified by this court in *DeRolph I* was blatant," she said. "During the late 1980s and early 1990s, the General Assembly simply funded all other departments first, and then funded education with what was left, with no regard to what the cost to fund education actually should have been." The legislature had replaced that with "cost-based budgeting" theoretically derived from the model that Augenblick had created from calculations of what it cost to educate a student in one of a group of "successful" Ohio districts. But Resnick didn't like the Augenblick model either. It was "obvious," she wrote, "that most of those 127 districts cannot in reality be termed successful." The flaws, his critics had said, lay both in Augenblick's methodology, which Rand researcher Stephen P. Klein in his testimony called "cherry picking" and at one point "junk science," and in the state's manipulation of the methodology. (During the hearings that led to the Moyer decision, the state had attacked Klein for, among other things, giving "his opinions without reviewing any of the testimony of the two experts who were actually involved in determining these weights.")[78]

The whole debate, Augenblick said later, illustrated the imprecision of adequacy as a constitutional standard. Should you use a straight average or an enrollment-weighted average to calculate the spending of the "successful" districts he used as models—one of the key points of contention in Ohio? Where in the constitution would you find the answer to that? Even his relatively brief time on the stand, he said later, had been a very unpleasant experience, and he'd decided he wasn't going to testify anymore. "This isn't supposed to be a murder trial. [But] the lawyers do anything they can to win." He said he didn't feel he'd been beaten up, "but I don't want to be the object of their attention anymore."[79]

The lack of precision was obvious, but so were the problems in the schools. The school construction program was moving along. The state hoped to spend $23 billion over the next twelve years and, according to officials at the Ohio School Facilities Commission, expected to be able to generate enough money with new bonds to pay for it.[80] Even so, at the rate it was going in 2000–2, it was managing barely one-third of that. More telling, perhaps, was a survey conducted by the E&A Coalition, in which superintendents in 46 percent of those model districts said they had no AP courses in math; 64 percent had none in science; 63 percent had none in social studies.

"Of the one hundred twenty-seven model districts," Resnick wrote, "only 8.5 percent offer all-day, everyday kindergarten for all students and less than fifty percent of the districts offer three foreign language courses for high school students. In addition, gifted students are not being adequately served in most of these districts, and many of the districts have one or more school buildings that have major problems."[81] And since "the state determines first how much it wishes to spend on education and then backs out from that the number to produce a formula that calls for spending that amount, the final result [became] more and more suspect." Predictably, "every time the state adjusted its sample the base amount was lowered." The whole calculation therefore was flawed. Ironically, moreover, House Speaker Jo Ann Davidson had justified the legislature's manipulations on the fact that Augenblick's amount "was calculated on inexact data. . . . Lower per-pupil funding would help make up revenues lost from scrapping the cigarette tax and expanding property tax relief."[82] Was this an adequacy formula, or was it just the familiar political process got up in costume?

It is apparent [Resnick wrote] that the state had no intention of actually establishing an adequate amount of state-provided funding, but instead tried to do the minimum amount it could, always with an eye to reducing spending whenever possible, in order to try to satisfy this court, rather than trying to legitimately mount an effort that complied with our Constitution. The result was a series of political bargains that established the state spending amount on education at a level the state felt it could get by on without cutting other programs too much and without raising significantly more revenue, and that had little, if any, relationship to the cost of an adequate education.

The Resnick dissent was tough talk from beginning to end. Although Douglas mused about whether the decision might show that they were afraid, Resnick didn't directly accuse her colleagues of cowardice. But she implied it, deploring not only what she saw as their "purely political motives" but their unwillingness to confront the tough question of what they would have done had they found that the system was still unconstitutional. Had the dissenters in the first cases—now the new majority—had their way, "our system of public schools would still be mired in the totally unsatisfactory condition it was in when this litigation began in 1991 [and] the unacceptable status quo would have endured."[83] As to the two who switched:

> Their professed fervor for the mandates of the Ohio Constitution, as expressed in the opinions in *DeRolph I* and *DeRolph II,* obviously has waned to the point that they are willing to enter into a political compromise that has little to do with the actual merits of this case. It is most remarkable that one of the justices who joins the majority's decision once expressed the opinion that education is a fundamental constitutional right and that, therefore, "[t]he state bears a heavy burden of demonstrating a compelling state interest for the wealth-based disparities inherent in Ohio's system of school funding."

It was at this point that Resnick brushed against the ominous possibility that must have made the majority's political compromise particularly tempting.

> With statewide standards and statewide testing, we should recognize that we have a state system of common schools. The state bears the ultimate responsibility to solve problems (in partnership with the local districts) that have been formerly viewed as local. Recognition of a statewide system of schools envisioned by the Constitution may take generations to fully implement.
>
> It is no wonder that people with the mindset that local problems are strictly local would resist this process. Those who are reasonably satisfied with the status quo within their own school districts fear that solutions to the problems of other local districts

will be at their expense. These views must be put aside, and a bipartisan effort must continue to ensure that every child in Ohio will receive a thorough and efficient education regardless of where he or she resides.

Resnick was partly right—eventually there might be a state system—and she was certainly right that there was enormous resistance to such an idea. But as Ohio's neighbors in Kentucky had shown, no major reform could be engineered by a court alone. The judicial process could help—it might even be indispensable in forcing the issue and, as Mark Rosenbaum hoped, shocking the conscience. But without a strong political effort, the result was more likely to be a truncated version of whatever systematic overhaul the constitution, good policy, and human decency required. In states where judges are elected in competitive races, it could also endanger the incumbents. Judges, as Phillis said, "don't have an army."

Even after Ohio raised its foundation spending—by 2002 it was well above the amount Augenblick had recommended four years earlier—Ohio districts with large numbers of poor children still had $400 less per student than those with the fewest; the very richest were spending two to three times as much as the poorest.[84] On the same day that Resnick lambasted her colleagues for capitulating on fiscal reform, Ohio state senate president Richard Finan was declaring he had no intention of putting up the additional $1.24 billion annually that it would take to fully comply and that the court's new majority was trusting the legislature to appropriate. When he was asked where the money would come from, he answered, "Let the court figure that out." Chief Justice Moyer quickly replied that he was surprised that Finan was upset. "I would think they would be pleased the court is out of the picture at this point," he said.[85] In the end, there was no getting around the political process.

In fact, the court was not out of the picture. In December 2001, an even ten years after the suit was first filed, the justices, having granted the state's motion to reconsider *DeRolph III*, appointed Howard S. Bellman, a professional mediator from Wisconsin, to try to settle the outstanding issues in the case. But three months later, after the court gave Bellman a couple of extensions, he sent Moyer a three-sentence letter saying that he'd failed; what, if anything, he told Moyer privately has to be left to conjecture. "He washed his hands of it," said one state official, "collected his money, and went home. These are decisions that courts are there to make, not hand off."

Bellman's failure meant that the court, which had made no secret of its wish to finally rid itself of *DeRolph*, still wasn't done with it. But since the impending retirement of Justice Andrew Douglas put a crucial seat up for grabs in the November 2002 election—the leading candidate was Lieutenant Governor Maureen O'Connor, a Republican and a protégé of Governor Bob Taft—there was a fair chance that the court might totally reverse itself. (O'Connor was reported to have said "she has no ethical problem casting a vote on the dispute despite her presence with an administration that strongly supports the present system.")[86] The race for the open seat, between O'Connor and a Democratic municipal court judge named Tom Black, and that between incumbent Evelyn Stratton, a conservative, and her Democratic opponent, Janet Burnside, promised to be the most expensive judicial races in the state's history, with tort reform and school funding again the paramount issues. By mid-October, the candidates had spent a record $5.5 million, not counting the estimated $5 to $7 million raised and spent, though not always officially reported, by independent committees on each side of the judicial fight. One, bankrolled by a far right Republican businessman named William Brennan, had stepped into the political breach left by the Chamber of Commerce's declaration that it would no longer run anonymously funded campaigns against Ohio judges. With the backing of House Speaker Larry Householder, the Brennan group prepared to do precisely that. It was named Informed Citizens of Ohio.[87]

The two conservatives, bolstered by strong support from insurance and other industry groups, and by the intense consulting-room lobbying by doctors fighting high malpractice insurance rates, won easily, making it appear likely that in Ohio, the judicial road to adequacy was nearing its end.[88] But before O'Connor could replace the retiring Douglas, the court, in a bizarre turn, changed course once again. In December 2002, barely seven weeks after the election, the justices, in yet another fractured decision—there were six opinions from the seven justices—declared that "we have changed our collective mind. Despite the many good aspects of *DeRolph III*, we now vacate it. Accordingly, *DeRolph I* and *II* are the law of the case, and the current school-funding system is unconstitutional." The decision in *DeRolph III*, the court said, was "in many ways, the result of impatience."

> To date, the principal legislative response to *DeRolph I* and *DeRolph II* [Pfeifer wrote for the court] has been to increase funding, which has benefited many schoolchildren. However, the General Assembly has not focused on the core constitutional directive of *DeRolph I:* "a complete systematic overhaul" of the school-funding system. Today we reiterate that that is what is needed, not further nibbling at the edges. Accordingly, we direct the General Assembly to enact a school-funding scheme that is thorough and efficient, as explained in *DeRolph I, DeRolph II,* and the accompanying concurrences. We are not unmindful of the difficulties facing the state, but those difficulties do not trump the constitution.[89]

As the justices no doubt knew, the chances that the Republican-dominated legislature would soon comply were no greater now than they had ever been, especially since the court, in what was obviously the quid for the quo of its reversal, was now formally withdrawing from the case. Taft, in fact, insisted that the court had ruled that the state didn't need to do anything.[90] He appointed a Blue Ribbon Task Force to propose "a better way of funding schools . . . that provides predictable funding, is affordable, spends money more efficiently, and supports student achievement," but its mandate did not address the court's demand for fundamental reform. In the face of the state's straitened finances, it wasn't surprising that he didn't offer the schools more money, but his failure to suggest more thorough reform had people like Phillis steaming. (Resnick, implicitly acknowledging the diminished prospects, suggested a constitutional amendment that would require the legislature to spend a fixed amount annually, calibrated to grow with the schools' needs, to meet the constitution's adequacy requirements.) The decision, nonetheless, was likely not only to add force to the extrajudicial campaigns that the adequacy fight had set in motion but to set the table for still further legal action in the future.

The *DeRolph* cases had already helped in raising the state's spending, getting major school construction under way, and partially protecting the schools from the huge budget cuts that had commonly hit them in economic bad times in the past. And with a membership of some five hundred superintendents and other school officials from every part of the state—together they represented 80 percent of the state's districts—Phillis's coalition had a political presence that had to be reckoned with. Nor was it alone. In September 2002, the Ohio School Boards Association passed a resolution that Ohio "does not have an adequate and equitable school funding system" and created a panel of tax experts, lawyers, school officials and people from various other education groups to "define the major problems with the current . . . system." The group was to develop proposals for change in governance and funding, determine what levels of funding were necessary, and "assess the possible success of a ballot issue implementing the appropriate language." Although the court, in its failure to retain jurisdiction, had backed away from the battle, the adequacy issue it had unleashed was not going away.[91] In Florida, they were about to pass an enormously expensive class-size reduction initiative, despite the high proportion of elderly people in the electorate, and despite the strong opposition of Governor Jeb Bush. Why not, Phillis said, a "rational funding system" in Ohio? "We're bloody on the ground, but we're not going away."

IV. Alabama: The Hard Ground of History

As the Ohio justices, searching for a gracious way out of the adequacy tangle, were tacking back and forth, the Alabama supreme court simply reversed itself. Nobody had formally asked for that reversal, at least nobody on the record. The nine-member court, dominated by a newly elected core of conservative Republicans, did it on its own motion. Among those new judges was Chief Justice Roy Moore, a circuit court judge in Gadsden who had gained national notoriety for hanging a carved "replica" of the Ten Commandments on the wall of his Etowah County courtroom.

Moore, running in 2000 for the open seat being vacated by the retirement of his predecessor, had been vastly outspent in the Republican primary by Harold See, an incumbent associate justice and the favorite of the business establishment, who was trying to move up. But in Christian conservative Alabama, the attention generated by the Ten Commandments drama, and particularly by Moore's defiance of another judge's order (prompted by an ACLU suit) to remove the carving, easily trumped the $1.1 million See had raised for his race. (Of that sum, at least $200,000 went to Karl Rove & Co., a campaign management firm owned by George W. Bush's chief political advisor, who before going with Bush to the White House ran a lot of judicial elections in the South.) "Of course, we give our first recognition to God," Moore told *New York Times* reporter Kevin Sack after his primary victory. "He has providence over us, and His will is something that can't be thwarted."[92] Friends of Bobby Segall, the Alabama ACLU lawyer who brought the suit, were fond of telling him that he was the one who got Moore elected.[93]

(Shortly after his election, Moore, without telling his fellow judges—he was by then known as "the Ten Commandments judge"—set up a two-and-a-half-ton block of granite engraved with the Ten Commandments and other references to God in the courthouse lobby, which quickly became a sort of shrine for busloads of believers. In November 2002, a federal judge named Myron Thompson found that the monument violated the establishment clause of the First Amendment. Thompson declared that he wasn't ruling out all displays of the Ten Commandments in government buildings. This monolith in the middle of the courthouse lobby, however, was—well—just a bit much. But with the expected appeals that will almost certainly not be the end of that story.)[94]

The court's reversal in the school case came in a suit, first brought in 1990 by the Alabama Coalition for Equity (ACE), a group of fourteen county school systems, and later linked to a suit filed by the ACLU on behalf of twenty students who didn't live in the ACE counties. Although its progress through the system was convoluted—even the name of the case changed frequently—the main story is clear enough. In 1993, Montgomery County circuit judge Eugene Reese, who tried the combined cases, had ruled that both the deep disparities between the state's spending on schools in rich communities and poor communities and the inadequate schooling in the poor communities violated the state constitution.[95] That couldn't have been news even to the people of Alabama, whose historically dismal support of schools and its large funding gaps between high- and low-poverty districts perfectly reflected (and no doubt contributed to) its low scores on national tests. The state's top ten districts generated an average of $3,355 per student in local revenues; the bottom ten raised an average of $453. Overall, the quarter of Alabama districts with the fewest students from poor families spent $6,250 per child in 1999–2000; the quarter of districts with the highest concentrations of poor kids spent $5,259—nearly $1,000 less. More than half of the 731,000 students in the state's schools qualified for free or reduced-price lunches; 37 percent were black.[96] Even in 2002, there were still Alabama K–12 schools where students hoping to get the academic diplomas necessary for college admission studied Spanish on their own because their school had no foreign language teacher, where one person tried to teach every science (without labs), and where the library had books that were not certain how the Vietnam War would end or about how long satellites could stay in orbit—would it be only twenty-four hours or as much as a hundred days?[97]

Alabama's state and local revenues were low not only because of the state's relatively low wealth but because it taxed itself at a lower rate than all but a half dozen other states. Worse, according to an analysis by PARCA, the nonpartisan Public Affairs Research Council of Alabama, the money it did raise (through a highly regressive tax structure heavily dependent on sales taxes) was spent so inefficiently because of the state's top-down "earmarking," either by statute or by constitutional provision, that it created "a formidable barrier to sound management of the money taxpayers invest in public services," schools not least among them.[98] In addition, the schools struggle with pressure from Christian fundamentalists on issues such as prayer and evolution; in 1995 those groups successfully pressured the state board of education to stick warning labels in the front of every biology textbook that evolution was "a controversial theory. . . . Instructional material associated with controversy should be approached with an open mind, studied carefully, and critically considered."[99]

By the time the ACE case came to trial, some Alabamians had been establishing their own school reform groups, most notably the A+ Coalition for Better Education, a group of business executives, community leaders, parents, and others that was modeled on Kentucky's Prichard Committee and that, as in Kentucky, understood the cost of the state's backwardness in education. A+ had produced a "Blueprint for Successful Alabama Schools" calling for broad school reform—higher standards, accountability, prekindergarten programs—and used it as the focus for a highly successful set of community forums in more than twenty towns and cities that drew an estimated twenty-three thousand people. It also received a great deal of supportive attention from a media establishment long embarrassed by Alabama's perennially low rankings, shared with its Deep South neighbors Mississippi and Louisiana, in almost any category anyone could think of. In effect, said A+ managing director Cathy Gassenheimer, the group was conducting a political campaign, working the media and, when Reese's 1993 decisions were announced, lobbying hard for the cluster of reforms that were common to its own blueprint, to Alabama First (Governor Jim Folsom's reform proposals), and to the court's order. Nor was A+ alone; there were a number of other groups in the same cause, among them Alabama Arise; Coalition of Alabamians Reforming Education (CARE), which was focused primarily on the state's black rural communities; and several others. The enthusiasm of those community meetings seemed irresistible.

But Alabama in 1993–4 wasn't Kentucky in 1989–90. The opposition coming from suburbanites fearing that their more-than-adequate schools might be damaged by reforms, and from the Alabama Education Association (AEA), the state's big teachers' union, objecting to reform provisions making it easier to fire consistently failing teachers, was no different from that found in other states. But a disproportionate number of its low-performing schools served poor and black children—this was still the Deep South—and its antitax, antireform conservatism and its populist majoritarianism were much more deeply entrenched, especially in the rural areas. There was no Bert Combs to charm the politicians, and the national political climate on the eve of Newt Gingrich's Republican sweep of 1994 was very different from what it had been just two or three years earlier. A year after its high-energy start, as A+ later acknowledged in a five-year report titled *For the Sake of Our Children*, issued in 1996, the whole reform effort had gone off track:

> Because it was an election year, overnight, school reform became inextricably linked to gubernatorial politics. Support for the *Blueprint* that developed in the original meetings splintered as AEA's Paul Hubbert declared his candidacy for governor and decided to oppose what had become the sitting governor's education reform package. By winter, traditional special interests and politicians jockeying for votes began to play on the public's natural anxiety about change. Opponents from the far right clouded the debate by making baseless and outrageous claims. Education associations and unions misled teachers and administrators by distorting tenure issues.
>
> Groups that traditionally oppose property taxes fanned the flames of opposition by incorrectly claiming the reform plan would cost an average Alabama family over $1,000 a year. Lost in the emotional rhetoric was meaningful deliberation and compromise around the core components in the *Blueprint*: tougher coursework, tougher testing and stricter accountability, coupled with more money for professional development, technology, and programs for at-risk students. Politics became the driving force, and helpful dialogue about how best to improve our schools became impossible. Support for the Alabama First Plan began to fade. It had become too much, too fast.[100]

Despite all that, said the report, A+ had a major impact in changing the discussion from fringe debates about distributing condoms in schools or dumbing down the curriculum to more fundamental reform issues. It raised expectations, produced a better understanding that it wasn't laws but minds and hearts that had to be changed, and created a large network of people who were committed to the cause. But in trying to rally the troops, the report struggled to make the best of what had been a major letdown. Even with the support of corporate leaders, reform in Alabama moved at a snail's pace, if at all.[101]

Judge Reese's 1993 decisions rested on a crucial ruling he made in 1991. Relying on the equal protection clause of the Fourteenth Amendment to the U.S. Constitution, he'd struck down Amendment 111, a segregation-era addition to the Alabama constitution approved by voters in 1956, two years after the *Brown* decision, that abolished the state's half-century-old guarantee of public education. If Amendment 111 had remained in place, there could have been no case.

Nothing in this Constitution [said Amendment 111] shall be construed as creating or recognizing any right to education or training at public expense nor as limiting the authority and duty of the legislature, in furthering or providing for education, to require or impose conditions or procedures deemed necessary to the preservation of peace and order. . . . To avoid confusion and disorder and promote effective and economical planning for education, the legislature may authorize the parents or guardians of minors who desire that such minors shall attend schools provided for their own race to make election to that end.[102]

(Predictably, some conservatives, including state supreme court justice J. Gorman Houston Jr., asked how a judge on one county court could declare part of the constitution unconstitutional. Houston saw no conflict between Amendment 111 and the Fourteenth Amendment.)[103]

In striking down Amendment 111, Reese selectively restored the race-neutral portions of the original constitutional provision, which mandated the legislature to "establish, organize, and maintain a liberal system of public schools throughout the state for the benefit of the children thereof between the ages of seven and twenty-one years." That, of course, had originally meant white children, but it would serve. And "liberal," in Reese's reading (later affirmed by the state supreme court), meant equitable and adequate, which, plainly, Alabama's education system was not.[104]

Reese's 1993 rulings were split into two parts—a liability order issued in April finding the state responsible for providing an equitable and adequate public school system and a remedy order signed in October. The latter was based on negotiations among the parties that required the state to provide full funding within six years for everything from equitable and adequate education meeting high academic standards to early childhood programs, special education, and professional development.[105]

In a series of subsequent decisions, culminating with two rulings in *Ex Parte James* (1997), the state supreme court upheld those orders. While the 1997 opinions, written by Justice Ralph Cook, deferred implementation of the remedy order, choosing instead to give the state a "reasonable time" to establish an equitable and adequate system— something it never did—the court reaffirmed its 1993 advisory opinion approving Reese's liability order holding the state responsible for creating a fair and adequate school finance system.[106] By then, the state's Judicial Inquiry Commission, while finding no evidence of "actual bias," had ordered Reese to recuse himself from any further involvement in the case. Reese, who ran for a supreme court seat in 1994 (he lost), had issued campaign literature proclaiming himself "the judge for educational reform" and declaring that "Gene Reese is a tough judge. Last year, he became famous for ruling Alabama's education system unconstitutional and telling a Governor and the Legislature to fix the problem. . . . Now, Gene Reese is running for Alabama Supreme Court— and he will be a tough Justice for change."[107]

Not surprisingly, the state's lawyers tried to use that recusal as evidence that Reese, driven by political ambition, had been biased and that all his rulings should therefore be thrown out. They also tried to counter the difficult fact that the state had never appealed the liability order, and so they argued that the farcical games of litigatory musical chairs attending the case, in which nominal defendants became plaintiffs and then defendants again, had prevented the state from getting its act together. That, the state's lawyers contended, hampered its case through what Justice Cook would call "an absence of adversity."

That contention was largely correct. Of the original defendants, several, including House Speaker Jimmy Clark, Lieutenant Governor Jim Folsom Jr., and the entire state Board of Education, had success-

fully petitioned the court to be redesignated as plaintiffs. To make
the situation still more bizarre, in 1993, just a month after Reese
issued the liability order, Governor Guy Hunt, another original plaintiff, was convicted of a felony for personal use of inaugural funds,
sentenced to five years' probation, and removed from office. That,
obviously, was a distraction, the lawyers argued, from the demands
of a vigorous defense.[108] In addition, some of those who were now
asking the court to throw out the remedy order, among them Governor Fob James—in 1994 he defeated Jim Folsom, who, as lieutenant
governor, had succeeded Hunt—were the successors of the people who
had negotiated the remedy order in the first place.

But the prime issue raised by the state's lawyers, an issue they'd
raised since the beginning of the case, was that the separation-of-
powers provisions of the Alabama constitution were so absolute that
the courts had no authority to intervene in the well-defined mandate
that the constitution gave the governor and legislature in areas such
as education. The language is rather charming:

> The legislative department [said Section 43] shall never exercise
> the executive and judicial powers, or either of them; the exec-
> utive shall never exercise the legislative and judicial powers, or
> either of them; the judicial shall never exercise the legislative
> and executive powers, or either of them; to the end that it may
> be a government of laws and not of men.

Cook, joined by four other members of the nine-member court—
with one judge recusing himself, it was a reasonable margin—rebuffed those challenges. As to the absence of adversity: well before
he was removed from office, as Cook pointed out, Governor Hunt,
despite his earlier denunciation of the suit as an attempt to throw
"more money into the same product," had said he would not appeal
the lower court rulings. Instead, he intended to name a task force "to
address the judge's order to overhaul the education system." Thus,
said Cook, the fact that "the present State parties may disagree more
personally and fundamentally with some aspects of this case than did
their predecessors does not deprive the court of jurisdiction."[109] As to
the separation-of-powers doctrine, "this objection to the exercise of

judicial review of the constitutionality of Alabama's public school system is tenuous at best. Long before Alabama acquired statehood, judicial decisions had recognized the power—as well as the duty—of
the judiciary to review and, if necessary, nullify acts of the legislature
it deemed to be inconsistent with the fundamental law of the land."
In similar cases, a dozen other state supreme courts had done precisely
what the Cook majority was now doing.[110]

In January 2002, when the Alabama Supreme Court, without being
asked, reopened the school funding case, Cook and the four justices
who voted with him in *Ex Parte James* were all gone, either by
resignation, retirement or defeat at the polls.[111] Cook himself had lost
to a Republican circuit court judge named Jacquelyn Stuart. Justice
Kenneth Ingram, another member of the Cook majority, had lost to
the Republican See in 1997. Two had retired, and another had resigned to enter private practice. He was replaced by John England, a
Democrat and another circuit court judge, who was appointed to his
seat by Governor Donald Siegelman. England also lost when he tried
to retain his seat in the election of 2000. Cook and England were the
only two blacks on the court.

The turnover wasn't prompted by the school case and probably
didn't have all that much to do with race. (Ralph Cook, back in
private practice, attributed his loss primarily to George Bush's Republican coattails, but that doesn't explain the judicial turnover of
1998, when Siegelman, a Democrat, was elected governor.)[112] The big
muscle in the elections belonged to the political parties, to the trial
lawyers, and to the insurance companies, corporations, and small-
business associations—Realtors, developers, auto dealers—that had
been chafing for years at what they regarded as Alabama's excessive
hospitality to big damage suits and even larger damage awards. Together, they poured enormous amounts into Alabama's partisan free-
for-all judicial politics.[113]

But in the 1998 and 2000 election cycles, when, according to the
nonpartisan Justice at Stake Campaign, the big players spent over $20
million in eight supreme court races, it was Republicans and corporations that prevailed.[114] In 1993, all nine justices were Democrats,
among them one who had been president of the Alabama Trial Lawyers Association. After the election of 2000, eight of the nine were

Republicans. (In 2000, Democrat Gene Reese, running for a seat on the state's Court of Civil Appeals, also lost.) For the business establishment, there could hardly have been a better investment. In the jury room, as in many other places, southern populism wasn't dead. Hitting corporations with large punitive damage awards was great fun. Alabama, said an out-of-state lawyer, had been "the tort capital of the nation."

When the new court decided in January 2002 to reopen the school case, now known as *ACE v. Siegelman*, it gave the parties just twenty-eight days to file briefs, and thus sent an unmistakable signal of what it intended to do. And by May 31 it had done it. In an unsigned sixteen-page opinion it booted the ten-year-old case out of court. "In Alabama," it ruled, "separation of powers is not merely an implicit 'doctrine' but rather an express command stated with a forcefulness rivaled by few, if any, similar provisions in constitutions of other sovereigns."[115] It then cited not just the constitutional section quoted earlier, that the "court shall never exercise the legislative and executive powers, or either of them, to the end that it may be a government of laws and not of men," but a constitutional amendment approved in 1996, and obviously aimed at rulings like Reese's, that "no order of a state court, which requires disbursement of state funds, shall be binding on the state or any state official until the order has been approved by a simple majority of both houses of the Legislature."[116]

In light of that, said the court in its unsigned 7–1 opinion, the "Equity Funding case has reached its end. . . . Because the duty to fund Alabama's public schools is a duty that—for 125 years—the people of this State have rested squarely upon the shoulders of the Legislature, it is the Legislature, not the courts, from which any further redress should be sought." And so "we complete our judicially prudent retreat from this province of the legislative branch."[117]

Justice Douglas Johnstone, the sole Democrat left on the court and the lone dissenter, argued, in effect, that the court's unbidden decision to reopen a case some four years after it issued a final ruling made it guilty of a level of judicial activism that made the rulings in the prior school finance cases seem benign. "The entirely unsolicited nature of the instant purported review of these equity funding cases exacerbates our lack of appellate jurisdiction," he wrote. "We do not want to become like the Iranian judges who roam the streets of Tehran ordering a whipping here and a jailing there. On the other hand, if this tardy and unsolicited purported review does prevail, I suppose the consolation will be that some old cases which I think or shall think grossly unfair will once again be subject to review."[118] The decision, said attorney Nancy Anderson of the Alabama Disabilities Advocacy Program, who represented handicapped children in the Alabama cases, "took the wind out of our sails."[119]

The overt message of the court's reversal had little to do with schools at all; the court's opinion barely mentions schools. It was related much more closely, first, to the business-friendly strict constructionism that had brought these judges to the court in the first place and, second, to what Jim Williams, who runs PARCA, calls the state's long history of "legislative tyranny." In Alabama—indeed, in much of the South—"legislatures have run everything since colonial times." This court was not going to run afoul of that history, nor did it need to. In effect, the court ruled that if there was a constitutional right to a decent public education, the courts had no authority to enforce it. But for the schools, of course, it meant everything.

The ten-year-long suit that culminated in the *ACE* reversal did have some impact, and continues to do so. Even as the decision was being handed down, the state's education leadership was pressing ahead with some ambitious school reform programs that had in large part been sparked by the *ACE* cases. The legislature had already approved some modest increases to the state's support of local schools, which hardly closed the gap but slightly narrowed it. The state had raised high school graduation requirements. It was touting the popular Alabama Reading Initiative to raise literacy levels through intensive reading instruction, especially in the lower grades—a program that brought in more reading specialists and was retraining thousands of teachers in two-week summer sessions in techniques "based on proven research." (The state remained agnostic in the ongoing dispute between phonics and whole-language instruction, which provided more choice in the schools but raised questions about what "proven research" meant.)[120] Siegelman had also developed an ambitious plan for a statewide prekindergarten program, part of which the governor hoped to fund with a state lottery.

But with the exception of some forty-three pilot preschool sites, the voters' rejection of the lottery and the sharp downturn in state revenues in 1999–2002 left the preschool plan high and dry, waiting for some lifting tide to return. And with his narrow defeat in 2002, Siegelman, one of the last Democratic governors in the South, was also gone. In the summer of 2002, two months after the justices kicked *ACE* out of court, state education superintendent Ed Richardson and the independently elected state Board of Education that appointed him formally unveiled an ambitious school finance program, citing Reese's 1993 decisions, which charged Alabama to develop a plan "to reach an adequate level in our schools." They'd been working on it with circuit judge Sally Greenhaw, who took over in 1995 after Reese was forced to remove himself from the case. Now dressed up as Realizing Every Alabama Child's Hopes (REACH), it called for $1.6 billion in new school funding, the equivalent of an additional $2,000-plus per year for each of the state's 731,000 students and roughly half again as much as the state itself was then spending to augment local school tax revenues. The money was to pay for additional teachers, guidance counselors, nurses, books, special education, and programs for at-risk students.[121]

If fully funded, said a state Department of Education promotional slide show, REACH would "ensure that every child will have an opportunity to succeed—no matter where they live or the wealth or circumstances of a student's family." Even so, as one local superintendent pointed out, it wouldn't do more than get Alabama to the average spending in the bottom tier of southeastern states. "I'm embarrassed and angry," Richardson had said earlier. "I've never in my life had to be just adequate."[122] In fact, REACH was not based on any systematic attempt to determine what it would cost to educate students adequately, or what adequacy meant. The plan, based on reaching parity with other southern states, was more a wish list of the education bureaucracy. Still, said Mitch Edwards, a spokesman for the Alabama Board of Education, "We probably wouldn't have done it without the lawsuit."

But even REACH was only a hope. It would first have to be approved by the legislature, never an easy thing in a state that was among the most tax-averse in the nation, and now, with the leverage of the court gone, more difficult still. Alabama had—has—one of the most unfair and unreliable tax systems in the nation. It rests heavily on sales taxes that include food and medicine and thus burden low-income people much more severely than the rich or the middle class. At the same time, sales taxes are always subject to wide fluctuations with the economy, even as real property, which is relatively stable, is greatly undertaxed. To fund REACH, that system would almost certainly have to be revamped, making the chances of it ever passing in anywhere near the proportions that Richardson and the board proposed slim, if indeed there was a chance at all. As to chances for a greater effort on local taxes, which Alabama was technically capable of, almost all of the state was served by countywide school districts, and rural people, in Williams's words, "vote everything down."

Unlike Kentucky, which completely revamped its school finance system, at least in part to attract new manufacturing industry, Alabama created what Jim Williams of PARCA calls "an alternative education system."[123] It got a shock when it lost a Saturn plant because Alabama was thought to produce too few skilled graduates and then got a few more when some employers, among them a steel corporation in Gadsden, announced their refusal to continue hiring local graduates because 70 percent of them tested below the eighth-grade level in reading.[124] But instead of radically upgrading the schools, the state cut special deals with Boeing, Honda, Hyundai, Lockheed, Mercedes, and other major manufacturers that established Alabama plants, creating an organization called Alabama Industrial Development Training (AIDT) to provide job-specific "customized training" at public expense for their new operations. ("Training services are offered in many areas," says AIDT, "and are free of charge to new and expanding industries throughout the State." Adequacy for corporate employers.)[125] Richardson still spoke hopefully about REACH, but even as he spoke, the legislature, squeezed by recession, was cutting spending, not raising it. A+, meanwhile, had deferred its objectives from fundamental reform to an agenda of gradualism, working, as one analysis said, "to help schools build their own capacity to succeed."[126] Some of the other organizations, deciding that school reform was a dead end in the state's political climate, had turned to other causes.

"In the more than ten years since the original lawsuit was filed," Gassenheimer wrote in a piece published after *ACE* was finally thrown out, "a generation of students has graduated, many of whom attended substandard schools without the resources to offer the rigorous instruction they needed. During this decade, we have ignored our responsibility to adequately fund our schools. Students in a few, mostly prosperous areas of Alabama attend schools that are funded at competitive levels, but most ... go to schools that are funded well below the level that would make their educational programs effective."[127] In Alabama, that was the way it had always been.

V. North Carolina: Judge Manning's "Iron Hand"

The pattern in many suits based on constitutional education clauses is for the parties and/or the courts to link equity and adequacy, using the one, as in New Jersey, as (at least) a partial measure of the other. But a number of courts have explicitly declared that while the constitution requires adequacy, however defined, it does not require equity. Perhaps the clearest of those declarations came in North Carolina, where the Supreme Court in 1987 rejected a suit based on alleged disparities in spending and where, in *Leandro v. State of North Carolina* (1997), a case brought by students, parents, and school boards in some of the state's poorest counties, it embraced adequacy a decade later. In doing so, the court was blessed with what may be the most wonderful constitutional provision of them all:

> The people have a right to the privilege of education, and it is the duty of the State to guard and maintain that right.... The General Assembly shall provide by taxation and otherwise for a general and uniform system of free public schools, which shall be maintained at least nine months in every year, and wherein equal opportunities shall be provided for all students.[128]

Those provisions, wrote Chief Justice Burley B. Mitchell Jr. for the supreme court, guaranteed "a right to a sound basic education. An education that does not serve the purpose of preparing students to participate and compete in the society in which they live and work is devoid of substance and is constitutionally inadequate."[129] Then, echoing the Kentucky supreme court in its *Rose* decision, among others, Mitchell enumerated the general outlines of what his court had in mind:

> (1) sufficient ability to read, write, and speak the English language and a sufficient knowledge of fundamental mathematics and physical science to enable the student to function in a complex and rapidly changing society; (2) sufficient fundamental knowledge of geography, history, and basic economic and political systems to enable the student to make informed choices with regard to issues that affect the student personally or affect the student's community, state, and nation; (3) sufficient academic and vocational skills to enable the student to successfully engage in post-secondary education or vocational training; and (4) sufficient academic and vocational skills to enable the student to compete on an equal basis with others in further formal education or gainful employment in contemporary society.

With certain variations, those phrases had found their way into any number of adequacy decisions and would find their way into more. What they said, at bottom, was that you can't just keep the doors open and put a warm adult body in every classroom; you have to try earnestly to accomplish not just something, but something pretty ambitious.

Justice Mitchell, quoting the North Carolina constitution's equal opportunity language, which was added in 1970, remarkably early for a southern state, nonetheless rejected the equity claim. Having considered the provision's history, the judges concluded that it "does not require substantially equal funding or educational advantages in all school districts." Therefore even if the county-based financed system resulted in unequal spending, it didn't violate the constitution. They then went on to cite a list of cases in other states where equity cases produced "substantial problems" and to warn that "even greater problems of protracted litigation resulting in unworkable remedies would occur if we were to recognize the purported right to equal educational opportunities in every one of the state's districts." Clearly, "the framers of our Constitution did not intend to set such an impractical or unattainable goal. Instead, their focus was upon ensuring that the children of the state have the opportunity to receive a sound basic education."

The court seemed to understand well enough the importance of the distinctions it made. It meant that a trial judge trying to assess the details of an adequacy claim, said Justice Mitchell, could use the state's own academic standards as a measure, though not necessarily a dispositive one. He or she could also look at the scores on standardized achievement tests and other outcomes, always with the caveat that "the value of standardized tests is the subject of much debate" and therefore shouldn't be "treated as absolutely authoritative" either. State funding levels could also be used as a measure, but that gauge, too, had its limitations, especially since "one of the major sources of controversy concerns the extent to which there is a demonstrable correlation between educational expenditures and the quality of education."

Mitchell cited William H. Clune of the University of Wisconsin, who had been the third member of the old Coons-Sugarman team that created the original theory of tax wealth inequities that led to the California *Serrano* cases of the 1970s and who had since jumped the fence from equity to adequacy. There was research out there, said the court, quoting Clune, suggesting that in some places "substantial increases in funding produce only modest gains in most schools." The court also cited the experience in Kansas City in the 1980s where the U.S. Supreme Court "expressly noted that despite massive court-ordered expenditures . . . which had provided students there with school 'facilities and opportunities not available anywhere else in the country,' the Kansas City students had not come close to reaching their potential, and 'learner outcomes' of those students were 'at or below national norms at many grade levels.' "[130]

The North Carolina case had begun in Wake County Superior Court in Raleigh—it went up before trial on an appeal of the lower court's refusal to dismiss it as constitutionally unfounded. Now the justices sent it back to the same court and the whimsical, affable (and often blunt) Judge Howard Manning Jr., the jurist who would want to know if those out-of-date globes in the Hoke County schools still showed Gaul. In a trial beginning in September 1999, one day before Hurricane Floyd hit the eastern part of the state—the proceedings were moved for three weeks to a federal courtroom—Manning heard forty-three witnesses and depositions from many more, and received 670 exhibits. (That was a pittance compared to the cases in California, New York, and New Jersey, although it would have amounted to a great deal more had the parties not agreed with Manning's decision to limit evidence to just one presumably representative rural system of the five that had joined the suit and one urban system of six.) Thus began one of the more extraordinary "conversations" ever held among judges, bureaucrats, and politicians.

The rural system Manning chose was Hoke County in the Carolina Sandhills ("Home of the North Carolina Turkey Festival"), one of the poorest in the state, though also one of the fastest-growing, whose thirty-five thousand people were 44 percent white, 38 percent black, and 11 percent American Indian and where one child in four was living below the poverty level, a rate roughly one-third higher than the state average. (School enrollment was 65 percent nonwhite; 62 percent qualified for free or reduced-price lunches.) There were no colleges or universities in Hoke County, no hospital, no pediatrician, and, with the exception of Friday night high school football in the fall, nothing much for kids to do.[131] And, of course, the schools were equally impoverished; in the first nine months of 1999, said a personnel officer of Unilever, which runs a Hoke County plant making deodorant and shampoo, the company hired twenty-five people from the county, none of whom was from Hoke High School. There was similar testimony from a representative of the Tar Heel Turkey Hatchery. The local graduates were too illiterate and innumerate, said their human resources people, even for the simple jobs that they were hiring for.[132]

But the evidence—about school performance and graduation rates, about low literacy levels, about the lack of qualified teachers and materials, about the weak academic records of Hoke County graduates at the University of North Carolina and other colleges, and about the persistent gaps between students from poor families, and those from

wealthier families—applied to a great many places other than Hoke
on North Carolina's educational landscape. Indeed, Manning believed
that it applied to all at-risk students, even those in the wealthier
districts. When he ultimately issued his expansive rulings in *Hoke v.
North Carolina,* a series of five decisions handed down over a period
of some eighteen months (from October 2000 to April 2002), it applied
to all poor North Carolina children at risk of educational failure, not
just those of the plaintiff counties.[133] But the logic of his analysis also
led him to conclude that "the disparity in local funding seems to
make no discernible difference in the academic achievement of the
at-risk populations."[134] "Sheer dollars," he said, wasn't the determining factor.

There was nothing subtle about those decisions. The state's contention, Manning wrote, that school performance at the basic level
satisfied the constitutional mandate of adequacy "flunks the smell test.
It flies in the face of common sense and reason that the Supreme
Court of North Carolina [intended] in defining the goals of a sound
basic education." That issue was reduced to its most awful dimensions
by an exchange between Manning and Deputy Attorney General Tom
Ziko, who represented the state in the case:

> Ziko: The state has far higher goals and always has had higher
> goals than providing a system which does nothing but provide
> a sound basic education.
>
> Manning: So . . . it's the difference between a Moped and a Cad-
> illac. The goals are a Cadillac goal and the minimum stan-
> dard, the minimum standard you're talking about, provides
> that child with a Moped, and if they can really achieve they
> get a Cadillac.
>
> Ziko: Yes.
>
> Manning: But the Constitution doesn't demand more than a
> Moped.
>
> Ziko: Right.[135]

"Adequate" had been roughly defined in the Supreme Court's
four-part *Leandro* test, which "mandates a quality education for all
children, sufficient for those who wish to go into the workforce, to

vocational school, to college, and to be able to meaningfully compete
with others in those endeavors." Although Manning left the means
up to the state, he ordered North Carolina officials to provide substantial extra help—and especially preschools—to all children at risk
of failure, even if that meant shifting resources from affluent to
needy kids:

> Economically disadvantaged children, more so than economically
> advantaged children, need opportunities and services over and
> above those provided to the general student population in order
> to put them in a position to obtain an equal opportunity to
> receive a sound basic education. These additional opportunities
> may include additional time on task, lower class sizes, early
> childhood education, individual tutoring, early intervention or
> supplementary instruction and materials. Enabling at-risk chil-
> dren to perform well in school requires more time and more
> resources.[136]

That statement was radical enough. But what really got attention
was the next part of his decision (*Hoke III*), issued March 21, 2001,
where he declared:

> The right to the equal opportunity to a sound basic education
> is only to the sound basic education, not the frills and whistles.
> The State Constitution does not require that children be pro-
> vided a prep school education, nor that children be provided the
> courses and experiences to enable them to go to Yale or Harvard.
> While there is no restriction on high-level electives, modern
> dance, advanced computer courses and multiple foreign language
> courses being taught or paid for by tax dollars in the public
> schools, the Constitutional guarantee of a sound basic education
> for each child must first be met.[137]

Although there would be no certainty until the appeals were decided, it was hard to imagine that North Carolina's supreme court
had that kind of redistributive strategy in its sights when it ruled

that the constitution's "right to the privilege of education" clause did not require equity. But the ruling made a lot of people uncomfortable who should, at worst, have been neutral on Hoke and who would probably have supported a general order to the state to ratchet up resources to needy areas. School superintendents in midlevel and relatively affluent districts quickly recognized that if the Robin Hood inferences of Manning's opinion became law, their own districts might well take a blow. "I don't think there's adequate funding available unless you do away with other programs," Johnston County superintendent James Causby told the *Raleigh News & Observer*. "What are you going to do away with?"[138] Causby's rapidly suburbanizing district, located not far from the state's big universities and the Raleigh Research Triangle, was among North Carolina's highest scoring school systems, and its voters were in the process of passing a series of school construction bonds totaling $300 million.

State school superintendent Mike Ward, though more guarded, said the same thing. "We can't do this with existing resources," he said. "We have to find additional funds to carry out our obligations to our most vulnerable children." In a place where a large part of operating funds already came from the state, judicial talk about possible redistribution wasn't helpful. "We reject the notion that money should be re-allocated from so-called frills," said Phil Kirk, who chaired the state board of education. "If resources are diverted from those programs, it will drive more of the brighter students away from public schools into private education."[139]

Manning, himself a Republican, called the response a political and educational "firestorm." But while it probably helped ensure the appeal that the state would file, it wasn't all that much of a conflagration. North Carolina, always the vanguard of what used to be called the New South and a national leader in school reform, was not going to jeopardize its progressive reputation and its appeal to the scientists, engineers, and technicians of its growing high-tech industry with rebel yells and mindless resistance. Its academic standards and school accountability programs were widely credited with putting the state among the nation's biggest gainers on NAEP and other measures of academic achievement; it had reduced the achievement gap in NAEP math scores between white and African American students; it was among the nation's leaders in Advanced Placement courses offered and AP exams taken.

By the time of his final formal ruling, handed down in April 2002, Manning himself seemed to be trying to pull back from the language that had caused the "firestorm." Advanced Placement courses and other programs to help students get into college, he said, are just as much part of a "sound basic education" as shop courses or vocational courses or (presumably) preschool for at-risk kids. There was even a touch of cranky defensiveness in his response to state board of education chairman Phil Kirk's published remarks about how Manning's language might drive some of the brighter students to private schools. "*Leandro,*" Manning wrote, "guarantees a sound basic educational opportunity to all children sufficiently substantial to permit those who can, including Chairman Kirk's 'best and brightest,' go to college." The Kirk remark, he said, was "a cruel scare." But Manning hadn't changed his position or softened on remedies. If necessary, said his 2002 ruling, the state had to "step in with an iron hand and get the mess straight."

> If it takes removing an ineffective superintendent, principal, teacher, or group of teachers and putting effective, competent ones in their place, so be it. If the deficiencies are due to a lack of effective management practices, then it is the State's responsibility to see that effective management practices are put in place.[140]

The state, in Manning's words, had argued that "if an individual [local district] is failing to provide any of its school children with the opportunity for a sound basic education, it is the [district's] fault, not the State's fault." But the constitution gave the state the ultimate responsibility. Indeed, Manning said pointedly, he wasn't sure that even the districts that were suing the state were allocating their existing resources strategically enough to provide the educational opportunity the constitution mandated. "It's how the resources are allocated that count[s]. Palatial central offices and high salaries for non teaching administrators and staff are not constitutionally mandated. The tax money that is spent must first be spent to properly educate the at-risk children that are failing to achieve grade level proficiency." Thus the plaintiff districts might themselves be candidates for the state's iron hand.[141]

The state, in fact, was trying to have it both ways. Even as he announced the appeal, Governor Mike Easley, a Democrat, also vowed to press ahead with efforts to broaden the state's preschool program and to address the other items on Manning's agenda. He named an Education First Task Force of school officials, businesspeople, and community leaders to pursue the goal of making the state's schools "superior and competitive," which turned out to be part substance, part the classic delaying tactic that such panels often were. By mid-2002, roughly a year after *Hoke III* and a bare ten weeks after Manning's final ruling, the state, responding to Manning's order that it report back on its implementation of his rulings, submitted Education First's proposals, along with a collection of stuff scraped from the files of the state's Department of Instruction that, in Manning's view, fell somewhere between unsatisfactory and insulting. He told the state that it wouldn't do. " "The task force is merely advisory," he wrote Deputy Attorney General Ziko and others. "In stark contrast, however, the court's orders in this case are not advisory. It appears clear to the court that the state, including the lawyers in the attorney general's office, has failed to appreciate this distinction and elected to do little if anything, in order to comply."

The Education First agenda nonetheless became a major blueprint, maybe even a weapon, for the courts as the battle continued. Although it never mentioned Manning or the lawsuit—the object, said one of its reports, was "to finish [North Carolina's] journey from the educational basement to the top floor"—it reflected both Manning's demands and school reform proposals that Easley himself had been making since his election in 2000.[142] Among its items: expand Easley's new More at Four prekindergarten program to serve every one of the state's forty thousand at-risk four-year-olds with "high-quality educational opportunities"; reduce class size in kindergarten and grades 1–3 to no more than eighteen students and no more than fifteen in classes in low-performing and high-poverty schools; continue to raise the state's teachers' salaries, which were already above the national average; intensify reading instruction in the early grades, including a "massive" teacher-training effort in the teaching of reading; improve training for principals and administrators.

All of that would involve money, including a $6.2 billion facilities bond, as well as an enhanced accountability system of "earned flexibility" in spending for successful schools, but tight "research-backed" constraints on how money was spent in low performing schools. The panel also called for a single funding stream for at-risk kids, rather than the uncoordinated categorical programs that characterized so much school funding. (Children, as Marian Wright Edelman of the Children's Defense Fund often said, do not come as separate parts, they come as whole people.) But the task force's estimated price tag— a total of $185 million in 2003–4—was often vague and, in the end, rather modest in a state with 1.2 million schoolchildren—an increase altogether of less than 3 percent. And, of course, as the *Hoke* plaintiffs pointed out, it was all just a task force proposal, not state policy, much less a legislatively enacted budget. At a time when the state's finances were squeezed, the distance even to such a budget seemed especially long.

In a document outlining its appeal of Manning's rulings—the document was filed in July 2002, almost at the same moment as the Education First reports—the state stubbornly returned to its original arguments. It contended that it was the local districts, not the state, that were ultimately responsible; denied that the constitution guaranteed a right to equal educational opportunity; and asserted once again that despite its own high academic and accountability standards, the state's lowest-achieving students were still getting an adequate education. It also charged that Manning had ordered remedies, including the "iron hand" order demanding greater state control over local personnel decisions, that the plaintiffs had never asked for, and that Manning's ruling intruded into the prerogatives of the governor and legislature and thus "violates the constitutional principle of separation of powers." All these things, the brief said, are nonjusticiable political questions. And where did the court get the power to grant four-year-olds the right to another year of public education?[143]

The sweep of the state's arguments, said Sheria Reid, who runs the North Carolina Education and Law Project, which was trying to organize a campaign to generate political support for the Manning reforms, "belie the avowed pro-education platform of our governor and legislative leadership." Easley, she said, was sincere, but either he and the attorney general "were dancing out of step" or they were playing a coordinated game of good cop/bad cop. What they'd affirmed in two decades of educational policy making—in the state's academic standards and testing and school accountability programs—and were now implicitly acknowledging in letters to Manning, they were denying in the appellate court. ("Just who is the state?" one of the *Hoke* lawyers wondered.) In any case, Reid said, they should have been embarrassed by the assertion in the appeal that students who were achieving below the level the state defined as acceptable for promotion were receiving an adequate education.[144]

The governor was in fact listening to the decisions that his attorney general was trying to repudiate and, at the very least, going through the motions of compliance. Despite the appeal, the state had not asked for a stay of Manning's decision. On July 24, 2002, two weeks after the release of the Education First report, and just two weeks after the attorney general filed the appeal, Easley issued an executive order to expand the More at Four preschool program for poor children from 1,600 to 7,600 (against an eligible pool of some 40,000), to reduce class size in kindergarten and first grade, and to hire hundreds more teachers, as his task force had proposed (and as Manning had demanded). He also promised local districts some $54 million in additional funds to pay for those programs. The order was accompanied by a letter to all members of the legislature citing Manning's decision and warning that the situation had reached a "crisis point" that required prompt action both on the budget and on a lottery proposal to help pay for Easley's initiatives. It wasn't at all clear that Easley had the constitutional authority to commit the funds—he said he wasn't usurping the General Assembly's power to appropriate money, merely complying with the court—but if he could get all the schools committed to the increases, it wasn't likely that the legislature would refuse them the money. "The court order," Easley said, "is not going away."[145]

In the face of a large budget deficit and a recalcitrant legislature, however, it was hardly a sure thing, particularly in the out years. But if the court order survived, it would, as Reid said, "put enormous pressure on the politicians." And that's just what Manning himself was already doing. In the summer of 2002, as the politicians were deadlocked on the budget, and as the plaintiff school districts complained that the state wasn't doing enough, he fired off letters to Ziko and state education officials telling them, "You may no longer stand back and point your fingers and deny responsibility." What the state had to do—and do now—was to help districts with large concentrations of at-risk students to "put in place, within their allocated and existing resources, effective educational methods and programs to help at-risk and other children achieve [a] sound basic education." So far, he said, the state's responses to his demand for quarterly progress reports had been "unacceptable."[146]

Here again, the dialogue would have its irony. The forces that made the state's responses so unacceptable—the holdouts in the legislature—were using Manning's own statements about ineffective allocation of resources to justify their resistance to Easley's demands for more funding. "Judge Manning said, as I read the opinion, that you can do it with existing dollars," said House Republican leader Leo Daughtry. "We're not going to move on the lottery or the sales tax."[147] Did that mean that they, too, favored a little redistribution from the frills and whistles of North Carolina's relatively well-funded schools to the urban and rural schools of the poor? Since the frills-and-whistles schools were the places to which most of their suburban constituents sent their children, it was hardly likely. But in this multicornered and very complicated political dialogue, it was Manning, *Hoke,* and *Leandro* that were driving the agenda.

VI. Maryland: Barbara Hoffman's Victory

On April 4, 2002, the same day Howard Manning issued his iron hand decision in North Carolina, there was a minor miracle in Maryland. On that day, the state's House of Delegates approved SB 856, a sweeping school reform bill passed by the state senate the day before. Within six years, the new law was to provide for an additional $1.3 billion on top of the $2.9 billion state taxpayers were then spending on K–12 education and bring the state's share of local school support from $3,500 per child to $5,600. Although the state raised cigarette and other tobacco taxes (from 64 cents a pack to $1.00) to pay for the initial stages of the sweeping new program it created, no one knew where the money was going to come from in the out years, when the new system was fully implemented. This was really betting on the come.

But while it was an enormous and perhaps risky commitment, the public's generally strong support of public education, even if it cost more money, would probably make it difficult for politicians to break. Major chunks of that new money would go to Baltimore and other school districts that were educating the highest concentrations of poor children, and most particularly to the kindergarten and preschool programs that were—and are—widely believed to be so crucial if disadvantaged kids were to get a relatively even start in school. More important, the bill mandated full-day kindergarten for all Maryland children and preschool services for all its low-income children by 2007. It also required each district to go through a master planning process "to determine [as its chief sponsor said] its own unique needs" and thus replace a lot of top-down mandates with local flexibility— but always within the state's academic standards. Where districts did not make progress or failed to develop an adequate plan, the state would step in to review, order changes in the plan, and where necessary withhold funding to get the locals' attention.

The Maryland bill, which Governor Parris Glendening would sign a month later, was based on the recommendations of a high-profile state commission of educators, legislators, and businesspeople appointed by Glendening and headed by Alvin Thornton, the chairman of the political science department at Howard University. The commission relied on an extensive adequacy study (ultimately a melding of two studies), called in Maryland "costing-out studies," by two of the major consultancies in the field—Augenblick and Myers of Denver and the California-based Management Analysis and Planning (MAP). Those studies were in turn analyzed and modified by the commission, which pegged the base cost per pupil (in 2002) at just below $6,000, with extra "weights" given to students with special needs. Every special-education student was given a weight of 1.17, meaning a district would get its base plus 117 percent of the base;

each economically disadvantaged student was weighted at 1.1; every limited-English-proficiency student was weighted at 1.0. Those numbers were then further adjusted with the use of the Geographic Cost of Education Index (GCEI) for the cost of living in the local area.[148]

The formulas were not hard science; indeed, as countless public officials, educators, and economists (plus Howard Manning) knew, the connection between raw dollars and student achievement is itself a subject of endless dispute. Nor was it quite clear from where the cavalry of educational wisdom would ride in when districts failed to make the grade. In state after state, governors and legislatures were fond of decreeing accountability schemes that included takeovers of failing schools that later turned out to be less than the shining successes their sponsors imagined. (The same was often true of local measures to "reconstitute" schools by reassigning their entire staff and bringing in a new team. Sometimes it worked; sometimes it just meant two more years of chaos as the new crew, which was often not much wiser than the people it replaced, tried to find its way through its inherited labyrinth.) In California, the state's list of approved consultants for failing schools included any number of ex-administrators of other problem schools or districts.

But it was nonetheless the Thornton Commission that shaped and gave legitimacy to what, by the standards of most state school finance systems, was a huge and often radical departure. Part of the commission's clout came from the stature of its members, part from the extensive public hearing schedule it pursued, and part from the revealing data it produced—figures that, in turn, became the core of the legislature's own analyses—and beyond that from the powerful conclusions it drew from it. "Maryland," said a legislative analysis of SB 856, "has set high performance standards and has established a nationally recognized accountability system. The State has not, however, linked its school financing system to expected student outcomes."

The legislature's analysis, using the commission's data, produced a comparison of the "adequacy costs" and available per-pupil revenues for each of Maryland's twenty-four county and city districts, along with the "adequacy gap" for each. For Baltimore in 2002, for example, the gap was $3,383 per pupil above the $8,564 the district had available, a difference of 40 percent. Caroline County, a poor rural area on the Eastern Shore, where the median family income was roughly half what it was in wealthy Montgomery County and the child poverty rate ran 50 percent higher than the state's, was spending $6,112 and had a revenue gap of $3,182.[149] That meant that in order to meet the adequacy definitions of the commission and its consultants, it would have to spend half again as much as it had available. With some exceptions, the commission found, as the adequacy gap went up from district to district, so did the "achievement gap" on the state's tests—the difference between the state's official academic expectations on the lengthy Maryland School Performance Assessment Program (MSPAP, now replaced by MSA, the Maryland School Assessment, a shorter, nationally standardized multiple-choice test)—and the actual performance of the average student.[150]

The hero of the moment was a veteran state senator from Baltimore named Barbara A. Hoffman—she was first elected in 1982—who was the longtime chair of the senate's Budget and Taxation Committee. Since the bill, SB 856, that she negotiated through the legislature not only had to find its way through the brambles of local funding formulas and the attendant local demands, suspicions, and jealousies but also involved major new funds during a recession when budgets were being cut and no one seriously expected such a breakthrough, its passage was an especially stunning achievement. It was "one of the finest hours of my career," Hoffman said at the time, "as well as that of my colleagues in the Senate and the House." But as she would say later, in her two decades in budget politics, she had learned that "governors [the real drivers of the budget process in most states] fund what governors care about. We'd spent a huge amount on open space. It's not rocket science. We just needed to make it happen." Somehow, as any number of people in Maryland reported, she had the determination to do that.[151]

As in North Carolina, this trail also began with a succession of lawsuits dating back nearly twenty years. In one of those cases, *Hornbeck v. Somerset County Board of Education* (1983), the Maryland Court of Appeals, the state's highest tribunal, rejected an equity claim—the Maryland constitution did not require equity in spending, it ruled—but indicated that the state constitution's "thorough and efficient" education clause did guarantee the right to an education "which by contemporary standards was full, complete and effective in every part of the State."[152] Those standards, the court said, were partially defined by the state's own academic requirements.

In the second case, *Bradford v. Maryland State Board of Education,* brought on their behalf by the ACLU in 1994, a group of Baltimore students and parents charged that the city's schools were so badly underfunded that they could not provide an education that satisfied the constitution's mandate as defined by *Hornbeck.* In 1996, the case, which had been consolidated with a similar suit brought by the Baltimore Board of School Commissioners, the city council, and the mayor, was settled by a consent decree.

The result was a "Partnership Agreement" that provided moderate funding increases for the Baltimore schools in return for a takeover by the mayor and governor of the city's dysfunctional system. But when the state failed to provide the additional funding that the new board had a right to request under the consent decree, the plaintiffs returned to the trial court, as the decree allowed, and got a decision (in 2000) from Judge Joseph H. H. Kaplan that the state was still underfunding the city's schools. Kaplan noted, among other things, that the state was proposing to pay Edison Schools, the private for-profit school venture, an average of nearly $2,000 more per pupil to manage three "reconstituted" Baltimore city schools than it was putting into similar public schools. If the state gave the public schools the same amount, Baltimore would have nearly $200 million more a year. Three pages further on, Kaplan told the state to do precisely that: pony up an additional $2,000 to $2,600 more per pupil per year.[153]

What the judge asked for, however, was more nudge than command. "Having found that the State is not fulfilling its obligations under . . . the Maryland Constitution as well as under the Consent Decree," Kaplan said, "the Court trusts that the State will act to bring itself into compliance with its constitutional and contractual obligations under the Consent Decree . . . without the need for Plaintiffs to take further action." That trust seemed to derive primarily from the fact that the dialogue that the court had set in motion among the various players was so intense and complex and had so much independent energy that any specificity might just have confused things.

In the prior year, there had been constant meetings (in various combinations) among members of the Baltimore school commissioners (all appointed by the Governor Glendening and Mayor Martin O'Malley) and between the commissioners and key members of the legislature, including Barbara Hoffman; between school commissioners and the state Department of Budget and Management; and between Hoffman and other legislators and the governor. There was a working group that included Baltimore school officials, ACLU officers as representatives of the students, and others to develop and negotiate a remedy plan for the district. There were discussions with Lieutenant Governor Kathleen Kennedy Townsend, who was getting ready to run for governor herself, state education commissioner Nancy Grasmick, and members of the governor's staff, all accompanied by declarations that if Maryland failed to act, the state would be hauled into court again. There was talk that if more money wasn't forthcoming, the state's rural districts would file their own suit. And there was the Thornton Commission, which had been established in the fall of 1999 and whose members included many of the same big players, Hoffman and her Republican senate colleague Robert Neall paramount among them. Much of Kaplan's twenty-six-page opinion in 2000 was devoted to a list of those meetings.[154]

For a painfully long time, all that negotiating produced so little that Hoffman and Howard Rawlings, chair of the House Appropriations Committee, wrote the governor early in 2000 complaining how "in a year of plenty, Baltimore City is like the starving Little Match Girl with her nose pressed up against the window of the grocery store. The proprietor (the Governor) is cheerfully doling out goodies to the mostly prosperous while the destitute (Baltimore) sinks further into despair." Hoffman later recalled a meeting with "a young man from the lieutenant governor's office" who'd been sent to say the time wasn't right for real reform—was it ever?—and to negotiate an anemic compromise; she recalled Governor Glendening's own lack of enthusiasm for what was likely to be a complex and expensive solution.[155]

Yet slowly a lot of things were coming together: a coalition composed of major children's advocacy groups, the state PTA, the ACLU, the Maryland Caucus of Black School Board members, the teachers'

unions, and others that helped reinforce an already strong public in-
clination to put more into schools and would hand-deliver twenty-
five thousand letters to legislators demanding action; the ongoing talks
among state leaders and, most particularly, the Thornton recommendations, which were carefully crafted so that while many districts—
poor and average, urban and rural—would be winners, none would
be a loser.

This was not Howard Manning's raid on the bells and whistles of
the rich people's schools; this was adequacy based on the analysis and
calculations of the best people in the field. And since the commission,
translating the experts' studies into clear standards, had spelled out
just how much each county would get, the coalition could not merely
explain the proposals to legislators but had to generate grassroots support by showing local voters, taxpayers, and parents the precise benefits for their own schools. And to make things a bit more persuasive,
not only had Baltimore's once notoriously chaotic schools been reor-
ganized, but Maryland now had the rising test scores from Baltimore
students, which were not necessarily the last word on student achievement but were still real enough, to persuade people that the schools
were shaping up. Not long before, any mention of Baltimore schools
would have been met with scorn and raised eyebrows, said the ACLU's
Bebe Verdery, one of the leaders of the coalition. But the rising scores
(which were going up even as the state average dipped slightly) ended
the derision. With the 2002 election only a few months off, how could
any member vote against money for his or her own district?

Whenever it appeared that nothing would happen, Verdery said,
"I'd tell people, 'We're going to do this.' " At one of the advocates'
press conferences at the state capitol, she said, "the Speaker of the
House walked by, and of course all the reporters grabbed him, and
he said, 'It's dead on arrival.' But that just reinforced everybody's
determination to show it wasn't dead."[156]

In the end, however, it was Barbara Hoffman, with help from
Bobby Neall and a rising Montgomery County legislator named Chris
Van Hollen (who would soon be elected to Congress), who almost by
force of will drove the reform bill through the legislature and past
the rocks and shoals that stood in its way. On one hand, there were
members who argued that it was irresponsible to make long-term

funding commitments without knowing where the money would come from. In the words of a person who sat through those sessions, "They just kept saying, 'It's too expensive, it's too expensive.'" On the other hand, there were the Washington suburbs in affluent Montgomery County, which has some of the best schools in the state, but where members were under pressure, as one legislative staffer said, "to bring home more of the bacon." Although they argued that the county's own costs were rising, particularly because of its growing numbers of limited-English-proficiency students, the bill also was a large opportunity to get a little more of that bacon.

That became especially tempting because Montgomery County's liberal Democratic votes were needed to pass the cigarette tax increase that was to fund the initial (low-cost) years of the reform. The members who held those votes thus had to be satisfied with what Montgomery County schools were getting, which meant that the county executive had to be satisfied. There were the usual members with pet projects—programs for infants and toddlers, for example—who had to be given a few goodies. There were rural members looking for a little extra. And there was the special problem of the mismanaged Prince George's County schools, which were seen as a bottomless pit that needed to be restructured before any major new statewide fiscal formula could pass political muster. And since 63 percent of Prince George's County's residents were African American, the insult and injury of a bill that was subsequently enacted replacing the district's elected school board with an appointed one, thereby disenfranchising the county's voters, had to be assuaged with even more extra money than the county would be getting under the Thornton formula.[157] What the *New York Times* would call "a visionary plan for Maryland" was generated through the same political dealing that any other bill involved. This was no virgin birth.[158]

The reforms, said a Baltimore journalist who covered the story, almost didn't happen. Late on a Friday evening, when things in her Budget Committee appeared to be going nowhere, Hoffman, perhaps in a ploy, perhaps in frustration, started to pack up her stuff and walk out. Then somebody suggested a five-minute time-out, after which at least one of the crucial compromises was hammered out. In the end, Hoffman, who had presided over the legislative budget process for years, swallowed hard and gave the Montgomery County schools a larger share of the pie and thus got the crucial votes to get the cigarette tax passed. She had also negotiated the deal assuaging the members' concern about the lack of an identifiable funding source in the out years. In 2004–5, when the cigarette tax would no longer be sufficient to pay for the rising costs of the reforms, legislators would have to approve a joint resolution if the funding increases were to continue. If they did not, funding increases would continue but at a much lower level. SB 856 funding would in effect be suspended.

Since schools would almost necessarily make the SB 856 money an important part of their budgets, any sudden curtailment of the expected funding would create havoc. But that very possibility led to the general expectation that somewhere, somehow, the legislature would find the money. What made that particularly likely is that the reforms were themselves based on legislative acceptance of the adequacy principles and formulas that the Thornton Commission developed. That created not only a powerful political imperative—how could anyone vote for a budget that, by the state's own definition, was inadequate?—it also imbued the constitutional mandates and the judicial decisions that followed it with great specificity and thus imposed on the legislature a far greater burden of proof in any future adequacy suit. If the courts had previously conjured adequacy out of old provisions like the "thorough and efficient" clause, bills such as SB 856 defined it in very concrete terms, put numbers on it, and thus, in effect, wrote the principle into the constitution in the boldest possible letters. That didn't ensure anything, especially in the face of tight budgets, but it certainly ratcheted up the goals.

For Barbara Hoffman, the legislative future of her great bill soon ceased to be an official concern. There was, in fact, plenty left to do—not merely finding the long-term money to support the adequacy standards in Hoffman's bill, but renovating the state's decaying school public school buildings, giving schools more flexibility from contract restrictions in placing teachers where they'd be most effective, generating greater public engagement, and, perhaps most difficult of all, getting the state's ed schools to move beyond their stubborn resistance, abandon their research-bereft pedagogical theorizing, and begin training people who knew how to teach reading and math. But on

September 9, 2002, after a large part of her (white, Jewish) voter base was reapportioned out of her district, she lost the Democratic primary to House Delegate Lisa A. Gladden, a young African American lawyer and public defender who was much closer in background to the black voters who now made up a substantial majority of its residents.

Hoffman had had an opportunity to move to an open seat in an adjacent suburban district where she probably could have won. But she declined: she was a Baltimore girl, she told friends and supporters, and given the growing suburbanization of Maryland politics, Baltimore needed representatives of experience and seniority more than ever. But she couldn't sell that to her new voters: as often happens, identity politics easily trumped strategic advantage and district self-interest. In a campaign laced with racial overtones and which sometimes became blatantly anti-Semitic, virtually all of the city's black leaders, among them her close recent ally Howard Rawlings, endorsed Gladden. "Everyone's expecting dirty tricks from Barbara Hoffman," he told a reporter.[159] If the voters of her new district knew anything of her long string of battles for her community—the fight for schools, for help for drug-addicted babies—they didn't acknowledge it. After her loss, she said she'd be glad to have more time, be free of the endless constituent work, but still it must have hurt.[160] When she'd said just five months before that the passage of SB 856 was the finest hour in her Senate career, she had no way of knowing how really ironic that would turn out to be.

VII. New York: "Eight Is Not Enough"

On January 10, 2001, in a case called *Campaign for Fiscal Equity (CFE) v. New York,* Justice Leland DeGrasse of the New York State Supreme Court, a trial court in New York's confusingly labeled judicial structure, struck down the entire New York state school financing system. "The education provided New York City students," said DeGrasse, "is so deficient that it falls below the constitutional floor set by the Education Article of the New York State Constitution. The court also finds that the State's actions are a substantial cause of this constitutional violation."[161] He also ruled that the state's school finance system, in effectively discriminating against minority children, violated Title VI of the U.S. Civil Rights Act of 1964.

DeGrasse gave the state nine months to institute reforms that would ensure "sufficient numbers of qualified teachers, appropriate class sizes," adequate buildings, up-to-date textbooks and other materials, "suitable curricula," and "a safe orderly environment."[162] He also wanted accountability measures to make sure resources were effectively used. Finally, he "directed" the state to "examine the effects of racial isolation on many of the City's school children." Though his objectives could be inferred from his findings, he declined to be more specific—the legislature, with the expertise of the State Education Department and other agencies, was far better positioned to do that— but, he said, "the court will not hesitate to intervene if it finds that the legislative and/or executive branches fail to devise and implement necessary reform."[163]

Some seventeen months later, in a 4–1 decision, justices of the Appellate Division, the state's intermediate appeals court, wasted no courtesies in overturning DeGrasse, holding that he'd set his standards of adequacy far too high. The court ruled that New York City's 1.1 million schoolchildren, three-fourths of them black or Hispanic, 73 percent of them poor enough to qualify for free lunches, 40 percent of them on welfare, were getting as much in educational opportunity as the state constitution required, if not more. Anything beyond the eighth or (at most) ninth grade and preparation for minimum-wage jobs, the court said, was not a constitutional requirement. It was merely "aspirational."[164]

Both DeGrasse's decision and the Appellate Division ruling followed two earlier decisions by the Court of Appeals, New York's highest tribunal (which had first used the word *aspirational* in the context of this case). One, *Levittown v. Nyquist*, decided in 1982, held that the constitution's requirement that the state legislature "provide for the maintenance and support of free common schools wherein all the children of the state can be educated" did not guarantee equal educational facilities and services.[165] But in also saying that the constitution did give students the right to a "sound basic education," it opened the door to the adequacy suits that followed.

The other case, decided in 1995, went through that door, allowing

CFE to go to trial. New York's constitution, the court said, required "a sound basic education [which] should consist of the basic literacy, calculating, and verbal skills necessary to enable children to eventually function productively as civic participants capable of voting and serving on a jury."[166] Thus, children were entitled to "minimally adequate physical facilities and classrooms which provide enough light, space, heat and air to permit children to learn ... access to minimally adequate instrumentalities of learning such as desks, chairs, pencils, and reasonably current textbooks [and] minimally adequate teaching of reasonably up-to-date basic curricula such as reading, writing, mathematics, science and social studies, by sufficient personnel adequately trained to teach those subject areas."[167]

Among the most significant elements of the 1995 decision was that the court didn't limit adequacy measures to input, but allowed outcomes—academic achievement, graduation rates, dropouts—to be thrown into the adequacy mix, thereby (ironically) echoing arguments made for some two decades by educational conservatives such as Chester Finn, the chief educational policy thinker in the Reagan administration, that all education should be measured not by dollars spent on teacher salaries or class size but by what it produced. But the Court of Appeals' carefully crafted ambiguity, with all its "minimallys" and "reasonablys," still left a huge gap in defining what was legally, if not morally, required, and the two decisions, De-Grasse's and the Appellate Division ruling written by Justice Alfred D. Lerner that overturned it, found a world of room to disagree within it. Those disagreements, in turn, resonate with a universe of other educational and social questions—about how much difference money makes, about the powerful effects of socioeconomic background on learning and academic achievement, about what was basic and what, in the terms of the 1995 Court of Appeals decision, was only "aspirational," how much extra effort a society must make to provide an equal chance to poor and minority children—and, if one were prone to be broadly philosophical, whether a good society had the responsibility to provide not merely minimal but decent opportunities to all its children.

DeGrasse's answer, though invoking his own determination to use "prudence," was expansive. It came after 111 court days during a

7-month trial of antitrust proportions that heard 72 witnesses, among them many of the leading education finance experts in the country, and generated a 23,000 page transcript, with hundreds of exhibits, witness declarations, and other evidence—all told, some 4300 documents. Based in part on the state's new Regents Learning Standards— the toughened academic and graduation requirements that the state was imposing—DeGrasse's opinion followed the implicit logic that if New York was establishing these new requirements, then the constitutionally mandated "sound basic education" changed accordingly. Despite the state's minimalist claims to the contrary, he said, passing the state's watered-down Regents Competency Tests was not enough. The state itself regarded the Regents Competency Tests, which should not be confused with the more rigorous Regents Exams and which assumed only an eighth-grade reading level and sixth-grade math, as so weak that it was phasing them out.

Nor, in DeGrasse's view, were the poverty and minority status of the city's students any excuse for trimming. "Demography is not destiny," he said. "The amount of melanin in a student's skin, the home country of her antecedents, the amount of money in the family bank account, are not the inexorable determinants of academic success.... The court agrees that the State must only provide the opportunity for a sound basic education, but this opportunity must be placed within reach of all students. The court rejects the argument that the State is excused from its constitutional obligations when public school students present with socio-economic deficits." The classic alibi and the long-standing argument that socioeconomic disadvantage trumped everything that a system could do in the classroom was not acceptable. The idea of productive citizenship that the Court of Appeals included in its outline meant "more than just being qualified to vote or serve as a juror, but to do so capably and knowledgeably. It connotes civic engagement." In this age, moreover, adequacy also implied higher-order thinking skills "to evaluate complex issues, such as campaign finance reform, tax policy, and global warming ... [and] the verbal, math, science and socialization skills" to deal with complex questions and "determine questions of fact [about] DNA evidence, statistical analyses, and conventional financial fraud." And, of course, it included the high-level academic skills, including science and computer skills, necessary not just for any job but for "sustained competitive employment."[168]

It took barely a week for New York governor George Pataki to appeal the DeGrasse ruling. "You can't have a judge running an entire educational system," he said when he announced the appeal. "We will challenge that decision because we want to make sure that that responsibility rests with the elected officials."[169] If it was upheld on appeal, the DeGrasse decision could cost the state another $1 to $2 billion a year in addition to the $5 billion the state was already providing—not a happy prospect for politicians who'd watched what happened under vaguely similar circumstances after New Jersey governor Jim Florio and the New Jersey legislature had raised taxes to comply with the *Abbott* decision a few years before. Worse, in creating what could become autopilot funding formulas, it would take a lot of political muscle out of legislative and gubernatorial hands. On statehouse floors, education funding—always a subject of intense battles among well-funded interest groups, and thus a nice source of campaign cash—was like soybeans or pork bellies on the Chicago commodities markets, something that could be traded and thus converted to other assets. In any case, Pataki said, he was already addressing the issue. Pataki had, in fact, approved increases in school funding of more than 40 percent in his first six years in office. But New York City was still spending over $2,000 less than New York State districts with low percentages of poor kids. The measures Pataki mentioned that day didn't match, either in amount or in character, what DeGrasse wanted.

Justice Lerner's opinion for the Appellate Division flatly rejected not only the DeGrasse order but the principles on which it rested. While it might be desirable public policy to pursue the DeGrasse standard, Lerner held, that's not what the constitution required. "Rather," he said, "the ability to 'function productively' [the term used by the Court of Appeals] should be interpreted as the ability to get a job, and support oneself, and thereby not be a charge on the public fisc. Society needs workers in all levels of jobs, the majority of which may very well be low level."[170] DeGrasse's "aspirational" standards, therefore, were inconsistent with the Court of Appeals' declaration that the constitution only requires the "opportunity" for a "sound basic education" or a "minimally adequate ... education."

The same went for voting and jury duty. "The evidence at trial," Justice Lerner said, "established that the skills required to enable a person to obtain employment, vote, and serve on a jury, are imparted between grades 8 and 9, a level of skills which plaintiffs do not dispute is being provided." (Which, one observer said, raised the question of why we weren't allowing fourteen-year-olds to vote.) A "statement that the current system is inadequate and that more money is better is nothing more than an invitation for limitless litigation."[171] Training hamburger flippers who never went beyond the eighth grade, or maybe the ninth, the court seemed to say, was all the constitution required.

There was no ambiguity here. In case anyone might have missed the point, Justice David Saxe, the appellate panel's sole dissenter, made it absolutely clear. The trial revealed, he said, "an educational process that fails to offer far more than merely the skills to get a high-paying job; it fails to offer a large segment of its students the opportunity to obtain sufficient skills to 'function productively as civic participants' in any sense of those words. I do not accept the proposition that providing students with instruction by which they may achieve sixth-grade arithmetic skills and an eighth-grade reading level is sufficient to satisfy the constitutional requirement."[172]

The *New York Times* saw the decision as another example of blaming the victim. Michael Rebell, executive director of the foundation-funded Campaign for Fiscal Equity, which brought the case, called the decision "callous" and "shocking." But he also predicted that when it went up to the Court of Appeals, as all the lawyers knew it always would, DeGrasse would be upheld.

The process that led to the decisions in *Campaign for Fiscal Equity v. New York State (CFE)* began in 1992 when Robert Jackson, a parent and community board member (and now a member of the City Council), frustrated by frequent school budget cuts and wanting to sue for what he thought would be fair funding, sought out Rebell, who'd been active in school litigation for many years. Together they created the coalition of parent and high-visibility community groups, among them a dozen of New York's community school boards, that became CFE, and they got foundation funding to support the organization (and which now includes grants from the Ford Foundation, the Carnegie Corporation of New York, the Rockefeller Brothers Fund, and a dozen others). In 1993, having organized a legal team that included Rebell and Joseph Wayland and other lawyers from Simpson Thacher & Bartlett, one of New York's big downtown law firms, which was working pro-bono and would do most of the trial work, CFE filed suit. The case, which named New York schoolchildren among its plaintiffs, rested on a combination of equity and adequacy claims: uncredentialed teachers, lack of books and materials, and overcrowded and stultifying physical facilities, on one hand, and inadequate and inequitable state funding, on the other.

The prime force in getting the firm into the case was Simpson Thacher's chairman, Richard Beattie, a longtime public school advocate who was also the founder and chairman of New Visions, the city's largest and most prominent school reform organization. But clearly it was also a special cause for people such as Joe Wayland, a commercial and securities litigator, who spent over a year on *CFE* and felt "extraordinarily passionate about this case . . . a once-in-a-lifetime opportunity that most people don't get. The passion made me a better lawyer; it was the engine that drove everything." By the time the trial was over, Simpson Thacher had spent the equivalent of $15 million in legal fees on the case, plus another $3 million in expenses.[173]

To defend the case, the state used not only lawyers from the attorney general's office but a team of private attorneys headed by Alfred Lindseth of the Atlanta firm of Sutherland Asbill & Brennan, which had done extensive work representing districts trying to come out from under federal desegregation orders and which would ultimately collect about $11 million for its work. The selection of the Atlanta firm—the *Daily News* called them "the Dixie solicitors"—was a politically dubious decision in a suit that was almost entirely about the education of black and Hispanic kids in New York City. But what seemed most mystifying is why the state—presumably the governor's office—chose to fight the case when it probably could have won at least a set of extended delays. It could have made credible claims that it was working hard to provide more funding—and indeed had increased school funding substantially—and address the myriad management problems that had plagued the New York City schools for generations. It just needed more time to get on with it. The problem, Wayland said later, is that "[Assembly Speaker Sheldon] Silver, [Senate majority leader Joseph] Bruno and [Governor George] Pataki were so fixated on keeping their cozy little club going that they weren't willing to budge on anything."[174]

The plaintiffs' basic charge was that the state's allocations to local schools were insufficient and discriminatory. They were theoretically calculated through what CFE accurately described as "an over-complicated hodgepodge of formulas, grants and adjustments—mostly vestiges of past proposals designed for political gain" that few understood (and, of course, they weren't meant to be understood). But as most people in Albany already knew, the actual school funding was divvied up in annual political deals by "three men in a room"—the governor and the leaders of the two houses of the legislature, who negotiated the numbers that always left New York City with the short end of the stick. (As indeed, they negotiated almost all other major issues). Somehow, after supposedly crunching the numbers through all those formulas, in seven of the ten years before 1999–2000, the city got exactly 38.86 percent of the state's education budget—what Harold Levy, who would soon become the system's chancellor, called "the 38.86 percent dirty little secret." The deal would be made first and then, as New York University fiscal expert Robert Berne testified, "the formulas are worked backwards to determine how one gets to that agreed upon amount." (The real problem, in the belief of some New York politicians, was simply that upstate legislators cared more about schools because their communities and media paid more attention to it. "Upstate and suburban legislators are defined by whether they deliver the aid," a New York City Democrat told Steven R. Weisman of the *New York Times*. "It's politically less important for legislators from the city."[175]

What the plaintiffs now wanted, as Rebell said in his summation, is that [the state] be required simply to adopt some objective methodology. We're not pinpointing which one. But, instead of the hodgepodge charade of what is called the formula now that is merely a shares agreement, what is needed for adequate education, we believe what the constitution requires, is a focus on what resources are actually needed to provide a level of education that meets the sound basic education necessity.[176]

In many respects, New York wasn't doing all that badly. In selective high schools such as Bronx Science, Stuyvesant, and Brooklyn Tech, in Edward R. Murrow High School and Midwood, and in a number of others, it still had some of the very best public schools in the country, proud places of academic intensity with distinguished teachers. Midwood, in Brooklyn, was badly overcrowded, and there was South Shore High with plenty of empty seats nearby, but students still piled into Midwood because it was, and had long been, so good. New York City children, once predominantly Jewish, now disproportionately Asian, still took a large share of the Westinghouse (now Intel) Science Talent Search awards, sometimes described as a prep program for future Nobel laureates, in which the sophistication and elegance of the entries testified not only to the smarts and diligence of the students who created them but to the dedication and ability of the teachers who mentored the young people through two or three years of grueling work. (Since World War II, Bronx Science alone has produced five Nobel laureates.) New York City had tolerated and sometimes nurtured innovative schools such as Deborah Meier's Central Park East in East Harlem, which became an exemplar to community-based reformers everywhere.[177] It had open, progressive places such as P.S. 234, which produced high scores even though it didn't give grades to its students. It had high-poverty schools that through some combination of great leadership, dedicated teaching, and sheer chemistry were producing remarkable results. And even in the worst schools, there were teachers who, as Judge DeGrasse said, were real heroes.

Nor were the city's schools on the verge of financial destitution. Judged at least in raw dollars, as the state's lawyers were constantly reminding the court, and as its experts testified, New York City schools were doing rather well. According to the National Center for Education Statistics, in 1997–8 the city schools were spending just over $8,000 per child per year—it would go to roughly $10,000 three years later—which put it in the highest ranks in per-pupil spending among U.S. districts that had a hundred thousand or more students. Using different calculations, the New York City Budget Office put the number at just over $9,000.[178] Many American suburbs, even those in high-cost regions in California and the Pacific Northwest, would have happily settled for what New York City was spending. At the same time, however, the New York City Board of Education, which, unlike most other New York districts, had no taxing power of its own, and which was trying to educate what was perhaps the most disadvantaged group of students in one of the highest-cost places in the country, had less to spend per child than schools in New York's other major cities—$900 less than Buffalo, $700 less than Rochester, $2,600 less than Yonkers—and dramatically less than schools in the surrounding suburbs. It paid teachers less than neighboring districts, put them into tougher schools, and so was chronically short of qualified people.[179]

Of the teachers who came, some of the best and brightest soon left for other districts; more just quit for other lines of work. In the face of that, said former New York State education commissioner Thomas Sobol, the state and the city faced a Hobson's choice between hiring people who, despite legal requirements, hadn't passed the certification exams and hiring no one at all. "To insist on the letter of [the] law would mean an unacceptably large number of classrooms without teachers in the city."[180] Nearly 14 percent of New York City's teachers weren't certified in any subject they taught—in the rest of the state, it was 3.3 percent—and the percentages were higher in certain fields. DeGrasse also discussed at length Hamilton Lankford's findings that teachers with the weakest academic records of their own were disproportionately concentrated in the schools with the highest numbers of poor and minority students. Citing calculations from the Board of Education, the judge found that in the previous year, 59,500 New York City students "were taught high school biology by an uncertified teacher, 19,000 students were taught high school chemistry by an uncertified teacher, and 54,375 students were taught high school mathematics by an uncertified teacher."[181]

The surrounding suburbs and the rest of the state had far fewer problems finding qualified teachers. In New York City teachers had failed certification exams at many times the rate of the rest of the state. In the state as a whole, 3.2 percent of new teachers failed the basic qualifying test; in New York it was close to 23 percent. In high school math, 16.9 percent flunked statewide; in the city it was over 42 percent.

The state's lawyers pointed out that, unlike many other districts, the city offered no incentives to attract good teachers to low-performing schools, despite the various categorical state and federal funding streams that were designed for that purpose. Armed with a collection of reports from the Board of Education itself, Lindseth and his colleagues also argued that the city wasn't putting up as much school funding out of its own resources as its tax wealth permitted.[182] Worse, every time the politicians in Albany appropriated more money for schools, as they did in the years just before DeGrasse's ruling, the city backed out some of its own money to use for other purposes, something that New York Mayor Rudolph Giuliani readily admitted. When he was asked in the legislature whether any new funds the city got for schools would actually go to the schools and not simply replace money the city would use for other purposes, he said he couldn't make such a commitment:

> [We] have to deal with the entire budget of the City. . . . If we can solve our other problems, it is my desire to move as much money to the classrooms . . . as we possibly can. . . . The other side of it is it makes it very hard for me when I have to close the deficit to realize that if I put $1 into education, I lose about 50 cents on that dollar on wasted administration, whereas if I put a dollar into something else, I get 75, 80 cents out of that dollar, because it's a scandal what goes on in the bureaucracy of the New York City School System.[183]

If they would give him more authority over the schools, as his successor, Michael Bloomberg, eventually got, he could do a lot more for the schools. In effect, he said, he wasn't going to put more money into the system until he could control it.

The state's lawyers also seized on the confining restrictions in the United Federation of Teachers contract that made it nearly impossible to get rid of bad teachers or, under seniority rules, assign good ones to the schools that needed them most and that limited actual teaching to less than four hours a day.[184] As indicated earlier, the seniority rules also made it hard to hire any teacher until senior people had a chance to apply, by which time the best new candidates had often taken other jobs. (In his decision, DeGrasse would recognize that "to some degree, [the] concentration of uncertified teachers in low performing schools is enabled by the teachers' collective bargaining agreement with BOE [Board of Education]. With some restrictions, experienced teachers are able to transfer out of such schools pursuant to a contract provision that gives senior teachers priority in filling vacant positions in other schools."[185] But he quickly passed it by, as if it were an accident of nature, not a problem the system had created and thus might be able to address.)

This being New York City, there were, in fact, roadblocks and special deals everywhere you turned. The process of modernizing the schools' antiquated wiring to make it possible, among other things, to install computers and other technology was severely delayed by what a city administrator called the electricians' "choke point," the refusal of the union to allow the city to import electricians from elsewhere despite the serious shortage of local workers. There was the building custodians' "administrative wife-swapping" in which the custodians, who were both city employees and independent contractors who engaged their own help, hired each other's relatives to get around the nepotism rules. Some had what Harold Levy called no-show jobs; some were in charge of two or more buildings, bringing their incomes (during the 1970s and 1980s) to $90,000 a year. And, since they controlled after-school use of their buildings, they could charge extortionate fees to community groups who wanted to meet there.

Given the experience of New York investigators who on repeated visits (in 1992) could never find the custodian of P.S. 87 at his school, only to discover that he was running a thriving practice in real estate law, even the word *custodian* was a little misleading.[186] And, of course, there was the endemic politics. The first time he tried to remove a principal, said Rudolph Crew, who was chancellor from 1995 to 1999, he got a call from Representative Charlie Rangel, one of the powers of New York's congressional delegation, telling him he couldn't do that. The principal was a strong political supporter and Rangel didn't care how bad she was, and just in case Crew misunderstood, he reminded him how much clout he had. Crew stood his ground—"I don't tell you how to vote in Congress," he told Rangel—and Rangel backed off, but it helped teach Crew how the game was played. Other districts just beat you up and break your bones, said Crew, who'd been superintendent in Sacramento and Tacoma before going to New York. "This one breaks your heart."[187]

From the start, Lindseth and the state's other lawyers had a tough task: to somehow refute the long list of reports, many of them from the state itself—the State Education Department, the Regents, the various official commissions—documenting the mess the city's schools were in, and to disprove, as Wayland said, "what the state has admitted for years."[188] To do that, Lindseth and his colleagues called a long string of witnesses, among them Edward F. Stancik, the city's chief investigator into New York school corruption, to show that it was mismanagement and, in some parts of the system, what Lindseth called a "felonious culture" of nepotism and outright theft, not lack of money from Albany, that contributed to the shortages of teachers, the decrepit buildings, and the other undeniable shortcomings in New York City's classrooms.

Until 1996, when the system began to change, the chancellor had no authority over the thirty-two district superintendents, who were picked by the independent community boards and who, in turn, appointed the elementary and intermediate school principals within their districts. Although the boards were in theory elected by the local community, four or five of the thirty-two, among them the worst-performing districts in the system, were in fact controlled by local political machines and thus were powers unto themselves. After Rudy Crew, who became chancellor in 1995, called a meeting of the district superintendents and several failed to show up, he successfully lobbied the legislature to end the boards' control over personnel. But the boards' ability to make life difficult for the chancellor continued until they were defanged in 2002–3. Thus, as Deputy Chancellor Lewis Spence testified, there was a "history of deep division between [the] central office and the districts and schools."[189]

Moreover, of the 135,000 New York pupils listed as special-education students—the total bill for their schooling came to $2.5 billion annually, more than 25 percent of the system's entire budget—a large percentage were misclassified: special ed was another of the dumps to which the unwanted were consigned. If New York put them in regular classes, the defense lawyers contended, it would free hundreds of millions for other purposes. Perhaps more questionable still was the cost of the city's thirty thousand teacher aides, of which it had three times as many per child as other large districts and whose value in raising academic achievement had never been established. "These positions are wonderful sources of patronage," said New York Deputy Attorney General Herbert Bienstock in his closing, "but they don't do very much for our children." The city could do a lot just by getting rid of the "hidden administrators" and the patronage. "Simply assuming that more state money will improve education while turning a blind eye to the role of local actors," said the state's lawyers in a brief, "will not achieve this result."[190]

To drive the point home, they called expert witnesses David Armor of George Mason University and Eric Hanushek, then at the University of Rochester, now at the Hoover Institution. Hanushek, the nation's leading economist of education and certainly one of the most respected, presented data showing (in the words of the state's appeal brief) "that increased spending and resources do not correlate with improved student performance in general, and in New York City schools in particular." It appeared to him, Hanushek said in his testimony, "that spending 50 percent above the national mean would provide sufficient resources [for] a sound basic education." Even when adjusted for the cost of living, Hanushek said, New York's school spending was still in the top 10 percent among the nation's 463 largest districts—those with enrollments of fifteen thousand students or more.[191] At various stages of the case, the state's lawyers, bolstered by Armor's testimony, argued strenuously that socioeconomic background was still a major determinant of academic success—the schools couldn't do it all—and, perhaps more tellingly, as Bienstock said, that "pouring a lot of money into schools may not be the best way of addressing issues of poverty at all. We may be better off spending on prenatal care or child care or some other programs directed at parents and children instead of schools."[192]

Later, after DeGrasse ruled, the state's appeal sharply criticized him for "erroneously assum[ing] that it was the State's responsibility to fully compensate for all economic disadvantages of the city's student population rather than simply provide the opportunity for all students to learn basic skills."[193] That short statement was itself loaded with enormously complex and emotionally charged social and philosophical implications. In any case, as Deputy Attorney General Harriet Rosen argued in her opening statement in DeGrasse's court, world-class standards weren't the issue; nothing fancy was required. "Although State education leaders commendably tried to provide educational opportunities and set standards for educational achievements which go well beyond [the] minimal constitutional standards, there is no constitutional command that they do so and it is not a constitutional violation to fail to provide educational opportunities meeting higher standards."[194] That was the nub of the case.

The state's financial arguments, as its attorneys surely knew, were a little disingenuous. They were right in their charge that when Albany increased education funding (and thus raised the dollar value of New York City's 38.86 percent share), the city often backed out some of its money, in effect using education funds to help pay its extraordinarily high welfare and medical costs—costs that upstate legislators had no desire to underwrite any more than absolutely necessary. New York City's per-capita cost for welfare in 1996 was $100; in the rest of the state, according to David Rubenstein, deputy director of the city's Office of Management and Budget, the cost was between $30 and $40. For Medicaid, the city was forced to spend $400 per capita; the rest of the state spent an average of $100. New York's debt—principally what it owed on bonds issued for capital improvements and thus its amortization costs—was enormous compared to the rest of the state.

In 1999, the legislature, over the loud protests of the city, had also repealed the city's commuter tax—an income tax paid by nonresidents who worked in the city—which had been on the books for thirty years and which had generated about $500 million a year. It was thus hardly surprising that the city was trying to skim the incremental education funds that Albany provided.[195] More immediately, as DeGrasse found, the state's "wealth allocation" formula, through which the state was supposed to use its funds to make up for what a poor district couldn't generate from its own resources, failed to account for the sometimes large differences in districts' costs, particularly those stemming from the extra needs of poor students and those with limited English proficiency. The state's own calculations showed that New York City "receives substantially less state aid than districts with similar needs."[196]

Most of the state's arguments were predictable—even, perhaps, when they descended to the cavalier, as when the defense lawyers declared that "schools can increase capacity through overlapping or double sessions [which of course many already had]. Year-round schooling, transfers of students between districts, and shifting grades between elementary and middle schools . . . are also more cost-effective."[197] What had not been predictable was the state's astounding contention that the New York City schools, despite problems common to all schools, were doing just fine. Notwithstanding mounds of evidence submitted by the plaintiffs showing the large numbers of uncredentialed and poorly trained teachers—in the city nearly one teacher in seven was uncertified in any subject; in the state as a whole, it was fewer than one in thirty—the state's lawyers submitted numbers showing the large proportion of teachers who had master's degrees or other advanced degrees. They also introduced data showing that where New York had one teacher for every 14.1 students (many of whom were doing things other than teaching), Los Angeles had one for every 20.8 students.

The New York ratio, said defense expert and Management Analysis and Planning (MAP) president James R. Smith, who had once been California's deputy superintendent of public instruction, "is dramatically low. If New York City were a state, it would be in the top four or five states in pupil-teacher ratio." If classes were large—and the state's data showed they were substantially larger than the average for either the state or its other large cities—the problem wasn't the shortage of teachers but their deployment and the union contracts that gave them a shorter teaching day than other districts in the state. And if their experience wasn't as long on average as in other districts, the state argued, it was still impressive. (Both the numbers for master's degrees and for uncredentialed teachers were correct, but neither necessarily proved much about teacher quality. While large numbers of uncredentialed teachers were almost certainly a negative sign, having teachers with credentials, or master's degrees, as Justice DeGrasse recognized, didn't necessarily mean they were good.)[198] The state's lawyers then presented compilations of the district's own internal school performance reviews for the years 1995–7 showing that 99 percent of the teaching force had been rated "satisfactory" and that "on average, schools were performing between an 'exemplary' and 'approaching exemplary' standard in the area of instruction."

But, as is true for hundreds of other school district documents in countless other places, almost everything about those reports was misleading.[199] As testimony during the trial made clear, because rating teachers U (unsatisfactory) was so complicated and generated so many bureaucratic headaches—and might leave a principal without any teacher for that class—the U ratings were reserved, as one former New York district superintendent said, "for the worst of the worst, people who were actually endangering students . . . the absolute worst. If you had people who were mediocre or not the absolute worst, you didn't put energy into trying to remove them." [200] Teachers rated U by a principal had a right under the contract to remain in their schools. In the recollection of district superintendent Frank DeStefano:

We had a situation in one of my schools, Middle School 136. The principal wrote 21 U ratings on lateness and absences alone. Twenty-one U's in her first year in the school. That was the kind of faculty she faced. When it came time for her, under the rules of contract, to pick 50 percent of her faculty new, because they were being redesignated, she was informed those 21 teachers were exempt because they had U ratings and had a right to remain under their U ratings. She reversed every one of those ratings and [took them off the transfer list] because, again, the system didn't work to her advantage. Her job—her bottom line was to get good teachers for those kids. It was not to concern herself with loopholes in the contract.[201]

Something similar was true for the Performance Assessment in Schools Systemwide (PASS) reports, the internal self-evaluations conducted in each school by administrators, teachers, and parents from that school, plus (on occasion) one person from the Board of Education. But it was, as Deputy Chancellor Lewis Spence testified, a "highly subjective" process in which schools would "give themselves excellent ratings." And since local school administrators worried that the PASS survey would be used as an accountability mechanism—give yourself a bad rating and the fixers would ride in from downtown—"they would [in DeGrasse's words] paint a rosy, rather than a realistic, picture of their schools. Instead of engaging in internal assessment, schools use PASS for public relations."[202] Which, of course, is how school systems use a great many reports and purportedly objective surveys. In the course of the New York trial, school officials testified about the dismal conditions and inadequacies of certain resources—the libraries, the special programs, the professional development—that they'd lauded in their own prior reports.[203]

But that didn't keep the state's lawyers from trying to sanctify the PASS surveys with a halo of expertise. So they got Christine Rossell, a political science professor at Boston University and one of the state's experts, to testify that "by their own rating system, the quality of schools is very good." And then she went a step further. Comparisons of the internal PASS reviews of each school with the actual funding of that school, she testified, "show that the schools [that] get a little bit less money, do a little bit better . . . the higher the general education budget, the lower the average school quality rating." On cross-examination, she acknowledged the possibility that schools with serious problems might be getting more money for that very reason, but, she said, it still showed that there was no correlation between dollars and the quality of a school.

Later, in an interview, Rossell said that while she was impressed by the level of detail covered by the PASS surveys, she hadn't analyzed them. "I just got handed this stuff," she said, because the lawyers "needed someone to discuss it."[204] She didn't know how the thing worked, didn't know that the district never used the PASS reports to make decisions about school quality—that indeed the whole process was merely a sort of internal checklist. As to producing "civic participants capable of voting and serving on a jury," one of the elements in the Court of Appeals definition of a "sound basic education," Rossell testified that voters get most of their information from radio, television, and the newspapers. "What is on the ballot is unimportant to the voter's decision. They have made up their mind before they go in the voting booth."[205] As to the PASS surveys, DeGrasse said, Rossell "appeared to have little knowledge about how the reviews were actually conducted. Dr. Rossell apparently misunderstood the reviews' scoring system in attempting to aggregate the results of the reviews. Accordingly, her testimony is not probative."[206]

More improbable still, the state, using the city's own test scores, also contended that the average student was doing fine. (One witness testified that New York City students "performed much better on standardized tests than students in other large urban districts.")[207] Among the key exhibits was a Board of Education report celebrating the 1997 scores of New York elementary school students on McGraw-Hill's CTB Reading Test (CTB-R), a nationally normed reference test that, in theory, allowed comparisons with students in the same grades and subjects across the country. The report showed not only that New York's students had improved in grades 3–8 and had done so in all parts of the city but that they were just below the national average and, in one grade, above it. And "since the CTB-R test is more closely aligned with the new standards to which our students will be held, and with actual classroom instruction," the report said, "these results are promising."[208] The math scores the city reported for the same grades and that the state's lawyers touted were even higher.

No one seriously thought things were that rosy. The three testing experts interviewed for this book on this point, two of whom were familiar with New York's testing culture, were certain that officials at the New York Board of Education, in "aligning" the CTB-R to its own standards, had cherry-picked test questions from an item bank and revised some of the CTB-R questions to make them conform to its own cultural norms. More important, two years later, when the city began to use a different test from the same publisher, it showed that only 44.6 percent of New York students were reading at or above the national average, compared to 49.6 percent the year before. There was an even larger drop in math scores. Some of that decline was later attributed to gross testing company errors in scoring at least eighty-six hundred tests, but those errors hardly added confidence to the process, nor did a disagreement two years later in which the city accused the company of yet another set of errors, or the alleged company errors in 2002 in scoring a seventh-grade reading test. A few months later, the district's new chancellor, Joel I. Klein, dropped CTB/McGraw-Hill and contracted with Harcourt Brace to provide its reading tests.[209]

There were other problems as well. The board's positive testing report showed only 9,500 students absent out of the 465,000 who were in the pool to be tested, itself an unbelievably low number when the city's reported average daily elementary school absence rate hovered at around 10 percent. The number was particularly incredible in light of reports that, as in other places, many city principals, under pressure to raise scores, appeared to have followed the ancient practice of "recommended absences," in which the weaker students were invited to stay home on test day. And since the schools had almost total discretion on excluding LEP students (those with limited English proficiency)— any student deemed "to fall below specified language proficiency levels" was exempt—the gate to what one testing expert called "manipulation at various levels" was wide open. Students who were good readers were tested, regardless of their LEP status; those who were bad readers were, by definition, "below specified language levels." If one added up all the students who were not tested under regular conditions, or not tested at all—the alleged 9,500 absences, the 41,000 LEP students, and the 31,000 special-ed students who were tested separately—it meant that at least 20 percent of the population was not part of the regular count. From start to finish, said one of those experts, the process was "weird," the results "absolutely suspect."[210]

Nor did the CTB-R scores square with student achievement reports showing New York City students scoring well below average on the state's measures of reading and math proficiency. Their passing rate in many subjects on the state's Regents Examinations was no better than half the state's; on the biology examination, which 60 percent of the state's biology students passed, the passing rate in New York barely topped 17 percent. In Manhattan in 1998–9, to use another measure, 40 percent of students failed their core course in math, and more than a third of tenth graders failed more than three courses.[211] But that didn't prevent the state's lawyers from now using the CTB-R scores with an absolutely straight face. Since the city had been using the test scores to show success, said one of the defense lawyers, the Board of Education was being hoist by its own petard.

The CFE lawyers challenged the CTB-R results as meaningless because the test wasn't based on New York's own curricular standards (one of the rare times that such a challenge was issued because the scores were allegedly too *high*). "Almost 40 percent of the students are failing their math courses," said Simpson Thacher lawyer Joseph Wayland in his closing statement. "They are above average in the national norms, but they are failing their math courses. And 30 percent are failing their social studies and science courses. They can beat that norm group, but they can't do English." When they hit ninth grade, he added, 41 percent of "those above-average kids fail three or more courses. They are above the national norm, but they can't do the work."[212]

But in planning their strategy, Rebell and his colleagues had long ago decided they didn't want to fight a two-front war against both the New York City Board of Education and Albany. The board had originally filed its own suit, making almost identical claims, which the Court of Appeals had dismissed on the ground that the city, as a creature of the state, "could not challenge the constitutionality of the acts of its governmental parent." But Rebell still needed the board's help in making the case against the politicians upstate, later acknowledging that the plaintiffs were "somewhat aligned" with the board. Therefore any direct assault on the board's dubious testing practices was out.[213]

In fact, the connections were a lot closer. Some of the community boards—not the crooked ones—were members of the CFE coalition. Rudy Crew, who during a portion of the case was still chancellor in New York, sat on CFE's board of advisors and, as he later acknowledged, strongly supported the suit. CFE co-founder Robert Jackson, a member of one of the community boards, chaired the CFE board, and until DeGrasse dismissed them from the suit, some of the community boards were also among the named plaintiffs in the case. In his closing, Bienstock told the court that, according to a letter the state had uncovered, the "Board and the plaintiffs in this case literally coordinated trial strategy to win more money from the state. So the plaintiffs' lawyers sat down with the Board of Education and they coordinated trial strategy. They were of invaluable assistance."[214] Some of the state's lawyers were certain, indeed, that the Board of Education was the ventriloquist and CFE was no more than its talking dog.

But the underlying theme of the state's defense, which was ultimately embraced by Justice Lerner and the appellate court, was that the new high school graduation standards adopted by the state Board of Regents—including four years each of English and social studies and three years each of math and science, and the requirement that beginning in 2005, no student can get a diploma without passing the state's fairly rigorous Regents Exams in five major academic subjects— were unrealistically high for use as a gauge of what a "sound basic education" was. Those standards were wish lists, defense expert Jim Smith testified. "They are not only very high, but unrealistically high and probably unsustainable over time.... High standards, world-class standards and by whatever name they go are and ought to be aspirational standards. They should be the curriculum that is today, but it is unrealistic to believe that all students will be able to master these standards, and so we're talking about two different things."[215] It was that contention that informed the Lerner opinion.

In fact, as Crew often said, good schools had standards about which the Regents list said nothing: standards of civic literacy, occupational literacy, personal engagement, civility. Kids wore those baseball caps all the time, he said by way of illustration; they had no idea that that if they wore them to a job interview, they probably wouldn't get the job. In the system's three hundred high-performing schools, courtesy and respect were generally taken for granted; in its two hundred worst schools, as thousands of American teachers understood, they had barely started with them, and there they were the first and sometimes main order of business. That didn't mean Jim Smith was right, but it told you something about how tough the job was. What made it particularly tough is that it required care, patience, and even love, not dismissal or neglect or contempt.

It would have been hard to convince anyone in New York City that in the perennial upstate-downstate/Republican-Democratic battles that marked New York politics, the Big Apple wasn't constantly getting the short end of the stick in Albany—and in the end, that included Justice DeGrasse himself. Alfred Lindseth, one of those "Dixie solicitors," said he sometimes sensed outright hostility, especially from the media, though it wasn't clear whether the hostility was directed mostly to Albany or to Atlanta.[216] Some in the New York education community thought Lindseth's firm had been hired primarily because it had been highly successful in getting school districts out from under their federal desegregation orders. Some resented them for what they thought was the lawyers' plush lifestyle—the rumor was that they were staying at the Waldorf—when they were in New York (and which, of course, their state clients were supposedly paying for). In fact, none of that was true: they were staying in modest $184-a-night rooms at a hotel near the courthouse, cheap by New York standards. Some of the defense lawyers believed the rumors had been leaked by their opponents, who "did everything they could to get us out of the case."

Asked about the mismanagement issue later, New York State deputy solicitor general Mark Gimpel, the state's lead attorney in the appeal of DeGrasse's decision, said the state's obligation was funding. And while the state wrote rules governing school administration, "the state has no responsibility for mismanagement."[217] Yet ultimately the state was responsible for everything, and when the state wanted to it acted as if it were. A long string of reform measures both in Albany and at Gracie Mansion, culminating in the scheduled abolition of the community boards and, under Mayor Michael

Bloomberg, abolition of the quasi-independent Board of Education itself—it's the mayor alone who now appoints the chancellor and in
effect runs the system—had also made clear that nobody believed
that lack of money was the whole story.

For a half century the thing called "110 Livingston"—the longtime Brooklyn headquarters of the school administration, now moved
to Manhattan—had devoured an endless stream of school chancellors
and chewed up or simply ignored the cleverest reforms. Crew, who
was hired with the blessings of Mayor Rudolph Giuliani and was
pushed out by him four years later, and who was almost certainly
among the best of the city's long and ever-changing string of chancellors, described the whole place—the school district, the unions, the
local and state politicians, the community activists who constantly
used it for leverage—as a kind of science fiction monster. "You can't
find its head, you can't find its tail, but it's alive, it's moving. It can
take anything you feed it—insecticide, whatever—and use it for
food."[218]

Rebell and his colleagues asked that the state be required to create
"an effective accountability system," that would "include opportunities for public input, public engagement [and] to make sure the whole
system is open, that it's no longer a secret." If there is corruption and
waste, he said, "the state should do something about it."[219] But it was
all said sotto voce, almost an aside. Because of their separate peace
with the Board of Education, they were never really able to boldly
argue the position that it didn't matter whether it was the lack of
state funding or local mismanagement and corruption that were ultimately responsible for the bad conditions in the city's classrooms—
they couldn't make the systemic mess a central issue—and so the
whole case often seemed to be only about money. Whether the cause
was lack of money or mismanagement, or both, or something else
altogether, they could have argued, the kids were getting hurt and
under the constitution the state was ultimately responsible—indeed,
had been admitting responsibility for years. All they really had to
prove was the hurt.

Instead, the focus was on money, a decision that could turn out to
be the Achilles' heel of the case. While Justice Lerner and two other
members of the Appellate Division's four-justice majority casually ac-

cepted the state's crimped burger-flipper version of adequacy, Justice Peter Tom, the fourth member of the majority, seemed deeply troubled. In his decision in the trial court, DeGrasse had catalogued the whole sad litany of failure in New York's schools. Of the students who began high school, 30 percent never graduated and another 10 percent got a GED (General Equivalency Degree), which is often a ticket to nowhere. "The job prospects and lifetime earnings of the GED certificates," Henry Levin of Teachers College had testified, "is considerably less than [that those of] the high school graduate. In fact, it is equal or close to that of high school dropouts." The military didn't accept GED graduates, and of those who went to college only 2 percent graduated. Worse, of the 60 percent of New York students who were allowed to "walk" at graduation, fewer than one in five got a Regents diploma, which was generally regarded as adequate preparation for college; the rest were awarded a "local" diploma, which the state thought was so flabby that it was scheduled to be phased out by 2005. Of all New York high school graduates who entered the City University of New York in the 1990s, he noted, 80 percent needed remedial help in English or math; 50 percent needed help in both. "This evidence," DeGrasse said, "depicts a public school system that is foundering."[220]

Justice Tom picked up on that data. "A nascent educational crisis has been growing over the years," he wrote in his concurring opinion, "with roots decades deep, but with consequences that are taking on a new urgency." Plainly, he wasn't so confident that the students were getting anything close to an adequate education, although "plaintiffs have failed to prove a causal link between the State's funding mechanism and the deficiencies of City schools."

> The growing crisis, such as it is, results from a matrix of administrative, demographic, and economic factors which, one may fairly judge from the appellate record, are not presently resolvable by increased State spending. That is a short-term expedient rather than a realistic long-term solution to numerous problems which are not necessarily related to each other, and some of which may even be intractable from the standpoint of State funding.

One may reasonably take from plaintiffs' as well as the State's positions the apt point that the very complexity of the system requires either that its many problems be directly and innovatively addressed, or, alternatively, that a complete overhaul be undertaken. I offer no opinion on this, but only observe that State funding, itself, is not a magic bullet. Mere budgetary fixes, extracted from the State rather than from the City or even by shifting resources within the system itself, are not going to achieve a system-wide functionality that has evaded prior budgetary infusions and half-hearted administrative reforms over the years.

If the system contains serious flaws within the managerial level, one must worry whether an infusion of funding will only be absorbed into the system with minimal or no improvement in raising the educational achievements of students. Moreover, one must seriously wonder how a system that seems historically mismanaged and chronically unaccountable financially—accepting for the moment some of the characterizations in the record—is going to become miraculously better managed and more financially accountable just because more attractive funding can be extracted from Albany. Such a quick-fix approach seems better described as a two-dimensional numbers game being played out in a multi-dimensional system.[221]

Tom, obviously worried by the lack of qualified teachers, by the mismanagement and by the long list of other problems in the city's schools, came close to saying that while the plaintiffs had not proven their case, the situation was bad enough that it might soon raise constitutional issues:

A healthy educational system, it seems, should be able to rely on competition among more than enough qualified candidates for teaching positions, so that a system that faces chronic shortages of such candidates would be, almost by definition, unhealthy. Undoubtedly, at some point, the functioning of an unhealthy system spirals downward as desirable personnel, facing increasing responsibilities but decreasing satisfaction, continue to leave in response to their work environment. It does not take extraordinary imagination to conclude that such a system at some point cannot provide even a basic education.

Although it's dangerous to speculate about the real reason for any decision that's not specified in the opinion, it's not hard to imagine Justice Lerner and his colleagues throwing up their hands in horror at the political and policy morass that the DeGrasse decision seemed to lead to. The morass, of course, was not so much in the decision as in the educational and political systems it addressed. Still, the De-Grasse ruling seemed to look toward a standard—presumably, by the Court of Appeals' 1995 template, a "minimal" standard with "reasonable" resources—that was as politically and fiscally risky as it was philosophically and educationally inspiring.

Nonetheless, the appellate judges could have followed their colleague Peter Tom in his finding that the real problem wasn't money—and certainly not money alone—but the managerial mess that oozed into evidence during almost every day of the trial in Leland DeGrasse's courtroom. They could have found that the state had, in fact, been appropriating a lot more money of late and that New York, while it may have been funded less lavishly than other New York State districts, should not have been regarded as the financial basket case that DeGrasse seemed to think it was. They could have found that trial testimony revealed very little research showing that unless additional spending was targeted to very specific ends, providing more money beyond what New York City was already getting would produce significantly better results. They could also have found that in the reforms—in the new academic standards and the abolition of the community boards and the near-certain shift of control of the system to what promised to be the tight grip of the new mayor—the state and city were in fact addressing both the district's fiscal and managerial problems.

The Lerner court could, in brief, have proclaimed at least an interim victory, giving the players additional time to make further progress, as courts in other states had done, and left all concerned with at least half a loaf, if not a bit more. But somehow they blinked, and in their blinking revealed a peculiar combination of ignorance about

schools and insensitivity toward the many children and teachers con-
signed to attend and work in the worst of them that was quite stunning. If there was ever a modern equivalent of giving all men equal
rights to sleep under the bridge, a declaration that in the year 2002
there was no constitutional right to anything beyond an eighth-grade
education could well be its darkest example. There was certainly an
argument to be made that despite the state's high academic standards,
what was socially imperative in public education was not constitutionally required. But the court, in a special demonstration of its insensitivity, didn't even do that. And so it became the inadvertent
Maoist to its own cause, the master of the orphanage shrieking at
poor Oliver Twist and whacking him with the ladle for wanting more.
Make it sound bad enough and change had to be made.

Within hours of the release of the appellate decision in June 2002,
New York controller (and Democratic gubernatorial candidate)
H. Carl McCall denounced it with a phrase that was to become a
campaign slogan: "An eighth-grade education," he said, "is not
enough. We need to open the doors of opportunity to all our children,
not slam them in their faces. For eight years, Governor Pataki has
sat back and let the most inequitable school aid distribution in America be just another part of the political spoils system in Albany. For
eight years, the governor has been dodging and dealing. . . . Governor
Pataki has spent millions of dollars, hired lawyers, and gone to court
to fight to keep this failed system in place, instead of providing the
leadership to fix it."[222]

And then three months later, Pataki, who had ordered the appeal,
repudiated its result. In a speech at a United Federation of Teachers
(UFT) breakfast less than two months before the November election,
Pataki, who said he'd been pleased by the Lerner decision when it
was handed down, tried to put as much distance between it and himself as he could. "Anybody who thinks an eighth-grade education is
adequate," he said, "is 100 percent wrong. . . . It will never be the
policy of this state so long as I am governor of this state."[223] Asked if
that meant he'd settle the case, he wiggled. "Lawyers do what lawyers
do," he said in answer to a question. "I don't need a court to tell me

that we have to make sure we put the resources in every community in every school."

Pataki had, in fact, put substantial chunks of new money into the state's schools—up from $9.7 billion a year in 1995 to $12.8 billion in 2000, an increase in real dollars of 19 percent—although the fundamental changes that DeGrasse's order would require were nowhere in sight. But Pataki's flip indicated that the "eight is not enough" refrain in McCall's campaign literature might have had an impact: with support from friends like Justice Lerner, Pataki may well have thought, he hardly needed enemies. In addition, there was the pressure from Randi Weingarten, president of the eighty-thousand-member UFT, who was getting ready to engineer the union's endorsement of Pataki for a third term as governor and appeared to have extracted his statement—some thought she even wrote it—as the final condition of the endorsement.

Pataki, who, recognizing his state's drift toward the Democratic Party, had moved increasingly from his very conservative political beginnings toward the center, had found $400 million for a new, richer teacher contract. It meant "great strides," Weingarten said, "toward attracting and keeping qualified teachers—the number one resource Justice DeGrasse advocated in his seminal lower court CFE decision."[224] Pataki had also given the teachers—along with a number of other public sector unions—a lot of other things in the preceding four years, including automatic cost-of-living adjustments on pensions and school safety and discipline bills that the UFT had long sought. There was also the strong possibility that the UFT was looking for a winner. Even then, it was highly probable that Pataki would overwhelm McCall and his other opponent, the self-financed deep-pockets candidate Tom Golisano, and win a third term in November. But the Lerner decision gave the UFT a lever that seemed perfectly tailored to its needs.

A week after Pataki's UFT speech, CFE and its supporters held a press conference calling on Pataki to drop the case and settle on the basis of DeGrasse's decision. There was not much chance of that. Nonetheless, "exploratory talks" began a week or two later. CFE believed that Pataki's speech had been mostly a political device to get the UFT's support, not a serious commitment. McCall called the governor's statement shameless; Rebell said it was "political double talk." And in fact, less than a month after the election, the negotiations reached an impasse. But the talks ended on a far friendlier note than Rebell's "political double talk" remark started them with. Although there'd been an agreement not to discuss details, Rebell said, there had been "some progress in exploring ways to reform the current state education finance system, and we hope that we an continue to work with the governor and the legislature, even while the litigation proceeds, to start laying the foundation for a new funding structure."[225] And ten days later, the state's Board of Regents, not withstanding the $2 billion budget deficit the state was then facing, urged the legislature to increase education spending another $516 million and put most of the money into districts with high concentrations of poor children. Given New York's fiscal problems, there was not much chance of that occurring anytime soon, but it was another sign nonetheless of what CFE had accomplished. In fact, in late June 2003, in a 4-1 decision, the New York Court of Appeals, the state's highest court, upheld DeGrasse and ordered the state to begin major funding and accountability reforms. Yet even before that decision was handed down, what one state lawyer called the Appellate Division's "impolitic" inference that eight is enough may have had as much impact on New York's school policy debates as the original decision would have had if it had never been reversed.

CHAPTER FOUR

Does Money Matter?

The longest shadow in modern American education is the one cast by the late Johns Hopkins University sociologist James C. Coleman. Coleman was the principal author of *Equality of Educational Opportunity*, a massive report commissioned by Congress and published in 1966 that shook American education and social thought as nothing had since the publication in 1944 of *An American Dilemma*, Gunnar Myrdal's seminal study of American race relations—and as no report on education has since.[1] Based on data from six hundred thousand students and teachers, it found not what Johnson-era Great Society optimism then expected, what Horace Mann and the nation's other great believers in the power of schools to equalize social classes had always celebrated—and what the policy makers of the Johnson era took almost for granted. Instead it painted a far more ambivalent and, in many respects, much gloomier picture about how little even the best-designed schools and other public programs could accomplish in addressing the inequities, poverty, and educational failures that continued to plague the nation. If the Vietnam War fatally undermined the promise inherent in the great outpouring of domestic legislation Lyndon Johnson drove through Congress—the Civil Rights Act of 1964, the Voting Rights Act of 1965, the Elementary and Secondary Education Act of 1965, the War on Poverty—the Coleman Report seemed to cast doubt on the hopes and the social assumptions themselves.

The report's findings, the first to measure achievement of a national sample of students that included racial breakdowns, were complex and multifaceted enough that they were bound to be variously interpreted. For social reformers, they seemed to show that black children learned more in well-integrated classrooms and that busing was thus a promising answer to the continuing gap in achievement between black and white children. (As white flight from urban schools increased, Coleman himself would give up on the policies his study seemed to justify.) But for most, and particularly for tougher-minded individuals, the Coleman data indicated something more fundamental and, as it turned out, more depressingly lasting. Put most simply: children's socioeconomic background—their parents' income and education in particular, their peer culture and their social environment in general—was a far more important determinant of their academic success than anything their schools could do. To this day, that gloomy finding—that socioeconomic standing (SES) accounts for anywhere from two-thirds to 80 percent of school performance—is a nearly immutable element in the minds of most educators, policy makers, and educational researchers, the class-is-destiny constant of virtually all educational analyses and policy making.

Shortly after the Coleman Report was published, Eric Hanushek, a recent graduate of the Air Force Academy and then a young graduate student in economics at the Massachussetts Institute of Technology, joined a seminar that Daniel Patrick Moynihan was conducting at Harvard to rerun Coleman's numbers and reanalyze and reexamine his methodology and conclusions. (Moynihan's controversial subsequent call, as a Nixon administration official, for "benign neglect" also seemed to have been influenced by Coleman's findings.) Coleman thus became not only the subject of Hanushek's doctoral dissertation but the beginning of a long and enormously prolific career in an area of economic research that, until not too long ago, Hanushek had pretty much to himself. Hanushek says that Coleman's findings were always misinterpreted. It wasn't that schools don't matter. "The right interpretation, that has held up subsequently with lots of other work," he told an interviewer, "is that the measured aspects of schools don't seem to be systematically related to performance, but that there are huge differences across schools."[2] (What Hanushek didn't say was that a great deal of that "lots of other work" has been his). But the belief that socioeconomic background still trumped almost everything else stuck.

The core of Hanushek's argument, based on some thirty years of research, is that a generation of sharply increasing spending on schools, much of it for increased teacher salaries and reduced class sizes (plus a substantial chunk for special education for handicapped kids), has produced little if any measurable increases in student achievement. In 1960, the country spent $1,765 per student in 1990 dollars; in 1991–2, it was $5,421, an increase of 207 percent.[3] Some of that increase reflects the special market conditions in education (particularly the greatly expanded career choices available to women, who once had few options other than teaching or nursing), some the general rise in costs in labor-intensive industries. Yet no matter how that figure is adjusted, it still represents a major increase in education spending. Nonetheless, said Hanushek in 1997, "the close to 400 studies of student achievement demonstrate that there is not a strong or consistent relationship between student performance and school resources, at least after variations in family inputs are taken into account."[4]

For Hanushek and, indeed, for many other educational researchers, class size reduction, one of the largest items on that list of increased expenditures—and perhaps the most popular school reform of the past decade among both teachers and parents—is particularly suspect. In California, which, beginning in the mid-1990s, has thrown over $1.5 billion a year into across-the-board class size reduction (a maximum of twenty to one) in the primary (K–3) grades, a major four-year study found lots of parent and teacher enthusiasm but few measurable benefits in educational outcomes that could be traced to class size reduction—and, very possibly, considerable damage to urban schools forced to hire thousands of unqualified teachers both for all those new classes and to replace the better teachers who suddenly found more attractive offers in neighboring districts.[5] Nationally, Hanushek argues, as class size has gone down across the country—and gone down significantly, from an average teacher-pupil ratio of about twenty-seven to one in 1949–50 to seventeen to one in 1993–94—student test scores on measures such as the National Assessment of Educational Progress (NAEP), which began testing samples of American students in the early 1970s, hasn't shown any corresponding increase. Thus, "while policies to reduce class size may enjoy popular political appeal, such policies are very expensive and, according to the evidence, quite ineffective."[6]

The only substantial gains, in the 1970s and 1980s, were achieved by blacks and to a lesser degree by Hispanics, itself very possibly an effect, as the Coleman Report suggested, of school integration, not of school productivity—and they were not gains that continued to increase into the 1990s. But Hanushek consistently contends that overall, the record on NAEP, the most widely accepted measure the nation has and arguably the most reliable, was unimpressive: up in some fields, especially math, flat in reading, and sharply down in science. (Though he recognizes that the large expansion and diversification of the college-going population in the past two generations have made longitudinal comparisons in college entrance examination scores dubious, Hanushek has also traced per-pupil spending against the decline on the SAT.) "There is no evidence that the added resources have improved student performance," said Hanushek, "at least for the most recent three decades when it has been possible to compare quantitative outcomes directly."[7]

Hanushek is hardly alone in that conclusion. "However one looks at these data," said Lawrence O. Picus, a school finance expert at the University of Southern California, "student performance in [math, reading, science and writing] did not improve at the 22 percent rate of increase in spending during the 1970s, nor at the 48 percent rate of increase in the 1980s."[8]

Because NAEP scores for black and Hispanic students rose in all fields through the 1970s and 1980s (and then flattened and in some cases declined somewhat in the 1990s), the Hanushek data don't quite tell the whole story. And since there is an increasingly large proportion of poor and Latino students, and thus of students whose native language is something other than English, one would expect a general dampening effect on the overall score. Alan B. Krueger of Princeton also points out that even the overall gain has not been negligible: the student who is at the 50th percentile today, he says, would have been at the 56th percentile twenty-five years ago. The whole student population, in short, is doing better now than its fathers and mothers did a generation ago, a fact that's rarely recognized. In 1970, 79 percent of all Americans between the ages of twenty-five and twenty-nine had finished high school and 12 percent had graduated from college; by 2000, those numbers had risen to 94 percent and 34 percent respectively.[9] And while the gains still don't appear to be commensurate with the increased investment that Americans have made in their schools, it's impossible to calculate how much of that additional money has gone to essential noneducational purposes. That's particularly true for social services that most European nations provide in abundance outside of school and which this country has offered only at marginal levels, if at all. Schools serving the neediest students are constantly engaged in coping with the consequences of the nation's failure to provide those services.

For Hanushek, the macroeconomic data was only one part of the proof that money per se made little difference; the other was in the results of his review of the literature. "In close to 300 studies examining the influence of class size reduction on student performance," he wrote, "nearly equally balanced positive and negative effects were uncovered. The dearth of statistically significant results (14 percent on each side) also underscores the fact that the vast majority of these studies reveal no relationship at all."[10] Hanushek then went on to analyze comparative inputs and outcomes, concluding that in the generation between 1965 and 1990, there was a decline in school productivity running between 3 and 3.5 percent a year.[11] In essence, he was saying, the whole finance system was counterproductive.

Like most economists, Hanushek had long been interested in production functions—essentially, what any measured increase in inputs will produce in outcomes—but he was among the first to apply that discipline to schooling, both here and abroad. As much as anyone, he created a field that few good economists wanted to muck around in. Much of that work is highly technical, but Hanushek is no recluse either personally or intellectually—he's personally amiable and engaging—and has discussed his work in a huge list of papers, articles, and interviews and in close to a dozen appearances as a defense witness in suits by advocates, parents' groups, and school districts for increased state funding. One of those appearances, as noted earlier, was in New York's *CFE* case. After Justice DeGrasse ordered the state to provide more funding for the city, Hanushek warned that it

wouldn't work. "The performance of [New York City students] is unlikely to improve from simple infusions of resources," he said. "It is
not that resources never affect achievement. It is simply that the current incentives operating in public schools do little to promote higher
achievement. Without more fundamental changes to make improved
student achievement the centerpiece of rewards and punishments, little should be expected from judgments [like DeGrasse's]."[12]

In his work for the defense in the Alabama *ACE* and *Harper* cases
he found that if the state lifted per-pupil spending in all districts to
the level of Alabama's highest-spending districts—at a cost of roughly
$1 billion over the $2.4 billion the state was then spending, it would
increase student performance by only about 4 percent. In one instance,
according to Picus, "Hanushek actually predicted that the increased
spending would reduce student performance by 0.2 percent."[13] Similarly, in the New York case, a witness showed that by Hanushek's
data "you can save a lot of money by reducing school expenditures
and not hurt Regents diplomas. . . . If you believed that result, you
should really substantially reduce spending."[14]

But despite the slips into statistical absurdity, there was a telling
point. Hanushek said he had a "jaundiced view of adequacy in school
finance reform" that was based on the simple fact that since no one
had really related inputs to student performance, "discussions that
concentrate on the distribution of educational inputs bear little relationship to the distribution of educational outputs. This fundamental
problem makes a definition of 'adequacy' in funding and resources
virtually impossible."[15] Put another way, if a district didn't really
know what paid off, how would it know where to put the additional
money? Picus had done studies showing that when a district got extra
money, it usually spent it in pretty much the same proportions as it
was spending all its other funds. Thus, he concluded in a paper written with Allan Odden of the University of Wisconsin, "if additional
education revenues are spent in the same way as current education
revenues, student performance increases are unlikely to emerge."[16] In
such circumstances, Hanushek was probably right that putting more
money in was more an act of faith than of science. That observation
also raises broader questions about what the trade calls "capacity." If
more money suddenly flows in and the system doesn't have the

trained teachers and administrators to use it effectively, there may be no point in providing it.

Hanushek's message was nothing if not consistent. "My research," he said in one summary, "suggests that there is inefficiency in the provision of schooling; it does not indicate that schools do not matter. Nor does it indicate that money and resources never affect achievement. The accumulated research simply says that there is no clear systematic relationship between resources and student outcomes."[17] None of this, he said, trying to answer his critics, can be explained "by a worsening of students over time. While some family factors have worsened—increased child poverty and fewer two-parent families, others have improved—more educated parents and smaller families." But the growing focus on "observed performance and student outcomes" caused him to fear "the tendency for analysis to be intertwined with hopes, dreams, or normative views."[18] In education, it had rarely been any other way.

As might be expected, Hanushek has become a great favorite of conservatives: a man with impeccable credentials as a scholar who has lots of charts and graphs showing that just throwing money at the schools will not help—that (as he testified in New York) "how the money is spent is much more important than how much or adding more." Stanford's Hoover Institution, which is probably the nation's most respected conservative think tank and which attracted him away from the University of Rochester, where he'd taught for twenty-two years, has given him carte blanche: He is free to do anything he wants and never has to teach again. For the same reasons, there's little love lost for him on the left, a problem exacerbated by the fact that he's not a kook or crank, but an eminently reasonable man who's not easily gettable. The response has been not to berate him but to ignore him as much as possible. His answer to a recent question about how often he's asked to speak to conferences of establishment education organizations and whether leaders of school organizations talk to him was another question: "You mean civilly?"[19] Before CFE filed its suit in New York, Hanushek said, Mike Rebell sounded him out about his take on the issues. After Hanushek told him, he said, he never heard from Rebell again.

II

The inescapable subtext in Coleman's work, and to a lesser extent even in Hanushek's, is race—the apparently intractable black-white test score gap that runs with depressing consistency through virtually every academic measurement. In 1969, three years after the Coleman Report was issued, Arthur Jensen, a Berkeley psychology professor, published an article in the *Harvard Education Review* and subsequently a book called *Genetics and Education* (1972) arguing that Great Society compensatory education programs had failed and were a waste of money because the black-white gap was largely genetic in origin. "Accordingly, the ideal of equality of educational opportunity should not be interpreted as uniformity of facilities, instructional techniques, and educational aims for all children," Jensen said. "Diversity rather than uniformity of approaches and aims would seem to be the key to making education rewarding for children of different patterns of ability."[20] Although the ideological and theoretical foundations probably were very different, as social policy the consequences of Jensen's argument were not all that different either from Justice Lerner's opinion in New York or from those of civil rights groups and other liberal advocates convinced that uniform academic testing and standards discriminate against minority children. Bush would call it "the soft bigotry of low expectations."

For a time, Jensen had some high-profile company, most notably from Nobel laureate William Shockley, a solid-state physicist at Bell Labs, later a Stanford professor, who had played the key role in developing the first semiconductors. But Shockley became far better known for his articles and speeches on "dysgenics," his theory that blacks were genetically inferior in intelligence, that most social programs merely perpetuated the spread of inferior racial stock, and that anyone with an IQ below 100 should be paid to submit to voluntary sterilization. Shockley was also said to have been a frequent contributor to the so-called Nobel sperm bank and, late in life, ran for the U.S. Senate from California on the dysgenics platform (he came in eighth). Jensen's own thesis suffered a major blow when it was discovered that Cyril Burt, the British psychologist on whose studies of twins Jensen had based much of his work, had almost certainly faked large chunks of his data. Meanwhile, Shockley sued the *Atlanta Constitution* for $1.25 million, charging that a column comparing his eugenic theories to those of the Nazis had libeled him. The jurors found for Shockley but letting him know what they thought of him, they awarded him a token $1 in damages.

But the debate about the role of heredity in determining academic and intellectual success—and, conversely, the power of social and educational programs to produce it—continues to cast its shadow, apparent most obviously in such work as Charles Murray and Richard Herrnstein's *The Bell Curve* (1994),[21] more broadly in the ongoing problems of trying to close the black-white test gap, and beyond that in the political battles over how much to invest, and how, in providing adequate education for have-not children.[22] As already noted, the black-white gap, as measured by NAEP, narrowed significantly in the 1970s and 1980s, particularly for students in the previously segregated Southeast, who showed major gains in the classes that began school between 1968–72 and 1976–80. For reading and math combined, the gains for thirteen-year-old black students were the equivalent of an additional one and a half years of schooling. "Such large gains over such a short period are rare," said David Grissmer and a group of research colleagues at Rand, who reviewed the literature. "Indeed, they may be unprecedented. . . . Gains of this magnitude are unusual even in intensive programs explicitly aimed at raising test scores."[23]

No one is certain what produced those gains (which peaked with the classes starting school in the late 1970s and then started down, though not to their Jim Crow levels). Desegregation in the South can't explain all of it, since black students made gains elsewhere. But desegregation—plus various poverty and affirmative action programs— certainly had its impact. "All these changes," the Rand team observed, "may have signaled to black parents and students nationwide, and also to their teachers, that black children's education was a national priority that would be backed by both money and legal authority."[24] The Rand group, which also lists a number of other possibilities— improved family circumstances, better schools—remains agnostic in designating any prime cause. Its major point was to challenge people such as Hanushek. "The NAEP data [for gains by black students in the 1970s and 1980s] do not suggest that schools have squandered

money or that social and educational policies aimed at helping minorities have failed." Those who think otherwise "have an obligation
to explain rising NAEP scores, particularly for minorities." Again,
Hanushek had a theory. In his Texas studies, he said, he and his
colleagues found that the higher the concentration of black students
in a classroom, the worse even the best of the black students did.
Latinos were not affected to nearly the same extent, and whites hardly
at all. "Desegregation," he observed, "how little we know about its
impacts."[25]

What seems indisputable is that long after people such as Jensen
and Shockley are mostly forgotten, the racial issues continue subtly
to afflict all sides in these debates—both the academic disputes and
the fights in the political arena. To what extent does any argument,
like those advanced by Hanushek and David Armor, that seems to
question the connection between money and achievement automatically fall under Jensen and Shockley's dark light and thus become
easy for opponents to subtly join, however unfairly, with the theories
that eugenicists such as Francis Galton promulgated a century before
that? How close is any argument for affirmative action (as some of
its opponents charge) to a declaration that blacks or Latinos will never
be able to achieve at the same levels as white or Asians and thus, in
the name of social parity, need special consideration? Was it true, as
former New York schools chancellor Rudy Crew said, that New York
State hired its Atlanta lawyers because they had the chutzpah to say
(or at least imply) things about the limitations of poor kids that the
governor and other senior officials were afraid to utter? Even though
the case is now couched in the argument that it's social and cultural
factors that keep students from learning, is the policy outcome all that
different from Jensen saying that a search for equality of educational
opportunity is futile because—well—the kids are different? What's
most vexing is that even children of black professionals—lawyers,
doctors, teachers—seem to trail their white peers, a factor that Berkeley anthropologist John Ogbu, a Nigerian immigrant, attributes to
cultural attitudes. The core of those attitudes is the fear of "acting
white" and the failure of those students who, Ogbu says, look to
rappers and other entertainers as models, to understand how their
parents made it. Others, such as psychologist Claude Steele of Stan-

ford, believe the cause is black students' fear of failure, what he calls "stereotype threat"—the self-fulfilling fear of black students of being unable to perform as well as whites on tests.[26] But whether it's family that's destiny, or peers or genes or culture, there's the same implication that schools have only a marginal effect and the negative consequences for educational policy aren't likely to be all that different. As the percentage of minority students increases, those factors are likely to loom even larger.

III

By the mid-1990s, Hanushek no longer had the field to himself. More important, the conventional formulation of the Coleman findings that socioeconomic background will swamp anything the schools can do was under serious challenge. Hanushek's own belief that "there is not a strong or consistent relationship between student performance and school resources" or between class size and academic achievement was facing a growing number of well-credentialed critics: David Grissmer at Rand, Alan B. Krueger at Princeton, Ronald F. Ferguson at Harvard, and Robert Greenwald, Larry V. Hedges, and Richard D. Laine at the University of Chicago, among others.

Their approaches and arguments differ. Some focus on the fact that in his surveys of studies purporting to show the uncertain correlation between money and achievement, Hanushek engaged in what critics such as Krueger describe as a skewed method of "vote counting"— every study is supposed to be given the same weight, but Hanushek took any study that had multiple estimates and gave it multiple votes. Pursuing that track, Krueger pointed out that Hanushek took one study, based on a small sample, that yielded twenty-four different estimates for different groups and tests and gave it twenty-four times the weight of another, larger study with a single pooled estimate. Thus, said Krueger, "Hanushek's procedure assigns excessive weight to studies with unsystematic or negative results."[27] When studies like those used by Hanushek were calibrated using different statistical techniques, said Greenwald, Hedges, and Laine, "the analysis found that a broad range of resources were positively related to student outcomes, with effect sizes large enough to suggest that moderate increases in spending may be associated with significant increases in achievement."[28] Indeed, says Krueger, any of the alternatives to Hanushek's weighting scheme "point in the opposite direction of his findings: all three find that smaller class sizes are positively related to performance."

What really got the attention of policy makers, however, especially the large number already prone to support class size reduction, were the results of Project STAR (Student Teacher Achievement Ratio), a major longitudinal study in Tennessee showing a strong and apparently long-lasting effect of smaller classes, particularly for minority students, that Fred Mosteller, Moynihan's old Harvard colleague from the Coleman days, called "one of the great experiments in education in U.S. history."[29] This was the kind of study that most researchers can only dream about, "a large-scale experiment in which both teachers and students were randomized into classrooms within a broad range of participating schools," which gave it (in the jargon of the trade) "both high internal validity and considerable external validity."

In that great experiment involving nearly 12,000 students, conducted in 1985–9 but with follow-ups by others over a period of another half-dozen years, researchers Barbara Nye of Tennessee State University and Larry Hedges and Spyros Konstantopoulos of the University of Chicago found that students in primary-grade classes with thirteen to seventeen students quickly outperformed their peers in larger classes (of twenty-two to twenty-six students) in reading and math. More important, when those students returned to regular-size classes after grade three, they maintained those differences; they took more challenging courses, and their dropout rates were lower. But what Nye and her colleagues found most interesting was that the gains were larger for minority students. "Thus, small classes may be a way to benefit all students while reducing the gap in achievement between white and minority students."[30] In a further analysis, Krueger and Diane Whitmore of Princeton also found that small classes substantially raised the percentage of black students who would take college entrance exams. "If all students were assigned to a small class," they said, "the black-white gap in taking a college entrance exam would fall by an estimated 60 percent" and would significantly raise black students' scores on those tests.[31]

Hanushek disputes the sweep of the conclusions drawn from the STAR study and particularly the across-the-board class size reduction policies that have been based on it:

> The existing evidence suggests that any effects of overall class size reduction policies will be small and very expensive. A number of investigations appear to show some effect of class size on achievement for specific groups or circumstances, but the estimated effects are invariably small and insufficient to support any broad reduction policies. . . .
>
> The existing evidence does not say that class size reductions are never worthwhile and that they should never be taken. It does say that uniform, across-the-board policies—such as those in the current policy debate—are unlikely to be effective.[32]

The real challenge, Hanushek says, "is figuring which students, teachers or subject matters may be most affected by reduced class sizes and which would not be affected by increased class sizes." The data seem to indicate that reduced class size seems to have little effect on affluent students and that black students are "much more sensitive to reduced pupil-teacher ratios than are white students," suggesting that "if done, policy applications must focus on strategic use of reduced class sizes." Hanushek also believes that STAR itself may be as reflective of differences in teacher quality as of class size variations.[33] (In another study, conducted in Alabama, Ronald Ferguson and Helen Ladd found that while reading scores improve as class size diminishes from an average of twenty-nine students to between twenty-three and twenty-five students, further lowering class size produces no additional gains; in math however, the scores seem to keep rising indefinitely as pupil-teacher ratios go down.)[34]

On this count, in any case, Hanushek seems at least partly right. As the California researchers recommended, at the very least class size reduction programs should give local districts far more flexibility to concentrate their resources than the rigid twenty-to-one formula that

California imposed in the primary grades and the even more stringent K-12 class size formula called for in Amendment 9, a ballot measure that Florida voters passed (53–47 percent) in 2002, despite Governor Jeb Bush's intensive campaign warning about its variously estimated multibillion-dollar cost and the tax increases it may require. Amendment 9 caps student-teacher ratios at eighteen to one in the first four grades (K–3), twenty-two to one in grades 4–8, and twenty-five to one in high school, and requires the state to pay for it.

Such formulas are unfailingly popular with teachers, voters, and parents but involve costly trade-offs. For educationally disadvantaged students, classes of fifteen to seventeen may make a considerable difference; for others, classes of twenty may provide little advantage over classes of twenty-five to twenty-seven. In Wisconsin's Student Achievement Guarantee in Education (SAGE) program, which targets schools with high poverty rates, primary-grade classes of fifteen students, combined with rigorous curricula, intensive training for teachers, and before- and after-school programs produced significant increases in test scores, especially when teachers worked one-on-one with individual students to strengthen their basic skills.[35] It thus seemed to confirm the commonsense assumption that where teachers took advantage of smaller classes—and didn't simply keep doing what they'd been forced to do in larger classes—it would make a difference. What no one could accurately measure, of course, was the effect of large classes, especially those with one or more difficult students, on the attention of other students and on teacher morale and burnout.

The class size debate and the related disputes about whether and how money makes a difference have been played out not only in countless journal articles and in the rebuttals and rebuttals to rebuttals that almost inevitably follow; but in courtrooms in dozens of states, in legislative hearings, and (with considerably less *politesse*) in the corridors of professional seminars and conferences. And here the questions begin to accumulate, not merely about the Hanushek analyses but about the paucity of theory underlying them. In all of the counterintuitive conclusions—about the failure to find connections between money or class size and performance—there was little explanation. In New York, Hanushek found some kids doing very well in overcrowded schools. But there was no theory to explain it.

"If we take these results seriously," said Rand researcher David Griss-mer in his trial testimony, "you know, try to have more kids in the school and spending less money is the answer. It is possible that counterintuitive results enter into education and economics, but I have not heard a counterintuitive explanation as to why these results make sense.... You need to provide a reason why we are wasting money licensing teachers." None of this stuff, said Grissmer, was up to Rand's research standards.[36]

If you want to see Hanushek grimace, say Grissmer's name; if you want to get a sour note from Joe Wayland, the Simpson Thacher lawyer in the adequacy suit against the state of New York, just mention Hanushek.

Yet surprisingly enough, given the acrimony of the dispute, there's little substantive disagreement about three major sets of reports on the importance of quality teachers in student achievement. All three of those studies demonstrate what may have long been obvious to parents who annually shop for the best teachers: that teachers, whose pay and benefits represent far and away the largest single item in any school budget, make not just a large difference but potentially enough difference to overcome all the handicapping impact of poverty and the cultural effects that often come with it. All three thus challenge the conventional wisdom derived (not always accurately) from the Coleman Report and Hanushek's own conclusion that there's "no strong or consistent relationship between student performance and school resources."

The first of those studies comes from the Tennessee Value-Added Assessment System (TVAAS), which was created by the State of Tennessee to link the impact of individual schools and teachers to the gains pupils make in the state's tests in five subjects in grades 2–8. TVAAS, which rests on a huge database of student information, was designed by a University of Tennessee agricultural statistician named William L. Sanders not just to measure how high a student scored on a certain date; it was a value-added study to determine how much annual progress (in math) he or she had made in a given classroom and school. Reporting on a study of students who were second graders in 1991–92 and were followed through fifth grade three years later, Sanders and his collaborator, June Rivers, seemed almost in wonder at their own findings. The effects of both good and bad teachers, they found, were enormous, and were measurable two years later, "regardless of the effectiveness of teachers in the later grades." And no matter how well students had done previously, "students under the tutelage of teachers in the bottom quintile made unsatisfactory gains."

> Based upon these results, students benefiting from regular yearly assignment to more effective teachers (even if by chance) have an extreme advantage in terms of attaining higher levels of achievement. (The range of approximately 50 percentile points in student mathematics achievement as measured in this study is awesome!!!! Differences of this magnitude could determine future assignments of remedial versus accelerated courses.)[57]

This report, needless perhaps to say, wasn't published in a learned journal, where the word *awesome* with four exclamation points would almost surely have caused terminal meltdown, but its findings are consistent with those in the other major studies on teacher effectiveness, both from Texas, with its huge database of student records. One of them is Ronald Ferguson's findings that "hiring teachers with stronger literacy skills, hiring more teachers (when students-per-teacher exceed 18), retaining experienced teachers, and attracting more teachers with advanced training are all measures that produce higher test scores in exchange for more money."[38]

The other report comes from Hanushek's own studies, done with Steven G. Rivkin of Amherst College and John F. Kain of the University of Texas, showing "large differences among teachers in their impacts on achievement. Our estimates, which are based on just the within school variations in teacher quality, reveal the effects of teacher quality to be substantial even ignoring any variations across schools. They indicate that having a high quality teacher throughout elementary school can substantially offset or even eliminate the disadvantage of low socio-economic background."[39] Those differences, he says, are "impressive"—"huge." In effect, said Hanushek and his colleagues, "having five years of good teachers in a row would overcome the average achievement deficit between low income kids and others from higher income families. In other words, high quality teachers can make up for the typical deficits that we see in the preparation of kids from disadvantaged backgrounds."[40] And since these conclusions are based on a large sample of students, it's almost impossible to write them off as flukes of sampling or other statistical anomalies.

Hanushek says that to date there's no way to know what distinguishes good from bad teachers other than their consistent record in raising or dampening student achievement compared to other teachers with similar students in the same schools—the within-school variations. Like others, he's pointed out that merely having a master's degree or more college credits beyond the bachelor's degree, which is still tied to higher pay in most teachers' contracts, doesn't make much difference. (Since some of those credits were obtained by listening to a few lectures on South Sea Island cruises or other similarly intensive vacation study programs, and since many more were only vaguely related to the specific skills that are required to teach the established curricula in the classroom, the lack of correlation is hardly surprising.) But Ferguson, among others, has some pretty good ideas about what makes a difference—or at least what seems to predict it. The association of teacher verbal ability and student achievement goes back to the Coleman Report—Hanushek was among the first to take note of it—but as Ferguson noted, when a teacher scores high on almost any basic test of literacy skills, he or she seems to be more successful in raising student achievement. Ferguson's own work shows that when students have teachers through their school years who did well on the Texas Current Administrators and Teachers test (TECAT), the students will do well in twelfth grade regardless of where they tested academically in first grade; conversely, even students who tested very well in first grade will test much lower in twelfth grade if they've had TECAT losers through their school careers.[41]

Ferguson, contra an army of conservative skeptics, also concludes that certification makes a difference. It's by now a cliché that, as David Armor observed thirty years ago, "when schools are concerned with raising black student achievement, the black teachers who have the major responsibility for it suffer from the same [lack of literacy skill] as their students." When testing for literacy and basic math skills was introduced in the early 1980s as a requirement to get a teaching credential, the passing rates for black teaching applicants in some states fell by half—in California, some of those who failed the California Basic Educational Skills Test sued, arguing that basic literacy and math were not job-related—but it also reduced the gap between the college entrance examination scores of black and white teachers, which, Ferguson notes, will probably also screen out some good teachers. "However, the relevant question is whether students are, on average, better off with the policy in place. I think that the answer is yes."[42]

That's hardly the last word. While there's little disagreement about the importance of good teachers, the battles over what makes a good teacher, and particularly about what sort of training is required, continue with unabated ferocity. Like the combatants over the teaching of reading or math (whole language vs. phonics, constructivist math vs. direct instruction in math facts, bilingual education vs. English immersion), these people don't just disagree; anyone sampling the fusillades of e-mail among the various groups of partisans will quickly discover that they detest one another with a passion. To what extent, for example, can a state seeking to upgrade the quality of its reading and math teachers dictate how the ed schools should train their students and with what materials? And what difference does certification make? In 2000, Dan Goldhaber of the Urban Institute and Dominic Brewer of Rand produced a study concluding that, "contrary to conventional wisdom, mathematics and science students who have teachers with emergency credentials do no worse than students whose teachers have standard teaching credentials."[43] That, too, set off an extended battle, both about their conclusions and about the alleged inadequacy of their sample.

These are holy wars. Linda Darling-Hammond of Stanford, who, as the founding executive director of the National Commission on Teaching and America's Future and as the author of scores of studies, reports, and other materials, has become the doyenne of formal teacher training in America, lists five elements that she says seem to be related to student achievement: "1) general academic and verbal ability; 2) subject matter knowledge; 3) knowledge about teaching and learning as reflected in teacher education courses or preparation experiences; 4) teaching experience; and 5) the combined set of qualifications measured by teacher certification, which includes most of the preceding factors." Darling-Hammond also points out that "principals are particularly forceful in their conviction that teacher certification is an important indicator of teaching ability; the credential shows that teachers have education training of the kind they find valuable."[44] Darling-Hammond's list drives some critics—and not just conservatives—to distraction. To those critics, the formal credentialing requirements, and particularly the ed schools with their profusion of what they regard as fatuous methods courses, multiculturalism, vacuous research, and a virtual monopoly on the requisite training, are the nation's biggest barriers to the best and brightest in teaching and the greatest impediments to effective classroom reform. Conventional ed school programs, they maintain, screen out as many creative and imaginative people as incompetent people.

What's certain is that college education majors, who still constitute a large part of the teaching force—though hardly all of it—are disproportionately drawn from the lower ranks of their college classes; those from the upper ranks who go into teaching are less likely to stay and, once out of the teaching force, less likely to return. Those who do stay come disproportionately from the ranks of those who scored in the bottom quartile on the SAT or ACT college admission tests.[45] Whether that's because of the stultifying ed-school requirements, because of the pay differentials, or simply because of the low social status of the profession is itself a matter of endless dispute.

For conservatives such as Chester Finn, the former Reagan administration education official, the shining models are the young graduates of Ivy League and other selective colleges in Teach for America (TFA), most of whom wouldn't be caught dead in an ed school. They go into the classroom with strong academic backgrounds and lots of dedication but little formal training in managing rooms full of kids. To people such as Finn, and now to education secretary Rod Paige, they seem to demonstrate that with a few hours of classroom training, any bright person with a sound background in an academic subject can teach. TFA volunteers commit to two years in the classroom, after which a high proportion leave teaching, but even their classroom performance is subject to intense dispute. CREDO, the conservative Center for Research on Education Outcomes at the Hoover Institution at Stanford, claims, on the basis of studies done in Houston, that TFA teachers do better in raising student achievement than the regular teachers working in the same high-poverty schools to which most of them are assigned. Darling-Hammond's establishment-oriented National Commission on Teaching and America's Future replies with data showing that because the comparison group of teachers has such a high proportion of uncredentialed people, the Teach for America volunteers are doing about as well as "an extraordinarily unqualified group of new hires."[46]

There are other alternative routes, many run by individual school districts for midcareer adults, that appear to be producing strong teachers, though not in numbers anywhere as large as those turned out by the conventional teachers college route. Most are people looking to change professions—particularly people retiring from the military who have some training in math or electronics or engineering and are looking for a new career. Many are being trained in the school districts where they expect to teach, often in collaboration with—but not within—a nearby teachers college. They reflect the "manifesto" issued by Chester Finn's Thomas B. Fordham Foundation in 1999 and signed by a long list of conservatives that called on the states to "get rid of most hoops and hurdles" and the long list of ed-school courses required in many teacher-prep programs. Instead, the idea is to focus on command of subject matter and "test future teachers for their knowledge and skills. Allow principals to hire the teachers they need. Focus relentlessly on results."[47] In essence, deregulate teacher training, end the quasi-monopoly long held by the ed schools, choose teachers according to what they know, and reward them on the basis of how well they produce.

In its No Child Left Behind Act, passed in 2001, the Bush administration has in effect adopted the Fordham program by tilting strongly toward those alternative routes. In its requirement that all schools serving large concentrations of poor students have "highly

qualified teachers" in all their classrooms by 2004–5, the law empha-
sizes subject matter knowledge and general literacy in its definition.
Education secretary Rod Paige, in what the U.S. Department of Education described as "a call to action," urged states to radically trans-
form their teacher certification requirements by raising standards and
lowering barriers that keep many highly qualified candidates from
pursuing teaching careers.[48]

That brought an immediate rejoinder from Teachers College president Arthur Levine that Paige's recommendation "all but guarantees
that our poor and minority youngsters living in our inner cities will
be left behind." Suburbs with middle-class kids and high-paying
schools, he said, can be choosy and insist on highly skilled professionals; the inner cities can't. For poor and minority children, "we are
willing to accept something far less under the definition of a 'highly
qualified teacher'. . . . We will still have large numbers of students
whose teachers are unprepared to teach them."[49] If the president of
the United States declared that he was sending his newest recruits
into battle with some surplus World War II equipment and keeping
his best troops and materiel in London, Paris, and Tokyo, Levine said,
"you'd impeach the guy."[50] Certification, as Linda Darling-Hammond
points out, guarantees at least a minimum of competence and experience. Where there are large concentrations of uncredentialed
teachers, the rates of student failure are significantly higher, even
after controlling for poverty and other student characteristics. The
differences seem to be even greater for poor, black, and Latino students. And in areas such as algebra and other high school mathematics
courses, the difference between teachers certified in their field and
those who are not is enormous.[51] Certification is no guarantee that an
individual will be a good teacher, and it may discourage some excellent candidates, but it also screens out the weakest prospects.

The stakes here are more than academic. Lurking beneath the
fights is the fear among some in the ed-school establishment that the
right is bent on deprofessionalizing teaching, thus lowering pay and
destroying the unions (which are, among other things, a mainstay of
the Democratic Party). Darling-Hammond has spoken darkly about a
conservative agenda that wants "a compliant teacher force.' " "If

teacher education were really effective," she said a few years ago, "it would become politically radical." The right, therefore, would prefer to deskill the profession—"to keep them barefoot and pregnant."[52]

Even the most conservative argument supports the idea of differential pay for difficult duty or outstanding work. What's crucial here is not which path into the profession produces the better teachers, but how teaching quality and effectiveness are to be measured when adequacy issues are defined. (So far, the best measure appears to be those verbal skills.) In the past few years, a growing number of states, some under the pressure of court orders, some not, have sought ways to get better teachers into the schools serving the neediest children. That would be difficult even if there were a reliable way of determining who those teachers are. But other than perhaps tests of verbal ability and subject matter comprehension, so far there is no measure that can be applied across the board. So when states and school districts, responding to charges that a high proportion of new teachers in urban schools lack credentials—which, of course, is true—develop incentives and/or requirements that new teachers have all to be credentialed, the system may do little more than move to the next rank of mediocrity. The real key, as one major study points out, may not be the number of courses a teacher took, either in pedagogy or in the field taught, but his or her conceptual command of the subject.[53]

It may not do even that if, as in New York City's efforts to reduce the huge number of new uncertified teachers, the system raises the pay of entering teachers, but at the same time changes the requirements for the credential to require far less training, and then reports that its chronic shortage of credentialed applicants for new teaching jobs has been miraculously eliminated. Or, as in California's attempt to satisfy the new federal law, simply redefines "highly qualified" to include virtually every person standing before a class, regardless of credential, training, or experience, or when the Washington, D.C., schools, perhaps the nation's most famously dysfunctional district, reports to the Department of Education that no one in its classrooms is teaching on waivers.[54] Even where there is no fudging, the imposition of any across-the-board formula, whether it's universal class size reduction in the lower grades or universal pay raises for teachers, may turn out to be an investment producing relatively little in return.

IV

In the heyday of his department store business, John Wanamaker supposedly complained that he knew half his advertising was wasted, and if he knew which half, he'd cut it out. The business of education research, once dismissed as a "soggy waffle," sometimes faces similar difficulties. There are too many variables, too many intangibles, too many moving parts. What we knew for certain a half century ago, or in some instances even a decade ago, we aren't so certain about anymore. In different places and at different times, Americans sought to ban homework, or to limit it, then to require it, and then to limit it again. Social promotion was a good idea, either to foster self-esteem or to save money or both, and thus encouraged, or it was simply a fraud on students and thus prohibited (at least on paper and in the speeches of the politicians who sought to have it outlawed). Children, especially disadvantaged children, benefit most from direct instruction and drill, or they learn better through exploration and discovery... the list goes on.[55] The STAR experiments themselves don't endorse class sizes of twenty; their effects seem not to be apparent until the class gets down to between thirteen and seventeen, and even then, says Hanushek, the gains in kindergarten and perhaps first grade, while carried into the later grades, don't seem to be augmented by further achievement gains derived from small classes in the later grades.

Meanwhile another set of debates rolls on about the efficacy of varying "whole-school reform" programs, each with its loyal following: Accelerated Schools, created by Henry M. Levin, now at Columbia Teachers College, a highly focused program that, Levin says, treats all students as gifted; Robert Slavin's Success for All, which was the model for whole-school reform in New Jersey; James Comer's School Development Program ("to improve the educational experience of poor minority youth ... by building supportive bonds among children, parents, and school staff to promote a positive school climate"); E. D. Hirsch's Core Knowledge (of common culture facts and ideas); and a half dozen others, some tightly scripted, others progressive and exploratory. In addition, there are remedial programs such as Reading Recovery, a labor-intensive (and thus costly) system to reconstruct the reading skills of children who fall behind. All claim success based on various (often self-defined) measures, and most have been brought before judges in the adequacy cases as examples of what schools could be doing if they had sufficient resources. But all are controversial—subject to legitimate criticism from the field about what the research really shows—and thus difficult for the courts to judge.

These days, the hottest of the whole-school reforms may be the Knowledge Is Power Program (KIPP) schools, begun in 1994–95 by Michael Feinberg and David Levin, two Teach for America recruits in Houston, where Paige was superintendent at the time. One of the original KIPP schools is in Houston, the other in the Bronx. By 2002, there were fifteen KIPP schools in eleven states, and the program expected to launch another nineteen by 2003. All middle schools in low-income areas, they're set up either as charters or under contract with local districts, which allow them considerable latitude to run their programs free of normal bureaucratic constraints. Aimed at getting all their students into competitive high schools and college, they're founded on five "pillars" that include an extended school day, school week (sometimes including Saturday classes), and school year; "clearly defined and measurable high expectations for academic achievement and conduct that make no excuses based on the background of students"; and a requirement that parents, students, and teachers "make and uphold a commitment to the school and to each other to put in the time and effort required to achieve success."[56]

The first five schools in the program—all those in operation in the fall of 2001—appear to show academic gains by students that far outpace districtwide averages. Because of those gains, KIPP has drawn large chunks of federal and private money, including $23 million from Donald Fisher and his wife, Doris, founders of the Gap stores (who put a similar amount into the financial troubled for-profit Edison Schools); the Walton (of Wal-Mart) Family Foundation; and a number of other deep-pocket educational conservatives. Much of that money will go to opening new schools and training the school leaders to run them. It's too early yet—and there is still too much professional doubt that KIPP's success can be widely replicated—for the KIPP formula to have made it into the adequacy debates. Most particularly, there is the question about the extent to which KIPP's early success is due to the highly motivated (and self-selected) children and parents that its high demands attract (and, conversely, to the children and parents KIPP schools select out). But to the extent it succeeds, it is more likely to prove precisely what the adequacy movement contends: that poor and minority kids require significantly more resources to succeed than they're getting now.

Both the Tennessee STAR data and common sense would indicate that small classes may be far more necessary for at-risk kids than for affluent kids in the suburbs. But is the record powerful enough to overcome political resistance against any generalized financial system that favors the poor over the rich? Hanushek himself, while strongly committed to the idea that good teachers make a great deal of difference, acknowledges that he doesn't know what the trade-offs are between higher teacher salaries (and thus the power to be much more choosy about teacher quality) and larger classes. Is one good teacher in a class of fifty better than two mediocre ones in classes of twenty-five? Given his repeated assertions that class size can't be linked to any measurable outcome, one would expect him to leap at this choice, but he doesn't because there's no data to support it. It also takes you quickly to logical absurdities that make quite clear that at some point class size makes a huge difference. Hanushek's mantra is incentives—connecting rewards to performance—but how that can be most effectively done without undermining the collaborative efforts and the sense of common purpose that most successful schools seem to depend on is not entirely clear. In some states, cash bonuses for schools with improving scores go to all employees, including the janitors. Conversely, in many states, failing schools are subject to sanctions. But the downtown district bureaucrats who can be crucial either in impeding or encouraging school success often remain untouched by state accountability systems.

For schools, Wanamaker's question may be especially appropriate. Schools are not just marketing or manufacturing operations whose output can be measured in units sold or profits made, and children are not just units of production. Schools are social enterprises with a long list of concerns that defy measurement and, given the shortage of other social services, a mission that goes far beyond formal education: as teachers of manners and decorum, as health centers, as providers of what for many kids may be the best meal (and maybe the only real one) they get each day; as counseling centers, as child care providers and sources of stability where there may be no other.

That doesn't argue against measurement or accountability or against efforts to assess productivity, nor does it justify attempts to excuse academic failure with vague generalizations about self-esteem and cultural validation. But it does argue for caution about their limits. No parent or student should have to offer scientific proof that attractive schools with working toilets and decent classroom environments are more productive than those without. None should be asked how they knew that having rats in their classrooms impaired their ability to learn. Nor should any school have to justify good libraries and courses and after-school programs in art or music with test scores and college attendance rates.

What's perfectly clear is that where people can afford it, they opt for the schools with the rich resources, and often struggle (and sometimes lie and cheat) to get their children into the right schools. "The costs of changing teacher ratios, increasing average teacher experience, teachers' educational background and, of course, increasing average staff salary, are staggering," said the New Jersey Supreme Court in 1990. "For instance, a large urban district with 8000 pupils and a staff ratio of one teacher per thirty pupils would have to budget an extra $900,000 per year to bring that ratio down to one per twenty-five (assuming the teacher salary [1990] was the statutory minimum, $18,000). Improvement of each of the other factors [better curricula, arts and music classes, fully equipped labs, hands-on computer instruction, richer foreign language offerings] has a similarly high cost attached to it. . . . If these factors were not related to the quality of education, why are the richer districts willing to spend so much for them?"[57]

CHAPTER FIVE

Final Test

No generalization can be entirely accurate in an educational system—historically a nonsystem—as complex and diverse as America's. With 47 million students and 3.1 million teachers in 92,000 public schools within 15,000 districts in fifty different states, each with its own governance structure and its own curricula, traditions, and practices, and many with children from a wide spectrum of ethnic, cultural, and economic backgrounds, there are exceptions to almost everything. But with the widespread, fundamental changes of the two decades beginning in the early 1980s—a shift, toward increased state funding and thus increasing state control, coupled with the centralization of state-imposed academic standards and requirements that have driven and sometimes overwhelmed local school policy, and now a growing list of federal mandates—some conclusions are possible. The nonsystem is rapidly becoming, at the very least, a set of fifty state systems. Some people predict it will someday evolve into a single national school system.

In that evolution, the reciprocal responsibilities between those setting the standards and those who are supposed to carry them out have been recognized only slowly, and usually only after the fact. In the middle and late 1990s especially, the competition among state politicians to see who could demand the most stringent academic standards became a replacement for the tough-on-crime contests of the 1980s. In California, where there was pressure from the elected state superintendent of public instruction to require not merely one year of algebra for graduation but two, members of the state board of education, who had the ultimate responsibility for the decision, were reluctant to resist, fearing they'd be accused of being soft on standards. Every state and every legislator was going to have the toughest standards.

In the process of toughening, however, some educational conservatives and some traditional liberals suddenly (and perhaps accidentally) found themselves on common ground that linked accountability to additional funding. While it was sometimes shaky, it could hold everyone from George W. Bush and Chester Finn, the former Reagan education policy thinker, to Ted Kennedy, a co-sponsor of Bush's No Child Left Behind education bill, and John Cole, the head of the Texas Federation of Teachers, a man with as good a set of liberal and labor credentials as you can find. When Texas began rating schools not just on average test scores but on those of poor and minority children, it meant that the schools had to start paying attention to children they'd never seriously bothered with before.

The Texas Assessment of Academic Skills (TAAS), the Texas test, had plenty of flaws, and it may have increased (and its successor-testing program may still be increasing) the dropout rate. But it also meant that many Latino and black students were being taught (or at least drilled) for the first time instead of being ignored. For Cole, the Texas school reforms also brought more pay for teachers and ended the era when, in Cole's words, a school principal "used to be anybody with a master's degree and two losing seasons."[1] As the Education Trust's Kati Haycock points out, the standards and accountability systems may well represent the best hope for getting those children the teaching and the resources that they've never gotten. Haycock understood that conservative means could be the way to liberal ends. When Bush stole the slogan "No child left behind" from Marian Wright Edelman and the Children's Defense Fund, it was not just a gigantic act of chutzpah but a calculated effort to mine that common ground. The adequacy principle couldn't be a better fit.

But as the stories in the states make clear, nothing is simple. Despite the major changes of the past two decades, the struggle to better educational opportunities rarely follows a straight and easy path. Michael Rebell, who may be as thoughtful as anyone on this issue, says the adequacy argument "tends to invoke less political resistance at the remedial stage because rather than raising fears of 'leveling down' educational opportunities currently available to affluent students, it gives promise of 'leveling up' academic expectations for all other students. Although standards-based reforms would most dramatically improve the performance of the lowest achieving students, the reforms are comprehensive and intended to provide benefits to almost all students. Instead of threatening to shift money from rich districts to poor districts, therefore, adequacy offers the possibility of increasing the pie for all."[2]

The battles of the past decades demonstrate, however, that the courts are rarely great places to make educational policy. "The courts," as James Guthrie said, "constantly push us beyond the bounds of social science knowledge." They can declare a state fiscal structure unconstitutional and order the legislature to fix it, but where the political system is reluctant, as it has been in Ohio, that can be like trying to push string uphill. Where they try to detail specific remedies, as in New Jersey, the courts may soon find themselves deeper in the business of imposing across-the-board educational programs—sorting their way through Reading Recovery, Core Knowledge, Accelerated Schools, Success for All—than they're equipped to manage. Paradoxically, they may even be ordering states to appropriate more money, or to spend it faster, than local schools can effectively spend it. "I'm not sure," said John Augenblick, probably the nation's most active adequacy consultant, "that the courts can handle this."[3] But in their power to say no—and, if necessary, say no again and again—the courts have real clout, and increasingly they seem to be using it.

The states' new academic standards provide both a rationale and a benchmark for the courts and legislatures—in Rebell's words, the "tools that courts needed to deal with complex educational issues." Despite the implication of the perverse ruling of the New York appellate division that an eighth-grade education is enough, it's become difficult for states to claim that minimal resources and an elementary-school-level education is all their respective constitutions require. But the standards still leave large unanswered questions. What's adequate for handicapped children who sometimes need thousands of dollars in special educational help? What's adequate for students who come to school speaking little or no English? What's adequate for the budding scientific genius? Is whole-school reform, as ordered by the New Jersey courts, a necessary condition of adequacy? Where in the constitution do you find Success for All?

In a society dedicated to opportunity, adequacy could most simply be defined as giving every child a real chance to achieve up to his or her potential. But applying that standard to school policy or programs or finance, as a National Research Council committee observed, is an art, not a science. It still leaves a lot of room for imprecise political judgments. In Wyoming, as the legislature was determining what outcomes would be included in the adequacy basket of courses and objectives, it first decided that every child learn cardiopulmonary resuscitation. That was subsequently replaced by a unit on balancing a checkbook and managing a retirement portfolio.[4] "Public, and even scholarly debate about 'standards' (i.e. adequate outcomes)," said Guthrie and Rothstein, two of the field's most experienced practitioners, "suffers from a confusion between minimum and average goals, and between relative and absolute goals. This confusion becomes especially important if 'adequacy' is defined as the resources necessary to produce 'average' outcomes."[5] And does adequacy in policy terms necessarily mean the same thing in constitutional terms? "What constitutes an 'adequate' or 'sound' or even 'basic' education," wrote Wisconsin Supreme Court justice Diana Sykes, "is most emphatically not a question of constitutional law for this or any other court." The decision of New York's intermediate appellate court that an eighth-grade education was enough seemed as much as anything else an act of judicial surrender to the intimidating complexities of the issue.

Rebell points out that the courts are engaging the public and other branches of government in an ongoing "dialogue" to define the evolving standards of "a sound basic education." That occurred in Kentucky and Maryland, where the political ground had been prepared and where there were political forces that used either the fact or the possibility of court decisions to push the reform agenda that the plaintiffs in those cases—children, parents, school districts—were seeking. Nor is there much question that the adequacy principle—the belief that school funding should be based on the real cost of educating each student, not on the political wheeling and dealing that divides whatever money is on the table according to the clout of contending forces—is beginning to influence policy even in states where there's been no court order. In California in 2002, a joint legislative committee produced a new Master Plan for California Education that recognizes the state's own accountability in providing the resources required to enable children to meet the educational standards and pass the tests that it requires of them and called for the creation of a commission to define just what that requires of the state. Although funding awaits better times, when the state doesn't face unprecedented budget deficits, the legislature approved, and the governor signed, a bill creating such a panel. In Florida, where the courts rejected an adequacy suit, the voters in 1998 passed an initiative declaring

the education of children [to be] a fundamental value of the people of the State of Florida. It is, therefore, a paramount duty of the state to make adequate provision for the education of all children residing within its borders. Adequate provision shall be made by law for a uniform, efficient, safe, secure, and high quality system of free public schools that allows students to obtain a high quality education.[6]

In 1999, soon after approval of the initiative, a new suit was filed in Leon County Circuit Court by a coalition that includes the NAACP, the League of United Latin American Citizens (LULAC), the Haitian Refugee Center, and other groups charging that for many Florida children, the state is not providing a high-quality education.[7] The suit cites the *Rose* criteria in Kentucky as its standard. In 2002, moreover, Florida voters approved two additional ballot measures. One (cited earlier) sharply limits class size in all Florida schools and orders the state to pay the costs, disregarding Governor Jeb Bush's stern warnings of its $27 billion cost. The other requires the state to provide every Florida four-year-old with "a [free] high quality pre-kindergarten learning opportunity" by the year 2005. No one was certain where the money for either was going to come from.

But probably the best illustration of the extrajudicial impact of the adequacy principle is Oregon, where the courts rejected a series of tax equity suits, and where the voters, in an act combining progressivism

and antipathy to local property taxes, then started to do the job themselves, passing an initiative in 1991 to shift the lion's share of local
school funding from local property taxes to the state. (In 1971, more
than three-fourths of school funds came from local taxes; a generation
later the proportions were reversed.) Since then, commissions established by the legislature and the governor worked with the Management Analysis and Planning (MAP) consultants to create the Oregon
Quality Education Model (QEM), an adequacy-based blueprint for
"policy makers to estimate the costs of providing a high quality education to Oregon students and evaluate the tradeoffs inherent in
making policy decisions in an environment of limited resources."[8]

Recognizing the reciprocal obligations that high academic standards
placed on the state itself, the gubernatorial commission that created
QEM saw it as both a state policy tool—it included a recommended
20 percent increase in state funding—and as a model for local schools
and districts. QEM, not the political sausage machine, was to drive
school funding. QEM also includes forecasts of the hoped-for student
achievement when the plan is fully implemented, and thus, presumably, a gauge of its own effectiveness. By 2002–3, 90 percent of third
graders were to meet the state standard in reading and math; by
2009–10, all tenth graders were forecast to reach the same level. So
far, in the prosaic summary of the Education Commission of the
States, "the state has not yet incorporated the findings from this study
into the state education funding formula," meaning the state is already behind schedule.[9] But it's unlikely that the policy makers will
be able to ignore it for too long; the lawyers will certainly be paying
attention. "The environment has changed," Augenblick said. "Legislatures don't have to be prodded by plaintiffs. The states are moving
on their own." But he also recognized that the court decisions give
the legislatures cover to do things they wouldn't have dared do otherwise.

But what's possible in a small state such as Maryland, which has
only twenty-four school districts, or a relatively homogeneous state
such as Oregon, which is 86 percent white, may be much harder to
achieve in large, diverse states such as like California and New York.
As Thomas B. Timar, who studies school governance issues at the
University of California at Riverside, points out, large states with large

school districts such as New York City or Los Angeles have state or local school governance structures that are "neither rational, nor coherent, nor functional." In California, it thus may be hard to execute any effective remedy without major restructuring "because it is not possible to determine just who the 'state' is. The diffusion of responsibility among various state actors and the lack of coordination among them makes oversight either everyone's or no one's responsibility." In California,

> the State Legislature, particularly since imposition of term limits, has become increasingly proscriptive, limiting local autonomy and enmeshing schools in an increasing web of rules, regulations, reporting requirements, and student testing. Indeed, if the present trend continues, public education in the state will become a massive paper chase with reports flying about that no one will have time or inclination to read.

What may be necessary, therefore, is "institutional reconfiguration," a gentle phrase for tearing up the system and radically rebuilding it from the top down (or perhaps better yet, from the children and teachers up).

> The failure of policy makers to effect improvement in low performing schools is not because they did not hit upon the right combination of policies. As some researchers suggest, some problems associated with low performing schools are beyond the reach of policy. Instead of focusing on polices, policy makers need to think about institutional redesign. How should roles and responsibilities be allocated within a system of state-local education and what kind of institutional infrastructure best supports such a system.
>
> What is clear is that the institutional framework of governance needs to be radically reformed. Further tinkering with new policies to "shape up" schools is not likely to have the desired effect. Increasing regulations is unlikely to have the desired outcome.[10]

State officials have discovered that even the current (relatively limited) attempts to take over or restructure dysfunctional districts—as in Chicago, Philadelphia, Camden, Newark, Jersey City, or Compton—have to be multiyear efforts (if, indeed, they succeed at all). In Philadelphia, the gubernatorial takeover that led to a divisive contract with the financially troubled for-profit Edison Schools, to run twenty inner-city schools produced at least as many problems as it solved.[11] It's easy for the courts or the legislature to decree state takeovers or partial takeovers by mayors or outside monitors, or "reconstitutions" of schools. It's quite another thing to carry them out successfully, or even to know where the rescuing cavalry is supposed to come from. What that suggests—paradoxically, given the courts' limited capacity in such areas—is that more money alone, however important it may seem, is not enough. In most places a great deal more will be necessary. The court can be the spark, but other people—parents, legislators, local and state school board members, teachers, superintendents, principals—have to do the hard work, both in policy making and within the schools. And in communities such as Camden, where there is pervasive mismanagement and/or corruption, such people have been hard to find.

II

There are other questions. Court decisions—particularly those that seem to require states to provide ever-richer resources to underperforming children—will almost certainly run into increasing political resistance, on both financial and equity grounds. To what extent are middle-income and affluent voters, the people who come to the polls, willing to send their local and state tax dollars to support extra resources for other people's children, especially if they're poor, black, or Latino?

Rebell is correct that adequacy is not inherently a zero-sum game. Carried out effectively, it can produce many more winners than losers. But in New Jersey, where the court ordered the state to raise spending in the poorest urban districts to the level of the wealthy suburban districts, it left scores of midlevel districts unprotected against the budget cuts that inevitably followed when a state treasury that had been drained by Governor Christie Whitman's what-me-worry tax cuts of the 1990s was hit by the recession that began in 2000. The resulting cuts left the whole scheme open to a growing middle-class backlash and recurring talk of vouchers as a much cheaper alternative to the problems of inner-city kids. The parochial schools, said voucher advocates, would be delighted with half the $15,000 a year that the state was shoveling into Newark, Trenton, and other Abbott districts. That, of course, couldn't fairly be blamed on the court's remedy, but the backlash, which was there nonetheless, demonstrates that even the best plans aren't invulnerable to fiscal mismanagement.[12]

More broadly, to the extent that adequacy policies harden school spending in state budgets, they'll require either tax increases, especially in tight times when state revenues fall, or cuts in other state discretionary spending, particularly in community colleges and health and welfare—which, because of their relative lack of political clout, tend to be treated as far more expendable than law enforcement and corrections. Which is to say that the same low-income groups that may benefit in the educational system will lose in the social service system. These are powerful arguments for allowing legislatures to set priorities according to their own political judgment, however irrational the result may sometimes seem. The success of any policy may depend on how well the adequacy goals are meshed with government's traditional authority to set priorities and make choices.

There are, in addition, major questions about the extent to which favorable adequacy rulings and concomitant legislation will further centralize state control over local schools—curriculum, teaching methods, fiscal priorities, union contracts—and thus create other countervailing forces. With the imposition of state standards, testing, and accountability, that process was in motion long before adequacy arrived on the scene, and so was the backlash. In 2002, the California Teachers Association, the state's muscular teachers union, whose members feel they've been buffeted by too many state-mandated reforms, nearly succeeded in pushing a bill through the legislature expanding the scope of collective bargaining to cover virtually all local school policy, from text-book selection to the creation of parent councils, and it seems deter-mined to try again, maybe through the initiative.

Those tensions can only intensify, especially as the testing require-ments and school accountability pressures mandated by federal law begin to be felt. The law requires states to "reconstitute" consistently low-performing schools, to notify parents of children who don't have qualified teachers, and to allow transfers—and to pay for transporta-tion—out of such schools. Recessions probably mitigate those prob-lems by making teaching jobs more attractive. Once there are more job choices, those mandates are likely to make it even harder to draw teachers to difficult schools, much less keep them motivated.

Given the blatant maldistribution of teachers and administrators (and sometimes other resources) *within* school districts, there is no equity in dollars, much less adequacy, between high-poverty schools and schools serving the affluent. (In some cities, where the affluent live in the hills and the poor in the flats, you can roughly calibrate the quality of a school by the altitude of the building). If good teach-ers are to be attracted to the schools serving the poorest kids—and if they're to be retained there—it will almost certainly require revisions in union contracts giving districts more flexibility in assigning teach-ers and thus in seniority rules and in pay and working conditions. It means differential rather than unitary seniority-based salary scales and, as people such as Hanushek continually insist, extra pay for good performance and for teachers with skills that are in high demand, such as in math or science or special education. The problem may be even more acute for administrators, and especially in the national shortage of principals for inner-city and other low-performing schools. Pedagogically and morally, therefore, there may be ample justification for providing the most disadvantaged students with the extra resources that they require to catch up. But when resources are limited and powerful interests are threatened, there is only so far that the political system is likely to go.

What's certain is that the more money states put into local schools, and the more the courts require them to provide adequate resources, the more they will be forced to show that the money is not wasted or stolen. Thus they'll be pressed (at the very least) to exercise stringent oversight over local systems or, better, impose even more effective measures of accountability that gauge both inputs and outputs at the school level—ideally, outputs measured by a range of criteria, not tests alone. Making things more difficult is the inertia of many schools of education that, in the name of academic freedom, have resisted political demands that they train teachers in the new standards and in the use of the (often highly scripted) materials that the states have adopted in their attempts to meet those standards. Are they in the business of training confident professionals or are they simply producing reliable drones who follow somebody else's script?

And at what point does the whole system simply lapse into exhaustion? To the extent that political pressure and civil rights lawsuits brought by parents or other advocates succeed in rolling back or watering down exit exams, the case for adequate resources may be further attenuated. The same thing could happen if state legislatures, calculating the real cost of their academic standards and accountability systems, and faced with recession-driven budget shortfalls, use the cover of fairness and equal opportunity to quietly water down all the toughened requirements of the past decade and the associated adequacy demands and costs along with them. The country's historical ambivalence between unforgiving standards of merit and perpetual second chances for its young has produced an endless seesaw between progressives and liberals, on one hand, and educational conservatives, on the other. It would be surprising if that ended now. The poor economic times that began in the year 2000 and the accompanying crises in dozens of state budgets—a total state deficit of some $85 billion in the 2003 budget cycle alone—make the prospects for major infusions of new funds into schools particularly grim. Through much of that year, even the optimists were hoping for no more than the ability to hold the line.

Conversely, but just as portentously, Justice Lerner's appellate court decision in New York, the supreme court's reversal in Alabama, and the Ohio supreme court's departure from the battle there indicate that despite blatant inequities (and thus inadequacies) in resources, the adequacy argument doesn't automatically lead to the reform of inferior schools. It could even be used in their defense. When the North Carolina supreme court declared that the state's constitution "does not guarantee a right to equal educational opportunities in each of the various school districts of the state" as long as the state provides "a sound basic education," you could hear the echoes of a whole litany of Jim Crow–era arguments that some minimal schooling is all that's needed for poor or minority children.[13] For the moment, that's not where the courts or the legislatures are going, and one hopes they never do. But adequacy can mean a lot of things.

Finally, there is the Hanushek question: if there is to be significant new money, will it produce results—improved test scores, reduced dropout rates, higher college attendance, and (to add Rudy Crew's criteria) civic responsibility and engagement—that seem roughly commensurate with the investment? So far the returns are mixed, and often unclear. In Kentucky and West Virginia, among the earliest states to implement adequacy-based reforms, test scores are up significantly, and so are some other measures of achievement. In Wyoming, which used a consultant-developed adequacy model to sharply boost state school funding beginning in 1998, much of the money, according to one of those consultants, "is buried in little tiny school districts with classes of 16 kids" made necessary by the difficulties of busing kids long over long distances in the winter. In many states, including New Jersey, which began to implement fiscal and educational reforms beginning very late in the 1990s, it's probably early to ask for results. Making things still more uncertain in New Jersey is the fact that the state didn't participate in NAEP until the federal government began to require it in 2002, and so there's little reliable data of any kind. But to the extent that adequacy funding becomes the national pattern, and as it drives funding up, the question will be asked with increasing urgency. If the system is deemed to fail again, what conclusions will then be drawn? Would we get conscious policies of benign neglect in the education of poor children, just as we got them in social welfare thirty years ago?

III

And yet, given the huge battleship that is American education, it's striking how much it has turned. There *has* been a sort of dialogue, not only among the courts, the politicians, and the public, but between accountability and adequacy, the one driving the other, and vice versa—the two together helping to energize a broad range of school reforms. Even with the budget cuts brought on by the 2000–3 recession, per-pupil school funding since 1990 has increased more quickly than inflation—from $6,800 to $7,600 per pupil in 2000–1 dollars for current expenditures. (Professional salaries, responding to the growing national awareness of the importance of good teaching, have been rising in tandem, though rarely yet in such a way as to reflect a market in which, for example, math and special-ed teachers are especially scarce or to draw the best teachers to the neediest schools.) And because the growing national resentment of high property taxes has fused with specific court orders, as in Kentucky, Ohio, and New Jersey, and with adequacy-equity politics, the proportion of school funding coming from the states has increased, mitigating (though hardly ending) the inequities linked to the local property tax and, more important, increasing funding for schools in many poor neighborhoods.

Suddenly, moreover, a broad array of publicly funded preschool and before- and after-school programs—things that no one thirty years ago would have imagined coming to America on any large scale—have become a major part of the public agenda, particularly for children from disadvantaged backgrounds. The boom years of the late 1990s, welfare reform, the nation's changed economy, and the millions of working mothers have driven some of that. But middle-class working moms don't account for the emphasis—in Kentucky, in Maryland, in New Jersey, and in North Carolina, among others—on extraschool services for poor kids.

Nationally, it's still hard to make any conclusive link among increased funding, higher teacher salaries, smaller classes, and specific outcomes in test scores or other measures of school success. But there are encouraging indicators—the studies in Texas and Tennessee on the huge difference good teaching makes, the class size studies in Tennessee, the increase in NAEP scores in Kentucky—to show that if money is well spent, it can have a major impact. Even in California, where an expensive across-the-board class size reduction policy has shown little in the way of demonstrable benefits, the research team that evaluated the program had strong reasons to believe that if there was more flexibility, and if class size reductions were combined with other programs targeting low-income students, they could produce significant results. The success of the combination of small classes, before- and after-school programs, and the intensive instruction they made possible in Wisconsin's SAGE program seemed to reinforce that conclusion.

Even if these studies showed less promise, however, there's really nowhere else to go. Visit those schools, hear the stories, consider the enormous achievement gaps, and the issue comes down to a stark choice: engineer major changes to the system or watch it rot from the bottom. Support for vouchers in minority communities is already high; a few more years of failure and even the most ardent defenders of public schools will find it hard to resist the demands of black and Latino parents and community leaders pleading for alternatives. Adequacy suits are a bit like some voter initiatives—desperate measures to compel legislatures to act when all other attempts have failed. But unlike most initiatives, these cases address injustices and failures that have been festering forever. They are not just attempts to scratch the temporary itches of the politically enfranchised. Those failures damage not just whole generations of children but the nation's economic and social viability. For much of the twentieth century, as Hanushek said, "the expansion of the education system in the United States outpaced that around the world." But as other countries expand their own education systems, the era in which America had *quantitative* superiority—higher high school graduation and college attendance rates, for example—has come to an end. That doesn't mean blaming every economic dip on the schools. But "going into the future, the U.S. appears unlikely to continue dominating others in human capital unless it can improve on the quality dimension."[14]

The gap now is not just between the schools serving our most affluent kids—Masconomet Regional High School in exurban Boston, New Trier in suburban Chicago, or Palo Alto High School—or elite selective institutions such as Bronx Science or Lowell in San Francisco and the dysfunctional places serving many of our poorest students. There's a similar gap opening between the nation's increasing dependence on the education and training of black and Latino—and white—workers from low-income families and the stringent civic and economic demands of the future. In 1972, nearly 80 percent of U.S. public school students were white. In 2002, it was barely 60 percent, and the percentage is rapidly declining.[15] Many of those students are as successful as all their predecessors, despite weak schools. But many others are not. The workforce and the civil society of the next generation will necessarily come in large measure out of the ranks of today's poor and working-class children. The black-white and Hispanic-white test score gaps have shrunk considerably, but the rich-poor difference in achievement between schools in which fewer than 10 percent of students get free or reduced-price lunches and those where more than 75 percent get them is still enormous.[16] If those children are not educated—and educated well beyond the eighth grade—it's not just the economy that's in danger, it's democracy as well.

For many people, litigation seems to be a slow way to go. Direct political advocacy is the preferred route of Russlyn Ali, who runs the West Coast office of the Education Trust: "You get a decree," she said "and nothing happens." Yet much of the progress of the forty years after World War II, however slow, came from decrees, and much in the last decade has come from the shifting criteria and standards institutionalized by other decrees. Even Ali recognizes that litigation helps because "people don't know what happens on the other side of the freeway. We've walled things off." The courts help spur the legislatures, give politicians political cover, and get public attention.

The rats and the toilets are secondary issues, but they are powerful symbols—"they slam it in everybody's faces." In Texas and Kentucky, in West Virginia and New Hampshire, low-wealth districts that never had any money before now have a little. In many other states, where in a time of recession legislators would have had no hesitation about putting schools on the chopping block, there's been a special effort to protect education as much as possible. Adequacy standards can't be credited (or blamed) for all of that, but they have certainly contributed to the political climate that's moving schools into the same favored category as public safety. Perhaps New York Governor George Pataki would have agreed to the substantial increases in funding that New York City got for its schools and teachers in 2001–2 without the additional leverage that the CFE adequacy suit gave Randi Weingarten and the United Federation of Teachers. But that leverage certainly helped.

Even when there is no favorable court decision—or no court case at all—adequacy is energizing the political drive for better schools for poor and minority children as nothing has since the first decades after *Brown.* In Wisconsin, even as its supreme court was rejecting an equity challenge (despite ample evidence that districts were funded inequitably), it all but invited an adequacy suit, and the invitation may yet be accepted. In the summer of 2002, the independent Institute for Wisconsin's Future developed an adequacy model for the state that Karen Royster, its executive director, and Jack Norman, its research director, hope will eventually become the basis for a new school finance system. At the same time, the institute helped launch the broad-based Wisconsin Alliance for Excellent Schools, which planned to develop and push major reform legislation in 2003.[17] In Pennsylvania, where the courts have flatly rejected all school funding suits as matters constitutionally reserved to the legislature, educators, community leaders, and an interfaith group of clergy—Baptist, Episcopalian, Jewish, Lutheran—recently started a well-funded movement, Good Schools Pennsylvania, that's been campaigning with increasing vigor for adequacy-based funding, better accountability, and other fundamental school reforms. Shortly after the 2002 election, which brought former Philadelphia mayor Ed Rendell, a Democrat, into the state house, the group held press conferences and prayer vigils around the state to press Rendell for school funding reforms. For the clerics who started it, said Donna Cooper, the organization's director, this is the next front in the battle for civil rights.

There's incontrovertible logic, ethical, fiscal, and legal, in the tight two-way link between standards and adequate resources. If a state demands that schools and students be accountable—for meeting state standards, for passing exit exams and other tests—the state must be held equally accountable for providing the wherewithal to enable them to do it. That means calculations to determine the cost of those resources. The most mundane entrepreneur asks the same question: how much will it cost to produce each unit?

At best, says Wisconsin's Allan Odden, adequacy "integrates educational practice with finance." At the very least, adequacy standards defining a state's priorities will reduce the temptation of the legislatures to leap piecemeal into one untested reform program after another. In trying to determine what is adequate, it also asks conservative questions that are intrinsic to virtually all other sectors: how to allocate resources most effectively to get maximum results? What works? In states such as California or New York, with their jumbled and uncoordinated funding streams, where the state really has no idea of the resources that individual schools have to spend or how they spend them, a rationalized adequacy-based funding system could at the very least (in the words of one critic) "excavate" the way districts spend and often waste money now.

Children, of course, are more than just units of production (which is how the scientific management crowd saw them in the first decades of the twentieth century).[18] Therefore any financial system will mean investments that can't be precisely justified by any easy economic analysis. But the effort can be made and the political choices aired. At the same time, the research showing the strong tendency of local districts to spend new money in the same proportions as they spend the rest of their funds makes it even more imperative that states foster more effective spending through accountability systems that, as in Texas and California, measure not just the achievements of the general population of children but those of the subgroups—African Americans, Hispanics, limited English-speakers, poor children—who most need the additional services that adequacy-based programs should provide.

Policy experts such as Picus and Rothstein ask, in Picus's words, whether "we're spending money in the wrong place." Since a child's socioeconomic circumstances play such a large role in determining his or her chances of success, shouldn't a much larger share of the state's resources be put into child welfare and social services? "Why pay schools more?" goes the rhetorical argument. "Let's make these mothers middle-class." Should every child have an individual education plan, like the students in special education, that covers every facet of the child's development? The shortage of such services for both children and parents—nurses, counselors, family support programs—burdens the schools in an unimaginable number of ways. Rudy Crew, the former chancellor in New York, tells the story of a snowy night when he was trying to decide whether to close the schools the next morning. He realized that "if we closed the schools, a lot of kids wouldn't eat." So the schools were kept open to feed those who could get there. For millions of children and their families, the schools are the default social service system that attempts, as best as it can, to provide what other modern societies offer in abundance.

Given the nation's individualistic tradition and its frail social welfare system, the pursuit of massive new investments in such services—perhaps excepting only preschools—is likely to be a quixotic quest. The chances of political success, in any case, are far slimmer than they are in education. One of the great political achievements of Reagan-era conservatism was its ability to subtly persuade Americans that, with the possible exception of crime, virtually all of children's social problems—in welfare, health, housing, recreation, child care—should be seen as school problems. That was, and remains, one of the great subtle lies of the past generation. But it doesn't change history, make America into France or Scandinavia, or eliminate the nation's responsibility to try to make schools work for all children. It was the schools, after all, that since Horace Mann's day, and perhaps since Jefferson's, were to be the great democratic equalizer.

The adequacy challenge is likely to test that faith again, and perhaps in a wholly new way. Are we willing to really invest the resources that it takes to finally address those gaps? If we are not, then a host of other social questions rush in to demand attention. The standards-adequacy-accountability link may further reinforce questions, on both the right and the left, about whether the schools are really capable of closing the gaps that—depending on your point of view—economics, culture, or genetics seems to make so intractable. But if the schools can't do it, can it be done at all? "I'm in the business of apocalypse prevention," Russlyn Ali says. "What are other choice do we have? What other choice do I have?"

Before World War II, American schools were judged by their successes—children of immigrants just off the boat or city newcomers just off the farm who became doctors or artists or entrepreneurs or teachers. Those who didn't go past the sixth grade were absorbed by the great market for unskilled or semiskilled labor. They were not judged failures, either for the schools or anywhere else. Now, with that labor market gone, this country is trying to do something that's never been attempted anywhere on earth before: to take an enormously diverse population of children—a population of countless races, cultures, and classes, many of whom come to school speaking little or no English—and educate them all to a high level of academic, economic, and civic proficiency. The adequacy argument asserts that it can be done, or at least approached. And as it seeks to ensure the future, it also, as Judge Howard Manning ruled in North Carolina, underscores the need for things such as preschool programs and other additional help for disadvantaged kids that go beyond the traditional K-12 menu. In the long run, recognition of the importance of preschool and children's early development may even be a way of subverting the Reagan-era doctrine that makes the schools the answer to all of children's problems. To make schools work, a whole lot of other things have to work as well.

For all the questions it raises, the adequacy argument is also a sophisticated and passionate declaration of faith in the great promises of American society: equality, opportunity, and human and social betterment—a sine qua non for a modern technological democracy. The goal of "the standards based reform movement can't be merely aspirational," as Rebell said. "There really is no alternative to actual fulfillment of the vision that today the schools must ensure that virtually all students must meet high expectations and develop high level cognitive skills."[19] A lot of fateful questions hang on how well we succeed—questions about social will, about the extent to which schools can do the enormous tasks assigned to them, about human potential and the capability of all children to succeed regardless of cultural and economic background, about the sincerity of all those professions that children are our most valuable resource, and about democracy itself. As we approach the fiftieth anniversary of the *Brown* decision, surely the most crucial school policy case ever decided, adequacy looms as the next, increasingly important milestone. In the effort to realize the great promise of education, this may be our ultimate test.

Notes

INTRODUCTION

1. William L. Phillis, executive director of the Ohio Equity and Adequacy Coalition, "Memo to Superintendents, Principals, Treasurers and Other Interested Persons," Nov. 27, 2002.
2. Federal money, much of it awarded through a variety of categorical formulas to schools that serve large percentages of poor children, or for teacher training, and for intensive reading programs, amounts to an additional 6 or 7 percent of school budgets.
3. The states where affirmative action in college admissions is prohibited, by either voter initiative, court decision, or legislative action, are California, Washington, Texas, Florida, and Georgia. As this book went to press, the U.S. Supreme Court was deciding a Michigan case that may further curtail or end all race-based preferences.
4. In New York, those who can afford it are resigned to paying $20,000 a year, and sometimes a great deal more, for the right private nursery school for their four-year-olds, or pulling every string they can, personal and corporate, to get them in. Preschool is the first step to Harvard. Even in New York, though, the Jack Grubman story was a little extraordinary. Grubman, a star brokerage firm stock analyst, got Sanford Weill, his boss at Citicorp, to arrange a $1 million corporate gift to help him get his twin daughters into the exclusive nursery school run by the 92nd Street Y. The quid pro quo, according to a Grubman e-mail he later disavowed as a sort of joke, was Grubman's favorable rating on AT&T stock that he had previously been cool about. According to the *New York Times*, Weill at the time was seeking the support of AT&T

chairman Michael Armstrong in a boardroom battle. Gretchen Morgenson and Patrick McGeehan, "Wall St. and the Nursery School: A New York Story," *New York Times,* Nov. 14, 2002; Stephanie Strom, "Private Preschool Admissions: Grease and the City," *New York Times,* Nov. 16, 2002.

5. Arthur Levine, phone interview, Oct. 12, 2002.

6. The core of the adequacy idea can be traced back many decades. For a century, states have had foundation funding programs designed to ensure that even where a local community couldn't afford to provide some minimum of public education, there would be some state money to keep the schools open and to put a warm adult body in every classroom. But the new standards and the accompanying accountability systems have given the adequacy principle new muscle and meaning.

7. *Update: California's Education Reforms* (Palo Alto, CA: EdSource, 2002), www.edsource.org.

8. "Public school students receiving federally funded free or reduced price lunches . . . 1993–94," *Digest of Education Statistics* (Washington, D.C.: National Center for Education Statistics, 2001), Table 375. "Free and reduced-price eligibility and racial/ethnic composition as a percentage of school district membership, and percentage of schools for which characteristic is reported, in the 100 largest school districts in the United States: School year 1999–2000," *Characteristics of the 100 Largest Public Elementary and Secondary School Districts in the United States, 1999–2000* (Washington, D.C.: National Center for Education Statistics, 2001), Table 9.

9. The school conditions described in this book are those that existed when the adequacy cases that are the subject of Chapter 3 were filed or tried, generally in the period between 1997 and 2002—not necessarily as they were thereafter.

CHAPTER   1

1. *Williams et al. v. State of California,* Superior Court, City and County of San Francisco, No. 312236, deposition of Alondra Sharae Jones, May 16, 2001, pp. 35–50.

2. This and all other California academic achievement data from California Department of Education Academic Performance Index (API) Reports, http://api.cde.ca.gov/reports.html.

3. *Williams,* declaration of Lawrence Poon, July 31, 2000.

4. Bernice Yeung, "Hard Lessons," *San Francisco Weekly,* Oct. 11, 2000.

5. Alondra Jones deposition, pp. 116, 159. How did she know those were mouse droppings? she was asked in her deposition. "I hope it's a mouse," she answered. "Hope it's not more serious." Deposition, p. 128.

6. *Williams,* declaration of Alondra Jones, Aug. 14, 2000.

7. Teacher CyberGuide, *A Raisin in the Sun,* www.nashville.k12.tn.us/ CyberGuides; Shane Safir interview, Aug. 22, 2002.

8. Paulo Freire, *Pedagogy of the Oppressed* (New York: Continuum, 1968, 1970), p. 33; Safir interview.

9. "Making the Grade," KQED-TV documentary, 1999.

10. *Williams,* declaration of Shane Safir, June 27, 2000.

11. *Williams,* deposition of Alondra Jones, May 25, 2001, p. 393.

12. Patricia Gray interview at Balboa, June 6, 2002; *Williams,* deposition of Patricia Gray, July 18, 2001, pp. 282–85.

13. Gray interview; *Williams,* deposition of Patricia Gray, July 18, 2001, pp. 298, 323–25.

14. Alondra Jones deposition, pp. 348–49. Lowell is San Francisco's elite public high school.

15. Interview with ACLU attorney Catherine E. Lhamon, who was present at the deposition, Aug. 14, 2002.

16. Whack-a-mole is in fact more than a schoolhouse metaphor. In schools that have them, grass play areas are sometimes laced with gopher holes, which are dangerous for kids and thus require constant and rather costly efforts at what one former school board member called mole control. Maintenance crews don't whack them with mallets, but try to trap them and then destroy them. But it's a never-ending struggle.

17. *DeRolph v. State* (1997), 78 Ohio St. 3d 193.

18. *DeRolph,* p. 84.

19. *Campaign for Fiscal Equity v. State of New York (CFE II,* 2001), Supreme Court, County of New York, Part 25, no. 111070/93, p. 68.

20. *Williams,* deposition of Carlos Ramirez, June 21, 2001, p. 320. Malabed herself said that when she started teaching at Bryant, the principal told her and other teachers to flush the pipes every day by letting the water run since "there was something unsafe in the pipes that kids should not drink." *Williams,* declaration of Lily Malabed, Apr. 10, 2000; declaration of Cynthia Artiga-Faupusa, May 9, 2000.

21. List compiled from personal visits as well as various sources, including *Hoke County Board of Education v. State of North Carolina,* Wake County Superior Court, 95 CVS-1158, plaintiffs' proposed findings of fact, pp. 430–40; *Bradford v. Maryland State Board of Education,* Circuit Court for Baltimore County, no. 94340058/CE189672; *Williams,* dep-

osition of Marcia Hines, Aug. 10, 2001, pp. 465–66. "Sink" remark from *Williams,* declaration of Taoi Dao, July 21, 2000.

22. *Campaign for Fiscal Equity v. State of New York (CFE),* trial transcript, Oct. 13, 1999, pp. 287, 284.

23. "Work Order Backlog," memo from Bruce Bender to Patricia Zedalis, May 21, 1997, *CFE,* plaintiff's exhibit, Px 1490.

24. "Meeting New York State's Crisis in School Facilities Today: Report of the [New York State] Regents Advisory Committee on School Facilities," Aug. 30, 1996.

25. *Abbott v. Burke (Abbott II,* 1990) 119 N.J. 363.

26. *Williams,* declaration of Glauz Diego, Aug. 9, 2000; declaration of Cindy Diego, Aug. 9, 2000; declaration of D'Andre Lampkin, Aug. 11, 2000, p. 1; deposition of Marcia Hines, June 18, 2001, p. 82. See also Erika Hayasaki, "Pupils Shunted to Vocational Ed Fear It Can Derail College Dreams," *Los Angeles Times,* Mar. 27, 2002.

27. *Hoke,* trial transcript, Nov. 15, 1999, p. 138; plaintiffs' proposed findings of fact, p. 426. In Los Angeles, the travelers schlep their stuff, but that's not a North Carolina word.

28. *Statewide Profile of the Educational System,* New York State Education Department, Albany, Apr. 1999, p. 12.

29. *Campaign for Fiscal Equity v. State of New York (CFE),* witness statement of John Lee, plaintiff's exhibit, p. 2855. Some schools, such as Midwood in Brooklyn, however, which was built for 2,300 and now enrolls 4,000, and which has been on triple shifts, continue to maintain an extraordinary level of academic intensity. In 1999 the school produced more finalists in the Intel Science Talent Search than any other school in the country.

30. After having nearly abandoned the project after spending $154 million, in 2002 the Los Angeles school board, desperate for space, voted to do a multimillion-dollar cleanup and finish the work. The ultimate price tag was to be about $220–240 million, making it the most expensive public school ever built in this country. But late in 2002, engineers found an earthquake fault under the site. No one knew whether it was active or not, but the project was suspended again. See, e.g., Andrew Trotter, "Los Angeles Revives Beleaguered Belmont Project," *Education Week,* Mar. 20, 2002; Joetta L. Sack, "Romer Puts New Hold on Troubled Belmont Site," *Education Week,* Jan. 8, 2003.

31. Data from Ronald W. Bennett, president of School Services of California, a private consulting and lobbying firm that analyzes fiscal data for school systems and other clients. In many cases, teachers prefer the

newer portables because they are cleaner and have self-contained heating and air-conditioning that they can control.

32. *Williams*, declaration of Craig Gordon, Aug. 29, 2001, p. 5; Balfanz telephone interview, Aug. 22, 2002. Also, Robert Balfanz and Nettie Legters, "How Many Central City High Schools Have a Severe Dropout Problem, Where Are They Located, and Who Attends Them?" paper prepared for the Civil Rights Project at the Harvard Graduate School of Education and Achieve, Inc., Jan. 13, 2001. Also, Richard Lee Colvin, "A School Flails in a Sea of Chaos," *Los Angeles Times*, July 14, 2002.

33. Academic data from California Department of Education Academic Performance Index (API) reports. Description of track system and schedule from *Williams*, deposition of Margaret Rowland, June 20 and Aug. 2, 2001, and deposition of Marcia Hines, June 18 and Aug. 10, 2001. Also Los Angeles Unified School District, "Key School Calendar Dates, 2002–03 School Year," <www.lausd.k12.ca.us/lausd/offices/Office_of_Communications/dates.pdf>.

34. *Williams*, declaration of Abraham Osuna, May 25, 2001.

35. Bachrach phone interview, June 3, 2002. Also, Hamilton Lankford, James Wyckoff, and Frank Papa, *The Labor Market for Public School Teachers: A Descriptive Analysis of New York State's Teacher Workforce* (New York: The Education Finance Research Consortium, 2000).

36. *Williams*, deposition of Marcia Hines, June 18, 2001, p. 138.

37. *Williams*, Roland deposition, p. 283.

38. Hamilton Lankford, "A Descriptive Analysis of the New York State and New York City Teaching Force," *Campaign for Fiscal Equity v. State of New York*, plaintiff's exhibit 1482. Also, Lankford, Wyckoff, and Papa, *The Labor Market*.

39. *CFE*, trial transcript, testimony of John Murphy, p. 17439.

40. *CFE*, testimony of Frank DeStefano, superintendent of Community School District 15 in Brooklyn, trial transcript pp. 5434–5; testimony of Kathleen Cashin, superintendent of Community School District 23 in Brooklyn, trial transcript p. 333.

41. Stephanie Banchero and Ana Beatriz Cholo, "Many Uncertified Teachers Work in Worst Schools," *Chicago Tribune*, July 9, 2002.

42. For Maryland, *Bradford v. Maryland*, Circuit Court for Baltimore County Case no. 94340058/CE189672. For California, *The Status of the Teaching Profession, 2001* (Santa Cruz: The Center for the Future of Teaching and Learning, 2001), www.cftl.org/publications.html.

43. Craig D. Jerald, *All Talk, No Action: Putting an End to Out of Field Teaching* (Washington, D.C.: The Education Trust, 2002).

44. *Hoke,* trial transcript, Sept. 28, 1999, pp. 11–12.

45. *Hoke,* trial transcript, Sept. 28, 1999, p. 26. In many schools, of course, subs have been a joke forever because students know that they're usually placeholders who probably don't know the subject; unless they've been briefed by the regular teacher, as some are, they won't have any idea what's been going on in class and can be manipulated to death. No one knows, of course, how many teachers there still are who think their students believe, as they do, that reading or writing is punishment.

46. *Hoke v. North Carolina,* 95 CVS 1158, plaintiffs' proposed findings of fact, § 232–33, 237, 258.

47. *Meeting the Highly Qualified Teachers Challenge* (Washington, D.C.: U.S. Department of Education, 2002), www.title2.org/secReport.htm.

48. On attrition, see, e.g., "Teacher Induction Programs," *Policy Update,* National Association of State Boards of Education, April 2000. On recruiting, David J. Hoff, "Urban Districts Employing More Aggressive Hiring Tactics," *Education Week,* Oct. 3, 2001.

49. Arthur Levine, phone interview, Oct. 12, 2002

50. See, e.g., Peter Schrag, "California's 40,000 New 'Highly Qualified' Teachers," *Sacramento Bee,* Aug. 7, 2002. The board has since negotiated a compromise with the U.S. Department of Education that seems to have conceded as much to California as California conceded to the feds. Catherine Gewertz, "City Districts Seek Teachers with Licenses," *Education Week,* Sept. 11, 2002; Diana Jean Schemo, "Law Overhauling School Standards May Be Weakened," *New York Times,* Oct. 15, 2002.

51. Quoted in Linda Darling-Hammond, "Access to Quality Teaching: An Analysis of Inequality in California's Public Schools," unpublished paper prepared for plaintiffs in *Williams v. California.*

52. *CFE,* witness statement of Betty Rosa (a district superintendent in New York City), plaintiff's exhibit 2332A, pp. 12–13.

53. Interview with Russlyn Ali, executive director of the Education Trust–West, which calculated the number from data supplied by the Los Angeles school district, Aug. 20, 2002.

54. Gaston interview, July 15, 2002; also *The Status of the Teaching Profession,* p. 8.

55. Kathryn Whitaker, "Where Are the Principal Candidates? Perceptions of Superintendents," *NAASP Bulletin* 85 (625), pp. 82–92; *Williams,* declaration of Susan Carroll Boysal, July 27, 2000.

56. *Abbott v. Burke* (*Abbott II,* 1990), 119 N.J. 360, 361.

57. *DeRolph v. State,* Perry County Court of Common Pleas, Case 22043,

findings of fact, conclusions of law, order and memorandum of the Perry County Court of Common Pleas, July 1, 1994, 9, 77. She subsequently graduated from Ohio University in 1996 with degrees in psychology and accounting. Doug Oplinger and Dennis J. Willard, "Slow to Build," *Akron Beacon Journal,* May 22, 1996.

58. Adam Cohen interview, Sept. 19, 2002; Cohen, "After 10 Long Years, Alabama is Back Where It Started," *New York Times,* Mar. 11, 2002. Cohen is now a *Times* editorial writer. Jim Sanders, "For a Shabby Learning Experience, Try School Library," *Sacramento Bee,* Jan. 21, 1990.

59. Keith Ervin, "Students Protest Lack of Textbooks," *Seattle Times,* May 31, 2002.

60. *Hoke,* transcript, Nov. 15, 1999. pp. 149, 152.

61. *Williams,* declaration of Erika Cabrera, p. 1.

62. *Williams,* deposition of Marcia Hines, July 5, 2001, p. 201.

63. Lou Harris, "A Survey of the Status of Equality in Public Education in California," March 2002. In 2002, after many schools had eliminated student lockers as a security measure, the California legislature passed a bill that, in an effort to reduce the heavy loads that children had to carry in their backpacks, instructed the State Board of Education to find a way to limit the weight of textbooks.

64. In the past three or four years, some districts—Boston, for example— used what extra money they had to buy back some of the most restrictive seniority provisions in union contracts. In effect, they traded higher pay for contract modifications. Bess Keller, "Boston Contract: A Policy Blueprint," *Education Week,* Nov. 13, 2002.

65. *Williams,* deposition of Marcia Hines, July 5, 2001, p. 235.

66. *Campaign for Fiscal Equity (CFE) v. State of New York,* New York Supreme Court, part 25, no. 93/111070, testimony of Edward Stancik, trial transcript, Apr. 13, 2000, p. 20050. Also Lydia G. Segal et al., "Power, Politics and Patronage: Education in Community District 12," City of New York, Apr. 1993.

67. *CFE,* Stancik testimony, transcript, p. 21466; Robert M. Brenner et al., "From Chaos to Corruption: An Investigation into the 1993 Community School Board Election," City of New York, the Special Commissioner of Investigation for the New York City School District, Dec. 1993.

68. Sean Courtney et al., "Corruption in Community District 9 (Preliminary Report)," City of New York, the Special Commissioner of Investigation for the New York City School District, 1996.

69. Edward F. Stancik, "Grand Illusion: An Investigation into Enrollment and Attendance Manipulation at Brandeis High School," City of New

York, the Special Commissioner of Investigation for the New York City School District, March 2000, p. 2. Also Lynette Holloway, "Principal Is Accused of Inflating Attendance to Aid Career," *New York Times,* Mar. 17, 2000.

70. For a fuller discussion of Texas's claims, see Peter Schrag, "Too Good to Be True," *The American Prospect,* Jan. 3, 2000, pp. 46–49. The California claims are from California State Department of Education press release #02-14, Apr. 19, 2002. Official California data at http://data1.cde.ca.gov/dataquest/. The grade-to-grade calculations are also subject to error since students transfer and, in places like Texas and California, move back to Mexico. But in general, transfers in and transfers out should more or less balance.

71. Howard Blume and Dennis Dockstader, "Degrees of Deceit: How One Inner-City High School Played the Numbers Game and Made Its Dropout Rate Go Away," *LA Weekly,* July 19–25, 2002.

72. Kirk Johnson, "For New York, 25-Year Losing Streak," *New York Times,* Jan. 13, 1999.

73. Mary Musca interview, Sept. 4, 2002; Nancy Lederman, "Hit or Miss: Fitness and Sports Opportunities in the New York City Public Schools," Educational Frameworks, Inc. (for New Visions for Public Schools), 2001.

74. *Williams,* deposition of Marcia Hines, July 5, 2001, pp. 348–51.

75. *Williams,* deposition of Margaret Roland, Aug. 2, 2001, pp. 322–23, 205; deposition of Marcia Hines, Aug. 10, 2001, p. 507.

76. *Williams,* declaration of Magaly De Loza, May 5, 2000.

77. *Williams,* deposition of Marcia Hines, Aug. 10, 2001, p. 614. Former *Los Angeles Times* reporter Richard Colvin, now the director of the Hechinger Center at Columbia University, also found that new computers "disappeared as quickly as they were unpacked," presumably because someone inside the school opened it to thieves.

78. *Williams,* deposition of Marcia Hines, June 18, 2001, pp. 18, 109, and July 5, 2001, pp. 225, 382.

79. *Williams,* deposition of Marcia Hines, June 18, 2001, p. 131.

80. Colvin (see note 77) says that when he visited the school in the spring of 2002, it was stuffed with books after the district superintendent, probably in response to the lawsuit against the state in which students complained about a lack of books, ordered Fremont to spend all its discretionary money on texts. But a lot of students still had no books because the teachers decided that the students couldn't read well enough to use the books. So why risk the damage and loss? Conversation with Colvin, Aug. 28, 2002.

81. *Williams,* deposition of Marcia Hines, July 5, 2001, p. 403.

82. *Williams,* expert opinion of Michelle Fine, p. 4.

83. *Abbott v. Burke (Abbott II,* 1990), 119 N.J. 364.

84. *The College Bound Seniors: A Profile of SAT Program Test Takers* (New York: The College Board, 2001), http://www.collegeboard.com/sat/cbsenior/yr2001/pdf/NATL.pdf.

85. E. D. Hirsch Jr., *Cultural Literacy: What Every American Needs to Know* (Boston: Houghton Mifflin, 1987).

86. The data here are from the most recent survey, done in 1999. *TIMSS 1999: International Mathematics Report: Findings from IEA's Repeat of the Third International Mathematics and Science Study at the Eighth Grade,* http://timss.bc.edu/timss1999i/pdf/T99i_Math1.pdf. On Finn and Ravitch, *Educational Reform, 1995–6: A Report from the Educational Excellence Network to Its Education Policy Committee and the American People* (Indianapolis: The Hudson Institute, 1996). Also, Diane Ravitch and Chester Finn, *What Do Our 17-Year-Olds Know? A Report on the First National Assessment of History and Literature* (New York: Harper and Row, 1987).

87. The reference, of course, is to *A Prairie Home Companion,* radio host Garrison Keillor's gentle irony about the imaginary Minnesota town where, among many other wonderful things, all the kids are above average.

88. E.g., Chester Finn, "Federal Spending and Education Reform: How Sound an Investment?" testimony prepared for delivery to the Committee on the Budget, U.S. House of Representatives, Mar. 16, 1995. See also Harold W. Stevenson and James W. Stigler, *The Learning Gap: Why Our Schools Are Failing and What We Can Learn from Japanese and Chinese Education* (New York: Summit Books, 1992), pp. 100–1.

89. Various author conversations with Finn, 1985–2000.

90. See, for example, Gerald W. Bracey, "TIMSS, Rhymes With 'Dims,'" as in 'Witted,'" *Phi Delta Kappan,* May 1998, pp. 686–87; and Bracey, "Tinkering with TIMMS," *Phi Delta Kappan* (on-line article), 1998, http://www.pdkintl.org/kappan/kbra9809.htm.

91. *Hoke,* findings of fact, § 322.

92. Marguerite Roza, "Policy Inadvertently Robs Poor Schools to Benefit the Rich," *Seattle Post-Intelligencer,* Sept. 24, 2000.

93. Telephone interview, Marguerite Roza, Aug. 20, 2002. Paul Hill, Roza's colleague, who runs the Center on Reinventing Public Education at the University of Washington, says that if the federal government really enforced a policy that's supposed to prevent schools from using

federal funds designed for high-poverty schools to replace underfunding from state and local sources, the schools with inexperienced teachers would at least get more funding to add staff or to buy other resources.

94. Author observation, Austin, Nov. 1999; also, e.g., Altwood Homes, in Indian Springs: "Schools attended by Altwood families have received exemplary ratings, the highest rating awarded by the Texas Education Agency, every year since 1998" (www.altwoodhomes.com/neighborhood.html).

95. J. D. Sparks, "San Juan Argues Urgency of Bonds," *Sacramento Bee* (Neighbors section), Aug. 1, 2002 (about a middle-class suburban Sacramento school district where portable structures, some more than thirty years old, "are plagued by water damage, leaking roofs, insufficient electrical output for computers, ineffective or nonexistent heating and air-conditioning units, loose and missing floor tiles and worn carpeting." In one of the district's schools, where only 10 percent of the students are from poor families, and nearly all are native English-speakers, "four portable classrooms...are racked with mold, water damage, split seams and shoddy roofs.") The quotes about Costa Mesa come from the *Orange County Register,* Feb. 29, 2000.

CHAPTER 2

1. *Rose v. Council for Better Education,* 790 S.W. 2d 186 (Ky. 1989).

2. *Rose v. Council for Better Education,* Kentucky Supreme Court no. 88-SC-804-TG, brief for appellees, p. 2; Kit Wagar et al., "The Tax Man Gives Away the Store—and the Schools," *Lexington Herald-Leader,* Nov. 12, 1989.

3. Peter Schrag, *Voices in the Classroom* (Boston: Beacon Press, 1965), p. 146.

4. Jack Bramar et al., "Nepotism Is Common in Kentucky, Where Education Is a Family Affair," *Lexington Herald-Leader,* Dec. 10, 1989.

5. Moreland phone interview, July 29, 2002.

6. National Commission on Excellence in Education, *A Nation at Risk: The Imperative for Educational Reform,* April 1983, www.ed.gov/pubs/NatAtRisk.

7. Phone interview with Robert Sexton, then (as now) executive director of the Prichard Committee, July 17, 2002; phone interview with Cindy Heine, associate executive director of the Prichard Committee, July 16, 2002.

8. Tracy Campbell, *Short of the Glory: The Fall and Redemption of Edward F. Prichard, Jr.* (Lexington: University of Kentucky Press, 1998).
9. Ibid., p. 140.
10. Ibid., p. 227. But as Campbell points out, other Kentuckians, particularly Republicans, believed Prichard continued to represent "the very worst of modern politics."
11. Moreland interview; Sexton interview; phone interview with Debra Dawahare, July 18, 2002.
12. McCann phone interview, Aug. 7, 2002.
13. National Center for Education Statistics, *Digest of Education Statistics, 2001* (Washington, D.C.: U.S. Department of Education, 2002), tables 168, 128, http://nces.ed.gov/pubs2002/digest2001. Molly A. Hunter, "All Eyes Forward: Public Engagement and Educational Reform in Kentucky," *Journal of Law and Education.* 28, 4 (1999), p. 486.
14. Kentucky Constitution, section 183.
15. *Council for Better Education v. Wilkinson,* Franklin Circuit Court I, Civil Action 85-CI-1759 (1988), p. 2.
16. *Rose v. Council for Better Education,* Kentucky Supreme Court No. 88-SC-804-TG, brief for appellees.
17. *Council for Better Education v. Wilkinson,* p. 7.
18. Ibid., p. 17.
19. Ibid.
20. *Rose* (1989), p. 29.
21. Ibid., p. 212. The West Virginia cases were *Pauley v. Kelly,* 162 W.Va. 672, 255 S.E. 2d 859 (1979) and *Pauley v. Bailey,* 324 S.E. 2d 128 (W.V. 1984). They were part of a thirty-year struggle started by Appalachian parents in 1972 to get adequate schools for their children. If those decisions had quickly led to comprehensive reform, as *Rose* would in Kentucky, West Virginia would probably have been the model that Kentucky became.
22. Moreland interview. Combs died in an auto accident in 1991. Some people in Kentucky doubted that Stephens had actually written the opinion, which was literate and well constructed. Among those skeptics is a former Kentucky editor who said Stephens was sometimes known by his detractors as "buckethead." That gives the Combs remark a certain additional resonance. For an extended analysis of both the law and politics of the case, see Michael Paris, "Legal Mobilization and the Politics of Reform: Lessons from School Finance Litigation in Kentucky, 1984–95," *Law and Social Inquiry* 26, 3 (2001), pp. 631–84.
23. Leibson dissent, *Rose* p. 220.
24. Quoted in Paris, "Legal Mobilization," p. 666.

25. Sexton interview; "The Religion of KERA," *Kentucky Citizen Digest,* April 1998, www.tffky.org/articles/1998/199804de.htm.

26. Sexton interview; Campbell, *Short of the Glory,* p. 273.

27. Kentucky Department of Education (www.kde.state.ky.us/); Sexton interview; Debra Viadero, "A Living Laboratory," *Education Week,* January 14, 1998 (www.edweek.org); Hunter, "All Eyes Forward," pp. 496–501.

28. Test chart in *Kentucky School Updates,* Prichard Committee, Aug. 2001, p. 2.

29. Sexton interview; Prichard Committee, www.prichardcommittee.org/pubs/updates_governance.pdf. As discussed below, in 2000 the legislature somewhat weakened the nepotism rules but did not abolish them.

30. "Starting Over," *New York Times,* Apr. 8, 1990.

31. "The Religion of KERA"; Paul A. Minorini and Stephen D. Sugarman, "Educational Adequacy and the Courts: The Promise and Problems of Moving to a New Paradigm," in Helen F. Ladd, Rosemary Chalk, and Janet S. Hansen, eds., *Equity and Adequacy in Education Finance: Issues and Perspectives* (Washington, D.C.: National Academy Press, 1999).

32. See, e.g., *Claremont School District v. Gregg,* 138 N.H. 183, 635 A. 2d 1375 (1993).

33. Horace Mann, "Intellectual Education as a Means of Removing Poverty," Twelfth Annual Report (1848), *Annual Reports of the Board of Education of Massachusetts for the Years 1845–48* (Boston, 1891), pp. 246ff.

34. *Debates (of the Kentucky) Constitutional Convention,* 1890. Quoted in *Rose.*

35. Minorini and Sugarman, "Educational Adequacy and the Courts," p. 187; *Keyes v. School District No. 1,* 413 U.S. 189 (1973); *Milliken v. Bradley,* 418 U.S. 717 (1974).

36. *Report of the National Advisory Commission on Civil Disorders* (New York: Dutton, 1968).

37. Gary Orfield, *Schools More Separate: The Consequences of a Decade of Resegregation.* (Cambridge, MA: The Civil Rights Project, Harvard University, July 2001), table 9.

38. For a concise history of school finance and its problems, see John G. Augenblick, John L. Myers, and Amy Berk Anderson, "Equity and Adequacy in School Funding," *The Future of Children: Financing Schools,* 7, 3 (1997).

39. *Abbott v. Burke,* 119 N.J. 287, 575 A. 2d 359 (1990) (*Abbott II*) 382.

40. From Jefferson's letters to James Breckenridge, quoted in G. Alan Hickrod et al., "The Effect of Constitutional Litigation on Educational Finance: A Further Analysis," in William J. Fowler Jr., ed., *Selected Papers in School Finance, 1995*, NCES 97-536 (Washington, D.C.: U.S. Department of Education, 1997).

41. "School Finance: State Efforts to Reduce Funding Gaps Between Poor and Wealthy Districts," (letter report, Feb. 5, 1997, GAO/HEHS-97-31).

42. *The Funding Gap: Students Who Need the Most Get the Least.* (Washington, D.C.: The Education Trust, 2002).

43. *Serrano v. Priest*, 5 Cal. 3d 584 (1971) *(Serrano I)* and *Serrano v. Priest*, 18 Cal. 3d 728 (1976) *(Serrano II)*; interview with John Coons, July 23, 2002.

44. California Constitution, Article 9, section 5.

45. Coons interviews, July 23 and Aug. 5, 2002.

46. *Serrano II*, p. 600.

47. *San Antonio Independent School District v. Rodriguez*, 411 U.S. 1 (1973).

48. *Rodriguez*, 411 U.S. 1 (1973), pp. 23–24. In his expansive dissent, Justice Thurgood Marshall assailed the majority's "labored efforts to demonstrate that fundamental interests ... encompass only established rights which we are somehow bound to recognize from the text of the Constitution itself." Education, he argued, is inextricably related to the right of expressing and receiving information guaranteed by the First Amendment, and thus a fundamental right in itself. *Rodriguez*, p. 99.

49. *Rodriguez*, p. 56.

50. Peter Schrag, *Paradise Lost: California's Experience, America's Future* (New York: The New Press, 1998), p. 148. William Fischel, a tax economist at Dartmouth, has long maintained that *Serrano*, by decoupling funding of local schools from the local property tax, helped undermine the commitment of affluent districts to local taxation and thus brought on Proposition 13. In fact, it was an inflation-driven spike in local assessments and taxes in the mid-seventies that caused the tax-cut frenzy. But it's quite possible that *Serrano* did reduce resistance of suburbanites to the initiative. Fischel, "Did *Serrano* Cause Proposition 13?" *National Tax Journal*, December 1989, pp. 465–74; "How *Serrano* Caused Proposition 13," *Journal of Law and Politics*, fall 1996, pp. 607–36.

51. Schrag, *Paradise Lost*, pp. 66–87.

52. *Edgewood Independent School District v. Kirby*, 777 S.W. 2d 391 (1989); *Edgewood Independent School District v. Kirby*, 893 S.W. 2d 450 (1995), among others.

53. Far and away the best single portal for school finance cases in the states is CFE's ACCESS Network Web site, www.accessednetwork.org, from which much of this data is taken. The site has links to hundreds of local advocacy and research organization, to litigation and court decisions, and to related legislation.

54. ACCESS Network, www.accessednetwork.org/litigation/lit_mn.htm. A subsequent case, brought in 1995 by the NAACP, charging inadequate and unequal educational opportunities in Minneapolis, was settled with an agreement providing for a new accountability system.

55. See, e.g., Richard Rothstein, "Juggling 3 School Goals, Texas Trips," *New York Times,* Oct. 30, 2002.

56. Michael A. Rebell, "Education Adequacy, Democracy and the Courts," paper prepared for the National Academy of Sciences and the National Research Council, Apr. 2001, p. 18.

57. Marguerite Roza with Karen Hawley Miles, *A New Look at Inequities in School Funding: A Presentation on the Resource Variations Within Districts* (Seattle: Center on Reinventing Public Education, University of Washington, 2002).

58. Margaret Hadderman, "Equity and Adequacy in Educational Finance," *ERIC Digest* 129 (1999), http://eric.uoregon.edu/publications/digests/digest129.html.

59. Among the states: Alabama, Idaho, Massachusetts, New Hampshire, New Jersey, New York, North Carolina, Ohio, South Carolina, Wyoming. The groups they represent include the American Civil Liberties Union in California, Alabama, and Maryland; the Campaign for Fiscal Equity in New York; the Ohio Equity and Adequacy Coalition (Ohio E and A); and the Education Law Center of New Jersey.

60. *Vincent v. Voight,* 614 N.W. 2d 388 (2000), p. 112.

61. Ibid., p. 49.

62. Ibid., p. 87.

63. AIMS in Arizona, FCAT in Florida, ISAT in Illinois, TAKS (formerly TAAS) in Texas, MSPAP in Maryland (in 2003 replaced by a new, standardized test), MCAS in Massachusetts, MCT in Mississippi, STAR in California, MEAP in Michigan, LEAP in Louisiana, and an alphabet soup of others.

64. See, e.g., "50 Schools Can Send Students to Better Ones," *Chicago Sun-Times,* July 30, 2002. The Department of Education regulations to implement NCLB, issued in November 2002, were regarded as so stringent that many states couldn't possibly meet them. On another front, in 2002, shortly after the U.S. Supreme Court rejected the argument that a Cleveland school voucher program violated the church-state bar-

rier of the First Amendment, a state judge struck down the Florida law as a violation of the state's constitutional prohibition of even indirect state support to religious institutions.

65. See, e.g., Craig D. Jerald, *Dispelling the Myth Revisited: Preliminary Findings from a Nationwide Analysis of "High-Flying" Schools* (Washington, D.C.: The Education Trust, 2001).

66. Author interview, Nov. 1999.

67. *ESEA Myths and Realities: Answers to Common Questions About the New No Child Left Behind Act* (Washington, D.C.: The Education Trust. 2002), p. 7. Data from National Assessment of Educational Progress (NAEP) 1999, http://nces.ed.gov/nationsreportcard/tables/Ltt1999/.

68. Although the language varies, virtually all states, with their historic faith in public education, have constitutional provisions requiring the legislature, in the most common phrase, to maintain a "thorough and efficient" system of public schools, "a system of free common schools," or an "ample education." In New York, the legislature must "provide for the maintenance and support of free common schools wherein all the children of the state may be educated" (New York State Constitution, Article XI, section 1). In Washington, with perhaps the most expansive provision, it is "the paramount duty of the state to make ample provision for the education of all children residing within its borders." In Massachusetts, it's a clause, dating to 1780, calling for the "encouragement of literature . . . especially the university at Cambridge, public schools, and grammar schools in the towns" (Constitution of 1780, Chapter V, section II). For others, see William E. Thro, "The Role of Language of the State Education Clauses in School Finance Litigation," *Education Law Reporter* 79 (1993): pp. 19–31.

69. *Debra P. v. Turlington,* 474 F. Supp. 244 (M.D. Fla. 1979), 644 F. 2d 397 (5th Cir. 1981), 564 F. Supp. 177 (M.D. Fla. 1983).

70. Ibid.

71. *G. I. Forum et al. v. Texas Education Agency,* 87 F. Supp. 667 (W.D. Tex. 2000). In upholding the Texas exit exam, the court found that the schools were providing students sufficient resources and notice to pass the test, including well-publicized standards, books linked to the curriculum, multiple chances to pass, and mandatory remediation courses. Kevin G. Welner of the University of Colorado suggests that if future challenges under the *Debra P.* principle were to focus on the denial of opportunity to learn the material or on the tracking of students into low-level courses and not on the denial of diplomas attendant on test failure, they might bear fruit even in the federal courts.

Welner, "Tracking in an Era of Standards: Low-Expectation Classes Meet High-Expectation Laws," *Hastings Constitutional Law Quarterly* 28, 3 (2001), p. 734.

72. Susan Phillips phone interview, Aug. 8, 2002.

73. Minutes of the Texas State Board of Education, Nov. 7, 2001. The OTL challenge in Texas was decided in *G. I. Forum*.

74. With apologies to Justice Holmes, who said the common law is "not a brooding omnipresence in the sky but the articulate voice of some sovereign or quasi sovereign that can be identified." Mark DeWolfe Howe, ed., *Holmes-Laski Letters: The Correspondence of Mr. Justice Holmes and Harold J. Laski, 1916–1935* (Cambridge: Harvard University Press, 1953), p. 822.

75. Rebell, p. 29.

76. To be discussed more fully in Chapter 3 of this book.

77. *Campbell County School District v. State,* 907 P. 2d 1238 (Wyo. 1995).

78. James W. Guthrie and Richard Rothstein, "Enabling 'Adequacy' to Achieve Reality," in Helen F. Ladd, Rosemary Chalk, and Janet S. Hansen, eds., *Equity and Adequacy in Education Finance* (Washington, D.C.: National Academy Press, 1999), pp. 209–259.

79. Jay G. Chambers, "Public School Teacher Cost Differences Across the United States: Introduction to a Teacher Cost Index," in *Developments in School Finance* (Washington, D.C., National Center for Education Statistics, 1995).

80. Quoted in Guthrie and Rothstein, "Enabling 'Adequacy,' " p. 224

81. Adequacy "is still an opportunity concept, and, as such, compliance with the adequacy requirement is ultimately still a matter of inputs, albeit now more broadly conceived. . . . At the level of the moral claim, educational adequacy seems to be about what fairly ought to be provided, leaving it in the end to the student take advantage of that offering." Minorini and Sugarman, "Educational Adequacy and the Courts," p. 189.

82. William D. Duncombe and John M. Yinger, "Performance Standards and Educational Cost Indexes: You Can't Have One Without the Other," in Helen F. Ladd, Rosemary Chalk, and Janet S. Hansen, eds., *Equity and Adequacy in Education Finance* (Washington, D.C.: National Academy Press, 1999).

83. Interviews with Jim Payton and Matt Cohen, Ohio State Department of Education, Oct. 24–25, 2002; John Augenblick, Oct. 18, 2002; *DeRolph v. State,* 88 Ohio St. 3d. (2000); Michael Hawthorne, "Ohio Defends School Funding," *Cincinnati Inquirer,* Aug. 25, 1998. But even under the best of circumstances, the calculations are necessarily dy-

namic; adequate public education, as the New Hampshire Supreme Court held, "is not a static concept removed from the demands of an evolving world."

84. Guthrie phone interview, May 22, 2002; Helen F. Ladd and Janet S. Hansen, eds., *Making Money Matter: Financing America's Schools* (Washington, D.C.: National Academy Press, 1999), http://books.nap. edu/html/money_matter/).

85. See, e.g., *Abbott v. Burke,* 119 N.J. 287, 575 A. 2d 359 (1990) (*Abbott II*), 388; *DeRolph v. State,* 78 Ohio St. 3d 193, 677 N.E. 2d 733 (1997). At last count there were eight *Abbott* decisions, the latest coming in 2001, and four *DeRolph* decisions. A fuller account of the saga in New Jersey and Ohio will be found in Chapter 3.

86. Augenblick phone interview, July 22, 2002. There are one or two states like Maryland (about which more below) that have recently enacted major fiscal reforms without immediate legal prodding, but there aren't many. Paul A. Minorini and Stephen D. Sugarman, "School Finance Litigation in the Name of Educational Equity," in Helen F. Ladd, Rosemary Chalk, and Janet S. Hansen, eds., *Equity and Adequacy in Education Finance* (Washington, D.C.: National Academy Press, 1999), p. 58; Minorini and Sugarman, "Educational Adequacy and the Courts," p. 206.

87. *Digest of Education Statistics,* table 168.

88. Its main objections appeared to be based on its fear that the state would expand its control over local schools and curricula and, subsequently, on the open-ended nature of the testing.

89. Calculated from *Kentucky School and District Accountability Results* (CTBS Summary), 2001, and *Nonacademic Data,* Kentucky Department of Education, 2002, table I-4. Calculating dropout statistics is a squishy business, giving all the possible variables. My computation simply uses the difference between seventh-grade enrollment and the number of high school graduates six years later.

90. Susan Perkins Weston, "2000 Elementary Performance and Poverty" and "2000 High School Performance and Poverty" (unpublished memos), Kentucky Association of School Councils, 2001.

91. "Average Reading Scale Scores for States," http://nces.ed.gov/nations-reportcard/reading/statescales.asp; "Average Mathematics Scale Scores by State," http://nces.ed.gov/nationsreportcard/mathematics/results/stateavgscale-g4.asp.

92. David Grissmer, Ann Flanagan, Jennifer Kawata, and Stephanie Williamson, *Improving Student Achievement: What NAEP Test Scores Tell Us* (Santa Monica, Calif.: Rand, 2000), p. 62.

93. Minorini and Sugarman, "Educational Adequacy and the Courts," p. 201.
94. Although Covington superintendent Moreland acknowledges that in some counties, "I might hire your wife if you'll hire my wife."
95. Linda B. Blackford, "Patton Agrees with Educators Funding Is Low," *Lexington Herald-Leader*, July 31, 2002; Lonnie Harp, "Teacher Qualifications Plan Pared," *Louisville Courier-Journal*, April 16, 2000.
96. Moreland interview; "Districts Re-Examine Spending," *Perspectives* (newsletter of the Prichard Committee), summer 2002; David J. Hoff, "Activist Ky. School Leaders Back; Want New Aid," *Education Week*, Mar. 6, 2002.
97. Hoff, "Activist."

CHAPTER 3

1. *Williams v. California*, San Francisco County Superior Court, complaint for injunctive and declaratory relief, May 17, 2000.
2. *Williams v. California*, San Francisco County Superior Court, no. 312236, first amended complaint. The participating organizations in the suit, in addition to the ACLU, included Public Advocates of San Francisco, the Mexican American Legal Defense and Educational Fund, the Lawyers Committee for Civil Rights, the Center for Law in the Public Interest, and the Asian Pacific American Legal Center. Local districts were supposed to have public hearings on the availability of books, but those hearings, as UCLA professor Jeannie Oakes remarked, were "an outrage," brief and perfunctory discussions conducted by school boards without public notice late at night and sometimes in the early hours of the morning.
3. For a fuller analysis of those differences, see David Grissmer, Ann Flanagan, Jennifer Kawsata, and Stephanie Williamson, *Improving Student Achievement: What State NAEP Test Scores Tell Us* (Santa Monica: Rand, 2000), pp. xiii–xvii, 70–73. Some of those differences may also have been due to the different protocols the two states used for determining whom to exclude from the test, to the intense test-success pressure in Texas, and maybe to outright fudging in decisions on which students not to test. But the test experts believe that none of those things could explain all the score differences.
4. Linda Brown was the lead plaintiff in the 1954 *Brown* case.

5. *Williams v. California*, San Francisco County Superior Court, no. 312236, first amended complaint; author interview, May 20, 2000, and other dates. Mississippification quote in ACLU press release, May 17, 2000. The source of "dumbing down" was William Koski, a law professor at Stanford.

6. By 2002, the University of California had instituted a large list of admissions reforms and had succeeded in pressuring the College Board to revise its SAT testing program.

7. Letter from Bill Lockyer to Demetrious Boutris, the governor's secretary of legal affairs, July 22, 2000.

8. Exxon paid hefty criminal penalties and civil damages in the oil spill case, plus $2 billion (by Exxon's estimate) in cleanup costs. But in mid-2002, Exxon and Daum were still contesting the punitive damages that a federal jury had awarded in 1994 to some fourteen thousand fishermen and other individuals who lived or worked in the damaged area. In November 2001, Daum persuaded an appellate federal court to declare the $5 billion verdict too high and to send the case back to the Alaska trial court. Mary Pemberton, "Exxon Puts Damages in Millions: Company Says $5 Billion Award Is Excessive," AP story in *Anchorage Daily News*, June 13, 2002. Also, Natalie Phillips, "$5,000,000,000 Jury Sets Oil Spill Damages," *Anchorage Daily News*, Sept. 17, 1994; Claire Cooper, "Court Says Exxon Damages Too High," *Sacramento Bee*, Nov. 8, 2001.

9. Interview, Aug. 1999.

10. Broder, "No Magic for the Schools," *Washington Post*, Feb. 28, 1999.

11. Rosenbaum interviews, July 14, 2002, and various other dates, 2000–2.

12. *Williams*, defendants' memorandum of points and authorities in support of demurrer, Oct. 16, 2000, pp. 2–3, 17, 26.

13. *Butt v. State of California*, 4 Cal. 4th 668–669 (1992). There were four different opinions, but all concurred on the state's essential responsibility.

14. *Williams*, Busch order, Nov. 14, 2000, pp. 1, 2.

15. *Williams*, defendants' objections and motion to strike certain declarations, Sept. 25, 2000.

16. *Williams*, deposition of Manuel Ortiz, June 10, 2001, pp. 26, 403–4.

17. *Williams*, deposition of Carlos Ramirez, June 21, 2001, pp. 34–38.

18. *Williams*, deposition of Manuel Ortiz, pp. 47, 458.

19. *Williams*, deposition of Cindy Diego, May 26, 2001, pp. 139–142.

20. *Williams*, deposition of Alondra Jones, pp. 380–81.

21. Ibid., pp. 379, 387, 391.

22. Rosenbaum interview, July 13, 2002; Londen interview, July 14, 2002.

23. Londen and others at UCLA meetings; author interviews with Londen, Rosenbaum, and others at UCLA meeting, July 14, 2002.

24. Six months later, as the state's fiscal crisis deepened, education, though still getting favored treatment, would go on the chopping block as well.

25. Londen, however, warned that the state's academic content standards "can't be read into the constitution." The inadequacy and disparity arguments would have to be made at a more fundamental and broader level.

26. *Abbott v. Burke*, 100 N.J. 269, 495 A. 2d 376 (1985) (*Abbott I*); *Robinson v. Cahill*, 62 N.J. 473, 303 A. 2d 273 (1973).

27. Paul Tractenberg interview, Aug. 29, 2002; Craig R. McCoy, "M. J. Morheuser, Advocate for Equity in Schools, Dies," *Philadelphia Inquirer*, Oct. 24, 1995.

28. Steven Block, for many years the research director at ELC, is, among others, certain that Florio wouldn't have lost had he not tried to pay for part of a property tax relief measure by cutting the funds with which the state had been paying the employer's share of social security and pension benefits for local school employees. In the end, Block believes, it was angry teachers and school administrators who had been key members of Florio's constituency, not the taxpayers, who brought him down.

29. *Abbott v. Burke*, 119 N.J. 287, 575 A. 2d (1990) (*Abbott II*), 306, 334, 339, 357.

30. Ibid., 375.

31. Nancy Phillips, "Victor in School Suit Celebrates—in Jail," *Philadelphia Inquirer*, June 6, 1990; Phillips, "School Suit Plaintiff Looks Back," *Philadelphia Inquirer*, May 17, 1990.

32. Block phone interview, July 24, 2002.

33. *The Funding Gap: Low-Income and Minority Students Receive Fewer Dollars* (Washington, D.C.: The Education Trust, 2002), p. 3; *Digest of Education Statistics, 2001* (Washington, D.C.: National Center for Education Statistics, 2002), table 168.

34. *Abbott v. Burke*, 149 N.J. 145, 693 A. 2d 417 (1997) (*Abbott IV*).

35. *Abbott v. Burke*, 153 N.J. 480, 710 A. 2d 450 (1998) (*Abbott V*).

36. "Evolution of Whole School Reform in New Jersey," in *Guide for Implementing Urban Education Reform in Abbott Districts*, New Jersey Department of Education, Sept. 2000, www.state.nj.us/njded/abbotts/guide/section1.pdf.

37. Odden interview, Oct. 8, 2002.

38. *Abbott v. Burke*, 153 N.J. 480, 710 A. 2d 450 (1998) (*Abbott V*).

39. Ibid.

40. Richard Venezky, "An Alternative Perspective on Success for All," in

Kenneth K. Wong, ed., *Advances in Educational Policy*, vol. 4 (Greenwich, CT: JAI Press, n.d.).

41. Stanley Pogrow, "Success for All Does Not Produce Success for Students," *Phi Delta Kappan*, Sept. 2000, p. 67. See also Jay Mathews, "Success for Some," *Washington Post*, July 21, 2002.

42. Bari Anhalt Erlichson, Margaret Goertz, and Barbara Turnbull, *Implementing Whole School Reform in New Jersey: Year Two* (New Brunswick: Rutgers University Press, 2001), pp. x, xi.

43. Block phone interview, Aug. 27, 2002.

44. For Grade Eight Performance Assessment, High School Performance Assessment, and Elementary School Performance Assessment. The "weird sisters" analogy should be credited to Rich Vespucci, a spokesman for the state Department of Education. Note that the elementary school social studies test is given in fifth grade.

45. Sally E. Goldenberg, "Crash Course in Budget Math," *The Bergen Record*, Mar. 18, 2002.

46. "Testing Reform: Creating a New Vision of Assessment. Summary of Proposal," New Jersey Department of Education, Nov. 15, 2002; Catherine Gewertz, "Governor Takes N.J. Down Testing Road Less Traveled," *Education Week*, Dec. 4, 2002.

47. In the 1980s, New Jersey governor Thomas Kean, a moderate Republican, had made his state a leader in a range of school reforms, particularly in trying to break the hold of the ed schools on teacher training. But when Whitman arrived in Trenton, things went astray.

48. Excellent Education for Everyone, www.nje3.org/believe.html.

49. Schundler Web site, June 28, 2002, www.schundler.org.

50. Among them was former Newark mayor Kenneth Gibson. The federal charges against him included bribery of two school board members in Irvington. After a federal jury failed to reach a decision, Gibson, seeking to avoid another trial pleaded guilty to income tax evasion and his firm, which had been hired to manage a $50 million school construction project, pleaded guilty to one count of mail fraud. The aging Gibson was sentenced to three years' probation. William Kleinknecht, "Gibson Gets Three Years' Probation," *Newark Star Ledger*, Nov. 1, 2002; Fordham University Corruption Information Exchange, www.fordham.edu/economics/vinod/cie/usa_nj.htm. There are similar corruption stories in Atlantic City and Paterson.

51. "Judge Rejects Takeover of Camden Schools," New Jersey Capital Report (AP story), Aug. 6, 2002; Frank Kummer, Renee Winkler, and Kathy Matheson, "Milton Milan Sentenced to 7 Years," *Camden Cour-*

ier Post, June 16, 2001; Jon Van Til et al., *Associations as Assets in the Urban Community: A Study of Two Inner City Neighborhoods in Camden* (Camden: Rutgers University at Camden, 2000); Andrew Jacobs, "Add Betrayal and Death to the Political Saga in Camden," *New York Times*, July 12, 2001. Camden, of course, was not the only place in New Jersey with corruption.

52. Tractenberg interview, Aug. 29, 2002.

53. He probably never did say it. James C. Burke, "The Cherokee Cases: A Study in Law, Politics and Morality," *Stanford Law Review* 21 (1969): pp. 500–531.

54. "Judicial Selection in the States: Appellate and General Jurisdiction Courts," American Judicature Society, 2002, www.ajs.org.

55. Gerald F. Uelmen, "Crocodiles in the Bathtub: Maintaining the Independence of State Supreme Courts in the Era of Judicial Politicization," *Notre Dame Lawyer* 1133 (1997).

56. *DeRolph v. State*, 78 Ohio St. 3d 193, 677 N.E. 2d 733 (1997) (*DeRolph I*).

57. Molly A. Hunter, "Trying to Bridge the Gaps: Ohio's Search for an Education Finance Remedy," *Journal of Education Finance*, Summer 2000, pp. 66, 67.

58. Quoted in *DeRolph I.*

59. Doug Oplinger and Dennis J. Willard, "Slow to Build," *Akron Beacon Journal*, May 22, 1996.

60. *DeRolph I*, Pfeifer concurring opinion.

61. *DeRolph I.*

62. *DeRolph I*, concurring opinion of Justice Alice Robie Resnick.

63. *DeRolph v. State* (2000), 88 Ohio St. 3d. (*DeRolph II*), pp. 93–94.

64. "Voinovich Blasts Court in School Funding Case," *Toledo Blade*, March 26, 1997.

65. Phillis interview, Aug. 30, 2002.

66. Phillis interviews, July 29, Aug. 30, and Nov. 8, 2002.

67. Sandy Theis, "GOP Justice Awaits Retaliation," *Cincinnati Enquirer*, June 28, 1998.

68. All election data from the Ohio secretary of state, www.state.oh.us/sos/.

69. Michael Hawthorne, "Ohio Defends School Funding," *Cincinnati Enquirer*, Aug. 25, 1998. Sutton's Democratic Party counterpart said the system was more like Groucho Marx.

70. *DeRolph II*, 56.

71. Ibid., 42–43.

72. Ibid., 72.

73. T. C. Brown, "Court Ads Mislead, Experts Contend," *Cleveland Plain Dealer*, Nov. 2, 2000.

74. Joe Hallett, "Chamber Promises Positive Campaign," *Columbus Dispatch*, June 25, 2002; T. C. Brown, "Pro-Business Campaign Decides to Disclose All Donors, Amounts," *Cleveland Plain Dealer*, June 25, 2002; *Dayton Daily News*, Aug. 6, 2002. Under Ohio law, as under federal law, campaigns that don't specifically call for the election or defeat of a particular candidate aren't required to disclose contributors.

75. *DeRolph v. State* (2001), 93 Ohio St. 3d 309 (*DeRolph III*), Douglas concurring opinion. Although Douglas and Pfeifer switched, the recorded margin in each decision was 4–3. That's because Justice Deborah Cook, who believed from the start that the court had no business meddling in the legislature's domain, also dissented in *DeRolph III*. But she would have never supported any further attempts to make the legislature do anything. The margin, therefore, was really 5–2.

76. *DeRolph III*.

77. Ibid., 51.

78. *DeRolph v. State*, plaintiff's findings of fact, conclusions of law, order and ruling for the remand court, case 22043, pp. 88, 91; *DeRolph*, brief of state appellants, Aug. 2, 1999, p. 31.

79. Augenblick interview, Oct. 18, 2002.

80. Interview with Rich Savors of the Ohio School Facilities Commission, Nov. 14, 2002.

81. *DeRolph III*, 73.

82. *DeRolph II*, 37.

83. She couldn't resist pointing to the illogic of justices who in the first cases had argued that there was no constitutional problem but were now part of the majority that was ruling that after making improvements the state was on its way to compliance.

84. *The Funding Gap.* The gap is the difference between the average per-pupil spending in the 25 percent of districts with the most students getting free or reduced-price lunches and that in the 25 percent of districts with the fewest.

85. "Finan Says State Won't Raise Taxes or Cut Spending to Comply With DeRolph III; Moyer Surprised at Comments," Gongwer News Service Ohio Report, Sept. 6, 2001.

86. "Two Supreme Court Races Key for Rural Schools Coalition," *Columbus Dispatch*, Sept. 10, 2002.

87. "2002 Candidates for Ohio Supreme Court Justice," Ohio Citizen Action, Sept, 30, 2002; Dennis J. Willard and Doug Oplinger, "Secret Funding to Affect Elections," *Akron Beacon Journal*, July 30, 2002.

88. The election campaign was probably not as dirty as the campaign against Resnick in 2000. But considering the office involved, it was

still monumentally unappetizing. The incumbent attorney general, Betty Montgomery, whose office regularly argues cases in the high court, appeared in a TV commercial and raised money for Justice Stratton, as did Taft. (Under Ohio's term limits, Montgomery was ineligible for reelection and was getting ready to switch elected jobs with her fellow Republican, Auditor Jim Petro, who was likewise termed out and running for the attorney general's job. They would win by identical 65–35 margins.) At the same time, Stratton and O'Connor were being slammed in TV commercials sponsored by the labor- and lawyer-funded Citizens for an Independent Court as being enemies of working families and friends of corporations. Another commercial, paid for by AT&T, associated O'Connor and Stratton with lower phone rates. Meanwhile, Lieutenant Governor O'Connor, who hadn't served in any judicial post since 1995, was facing an appellate court disciplinary panel for appearing in a campaign commercial wearing judicial robes. Ohio Secretary of State's Office, 2002 election returns, www.state.oh.us/sos/; T. C. Brown, "Bar Association Asks Two Groups to Pull Campaign Ads," *Cleveland Plain Dealer,* Oct. 22, 2002; T. C. Brown, "Montgomery Raising Money for Justice on Supreme Court," *Cleveland Plain Dealer,* Oct. 23, 2002; T. C. Brown, "Independent Group Uses Ad to Target GOP's Stratton," *Cleveland Plain Dealer,* Oct. 23, 2002.

89. *DeRolph v. State,* 97 Ohio St. 3d (2002).

90. See, e.g., Michael Douglas, "*DeRolph* Is Dead," *Akron Beacon Journal,* Dec. 15, 2002. On Phillis, see "Message to Blue Ribbon Task Force on Financing Student Access," one of several e-mail messages to school superintendents, treasurers, and others from William Phillis. Feb. 4, 2003.

91. "OSBA Begins School Funding Study," resolution of Ohio School Boards Association Board of Trustees, Sept. 21, 2002; Brown, "Bar Association"; Brown, "Montgomery Raising Money"; Brown, "Independent Group Uses Ad."

92. Kevin Sack, "Ten Commandments' Defender Wins," *New York Times,* June 8, 2000. See himself had been temporarily suspended from office on charges that he ran misleading campaign ads against Moore: David White, "Justice See Suspended on Charges over Ads," *Birmingham News,* July 25, 2000.

93. Phone interview with Tuscaloosa attorney Stan Murphy, Aug, 8, 2002.

94. *Glassroth v. Moore,* U.S. District Court for the Middle District of Alabama, civil action no. 01-T-1268-N; Jeffrey Gettleman, "Judge's Biblical Monument Is Ruled Unconstitutional," *New York Times,* Nov. 19, 2002.

95. *Ex Parte James,* 713 So. 2d at 877; *Ex Parte James,* 713 So. 2d 869, 879 (Ala. 1997).

96. "Alabama Education: Quick Facts," Montgomery, Alabama Department of Education, 2002, www.alsde.edu/allreportcards/quick_facts.pdf; *The Funding Gap.*

97. Diana Jean Schemo, "Poor Rural Schools Must Strive to Meet New Federal Rules," *New York Times,* Dec. 2, 2002.

98. "How Alabama's Taxes Compare," *The PARCA Report,* no. 37, summer 1999.

99. See, e.g., "Evolution Warning Labels for Alabama Texts," *Eagle Forum Education Reporter,* December 1995, http://www.eagleforum.org/educate/1995/dec95/biology.html; "Counter Evolutionary," *Education Week,* Nov. 20, 1996; Julie Blair and David Hoff, "Evolution Restored to Kansas Standards, but Called 'Controversial' in Alabama's," *Education Week,* Feb. 21, 2001.

100. *For the Sake of Our Children: The Future of Alabama's Schools, A Five Year Report* (Montgomery, AL: A+ Research Foundation, n.d.).

101. Interview with Cathy Gassenheimer, Aug. 15, 2002; interview with Sally Howell, Alabama Association of School Boards, Sept. 3, 2002; Jeffrey Scott Berman and Drew Dunphy, "Building Plans for Reform: Alabama's School Finance Litigation," *Studies in Judicial Remedies and Public Engagement* 1, 4 (1998).

102. Ala. Const. amend. 111, § 256.

103. *ACE v. Siegelman* Sup. Ct. Ala. # 1950030, 1950031, 1950240, 1950241, 1950408, 1950409. (2002), 19.

104. *Pinto v. Alabama Coalition for Equity,* 662 So. 2d 894, 896 (Ala. 1995).

105. *ACE v. Hunt,* 1993 WL204083 (Ala. Cir. Ct. Montgomery County, Apr. 1, 1993); *ACE v. Folsom,* nos. CV-90-883-R, CV-91-0117 (Ala. Cir. Ct. Montgomery County, Oct. 22, 1993).

106. *Ex parte Governor Fob James* (Dec. 1997). The "reasonable time 'allowance,' " said an editorial in the *Birmingham News,* "was like holding a gun to lawmakers' heads that when you pull the trigger, a flag that says 'Bang!' pops out." "Supreme Buck-Passing," June 4, 2002.

107. *Ex Parte James,* 713 So. 2d 869, 879 (Ala. 1997). Reese, who was not the original judge on the case, took it over from Judge Mark Montiel, whom he beat and replaced in 1991.

108. See, e.g., "Alabama Governor Convicted on Ethics Charge," Associated Press, April 23, 1993. I'm also indebted to Sally Howell, assistant executive director of the Alabama Association of School Boards, for her chronology of the complex twists and turns of the Alabama cases and the shifting affiliations of many of the state's leaders.

109. His colleague Reneau Almon, concurring, put it even more starkly: "The following parties chose not to appeal from the Liability Order: then Governor of Alabama Guy Hunt; Speaker of the House of Representatives James Clark; then State Finance Director Robin Swift; and then Superintendent of Education Wayne Teague; and the members of the State Board of Education. It makes no legal difference to the finality of that order that other persons, who may disagree with that decision not to appeal, now hold those offices."

110. *Ex Parte James,* 713 So. 2d 869, 879 (Ala. 1997).

111. Cook himself had lost to a Republican circuit court judge named Jacquelyn Stuart. Justice Kenneth Ingram, another member of the Cook majority, had lost to Republican See in 1997. Justices Reneau Almon and Janie Shores had retired, and Justice Mark Kennedy had resigned to enter private practice. He was replaced by John England, a Democrat and another circuit court judge, who was appointed to his seat by Governor Donald Siegelman. England also lost when he tried to retain his seat in the election of 2000. Cook and England were the only two blacks on the court.

112. Interview with Ralph Cook, Sept. 3, 2002.

113. In 1996, a sitting judge, in what could have been a symbol of the process, ran an ad against his opponent with a picture of a skunk and the line "Some things you can smell a mile away."

114. figures and data from Justice at Stake, www.justiceatstake.org, and from the Alabama secretary of state, http://arc-sos.state.al.us/.

115. *ACE v. Siegelman* (2002), 3. The opinion was probably written by Houston, who had written the most vehement dissent in the 1997 cases; Houston also wrote his own concurrence in the 2002 decision.

116. Ala. Const. Amendment 582 (June 1996). It may not be necessary to point out that even in comparison to many other state constitutions, Alabama's is an enormously long document that includes everything from a declaration that navigable waters are free public highways and provisions on "the suppression of dueling" to sections on the promotion of the catfish industry.

117. *ACE v. Siegelman* (2002), 16.

118. Ibid., 178–79.

119. Nancy Anderson, phone interview, Aug. 12, 2002.

120. See, e.g., "The Alabama Reading Initiative," Alabama Department of Education, www.alsde.edu/. Also "Reading Is the Key: Alabama Reading Initiative," www.governor.state.al.us/news/2000-initiatives-ari.html.

121. "REACH: Realizing Every Alabama Child's Hopes," Alabama State Department of Education, 2002, www.alsde.edu/boe/REACH-EducationalAdequacy_files/frame.htm. Also Erin Sullivan, "Will School Funds Proposal Fizzle?" *Birmingham Post-Herald*, July 22, 2002.

122. "REACH"; Challen Stephens, "$1.4B Would Make Schools 'Adequate,' " *Huntsville Times*, Oct. 21, 2001.

123. Williams interview.

124. Martha I. Morgan, Adam S. Cohen, and Helen Hershkoff, "Establishing Program Inadequacy: The Alabama Example," *University of Michigan Journal of Law Reform*, spring 1995, p. 559.

125. Alabama Industrial Development Training, www.aidt.edu/index.html.

126. Berman and Dunphy, "Building Plans for Reform," p. 30.

127. Bill Smith, Caroline Novak, and Cathy Gassenheimer, "Our Children Are Still Waiting," *Mobile Register*, June 9, 2002.

128. N.C. Const. Art. I, § 15.

129. *Leandro v. State of North Carolina*, 346 N.C. 336, 488 S.E. 2d 249 (1997).

130. *Missouri v. Jenkins*, 515 U.S. 70 (1995), 88–89. The only disagreement in *Leandro* came from Justice Robert F. Orr, who believed that the state constitution required equity as well as adequacy.

131. U.S. Census, State and County Quick Facts, http://quickfacts.census.gov/qfd/states/37/37093.html; *Hoke*, March 21, 2001 (*Hoke III*), 6.

132. *Hoke III*, 29–30.

133. *Hoke County Board of Education et al. v. State of North Carolina*, Wake County Superior Court, 95 CVS 1158 (2000–2).

134. *Hoke*, March 21, 2001 (*Hoke III*), 37–38.

135. *Hoke*, April 4, 2002 (*Hoke V*), 13.

136. *Hoke*, Oct. 26, 2000 (*Hoke II*), 11.

137. *Hoke*, March 21, 2001 (*Hoke III*), 82.

138. Todd Silberman, "Mandate on At-Risk Students Welcomed," *Raleigh News & Observer*, Mar. 28, 2001.

139. Todd Silberman, "State to Appeal At-Risk Student Ruling," *Raleigh News & Observer*, Apr. 24, 2001.

140. *Hoke*, April 4, 2002 (*Hoke V*), 108. On Kirk, *Hoke V*, 18.

141. *Hoke V*, 7.

142. "Let's Finish the Job: Building a System of Superior Schools," report from the Governor's Education First Task Force, spring 2002.

143. *Hoke*, defendants' proposed record on appeal, July 10, 2002.

144. Reid interview, Sept. 9, 2002; Sheria Reid, "State Reveals Arguments on Appeal of *Leandro*," N.C. Education and Law Project, July 2002;

letter from Hampton Y. Dellinger, legal counsel to Gov. Easley, to Judge Manning, July 29, 2002. There was indeed something disorienting in the fact that while the state in its legal track was denying that the courts had any jurisdiction and that even minimum achievement was adequate, the governor and senior education officials were writing polite letters to Manning implicitly recognizing what they were denying in court.

145. Kathleen Kennedy Manzo, "Funding for N.C. Executive Order Snagged in Budget Battle," *Education Week*, Aug. 7, 2002; Amy Gardner and Todd Silberman, "Easley Demands Quick Action on Lottery," *Raleigh News & Observer*, July 23, 2002.

146. Todd Silberman, "Judge Orders School Action," *Raleigh News & Observer*, Aug. 16, 2002.

147. Gardner and Silberman, "Easley Demands Quick Action."

148. *Commission on Education Finance, Equity and Excellence: Final Report* [hereafter Thornton Report] (Annapolis: Office of Policy Analysis, Maryland Department of Legislative Services, 2002), http:// mlis.state.md.us/other/education/final/2002_final_report.pdf.

149. Census, State and County Quick Facts, http://quickfacts.census.gov/ qfd/states/24/24011.html.

150. Maryland General Assembly, Department of Legislative Service, Fiscal Note on Bridge to Excellence in Public Schools Act (SB 856) 2002, pp. 11–12; Thornton Report, p. 33.

151. Barbara Hoffmann, phone interview, Sept. 18, 2002.

152. *Hornbeck v. Somerset County Board of Education,* 295 Md. at 615, 458 A. 2d, 768.

153. *Bradford v. Maryland State Board of Education,* Circuit Court for Baltimore City, case no. 94340058/CE 189672, memorandum opinion, June 30, 2000. The figure was also based on a study that another consulting firm, Metis Associates, had done.

154. *Bradford,* memorandum opinion, June 30, 2000. Among the more impressive figures in the three-year process that led up to Hoffman's legislation was Baltimore school board chairman J. Tyson Tildon, retired associate dean for research and graduate studies at the University of Maryland School of Medicine, where he'd also been director of pediatric research and head of the school's research into sudden infant death syndrome. Since Tildon had been appointed to the board by Glendening after the takeover that was mandated by the consent decree, he should have had some you-owe-me claims on the governor. But Glendening kept his distance from the reform bill until the very end.

155. Hoffman interview, *Bradford* memorandum and opinion, pp. 19–20.

156. Verdery interview, Sept. 18, 2002.

157. Much of this material comes from background interviews with legislative staff members, journalists, and others who followed legislative politics in the SB 856 battles.

158. "A Visionary School Plan in Maryland," *New York Times,* Apr. 2, 2002.

159. Ivan Penn, "Negative Tactics Alleged in 41st," *Baltimore Sun,* Sept. 1, 2002.

160. Hoffman interview, Sept. 18, 2002.

161. *Campaign for Fiscal Equity v. State of New York* (*CFE II*) (2001), Supreme Court, County of New York, Part 25, no. 111070/93, p. 3.

162. The U.S. Supreme Court in *Alexander v. Sandoval,* 532 U.S. 275 (2001), in holding that "there is no private right of action to enforce disparate-impact regulations promulgated under Title VI," effectively cut the ground out from under DeGrasse's Title VI argument.

163. *CFE II,* 185.

164. *Campaign for Fiscal Equity v. State of New York* (*CFE III*) (2002), NY Slip. Op. 05327; *Digest of Education Statistics, 2001,* (Washington, D.C.: National Center for Education Statistics, 2002), table 92.

165. N.Y. Constitution, Article XI, Section 1.

166. *Board of Educ. Levittown Union Free School Dist. v. Nyquist,* 57 N.Y. 2d 127, 439, N.E. 2d 359 (1982); *Campaign for Fiscal Equity v. State of New York* (*CFE I*) (1995), 86 N.Y. 2nd 307.

167. *CFE I,* 31.

168. *CFE II,* 17, 18, 36, 104.

169. Richard Perez-Pena and Abby Goodnough, "Pataki Is Ready to File Appeal on School Aid," *New York Times,* Jan. 17, 2001.

170. *Campaign for Fiscal Equity v. State of New York* (*CFE III*) (2002), NY Slip. Op. 05327, 10.

171. Ibid., 11.

172. Ibid., 38.

173. Joseph Wayland interview, Sept. 23, 2002. In his decision, DeGrasse singled out Simpson Thacher for special (and extraordinary) commendation. "The firm expended enormous resources," he said, "and its lawyers brought to bear great talent and perseverance in support of plaintiffs' cause. The firm's commitment is an exemplar of the Bar's highest traditions."

174. Wayland, phone interview, Sept. 23, 2002.

175. *CFE II,* testimony of Robert Berne, trial transcript, pp. 11823, 11884; letter of Harold Levy to Deborah Cunningham, New York State Department of Education, Dec. 1, 1999; Steven R. Weisman, "Editorial

Observer: Machiavelli and New York's School-Aid Politics," *New York Times,* Jan. 18, 2001.

176. *CFE II,* trial transcript, p. 23067.

177. For one illustration, see Jonathan Schorr, *Hard Lessons: The Promise of an Inner City Charter School* (New York: Ballantine, 2002), pp. 16–17.

178. Revenues and expenditures of public school districts enrolling more than 15,000 pupils, by state, 1997–98, *Digest of Education Statistics, 2001* (Washington, D.C.: National Center for Education Statistics, 2002), table 93; *CFE III,* defendants' brief in the Appellate Division, Aug. 13, 2001, p. 24; "NYC Public School Funding," *Inside the Budget,* NYC Independent Budget Office, Nov. 22, 1999.

179. In 2002, the district negotiated a teacher pay increase in return for a longer workday that, the district claimed, sharply reduced the shortage of qualified applicants for new positions. But since it also included a significant reduction in the requirements for a credential, the district's glowing reports were quickly challenged.

180. *CFE II,* trial transcript, p. 1064.

181. *CFE II,* 41.

182. Which the plaintiffs vehemently denied, presenting charts showing that in every income bracket except the very lowest, state and local taxes as a percentage of household income in New York City were as high or higher than those in the neighboring states of Connecticut and New Jersey. *CFE II,* testimony of David Rubenstein, deputy director of the New York City Office of Management and Budget, trial transcript, pp. 11582–87; plaintiff's exhibit P2691.

183. Giuliani testimony, *CFE II,* defense exhibit 19626, pp. 413–15.

184. In a deal made in January 2002 that substantially increased the pay of New York City teachers, the union agreed to raise that limit by twenty minutes a day.

185. *CFE II,* 42. Under the UFT contract, if 75 percent of UFT members in a school agree, the school can create a School Based Option Committee that can consider qualifications other than seniority in hiring new teachers. At the time of the CFE trial, about 200 of the city's 1,100 schools had opted for this limited waiver.

186. *CFE II,* trial transcript, 11207; *CFE II,* Stancik report, defendants' exhibit, 10025–35, pp. 23–24.

187. Crew interview, Sept. 25, 2002.

188. *CFE II,* trial transcript, p. 22958.

189. *CFE II,* trial transcript, 2058; Crew interview. The thirty-year story of community control in New York is itself a drama of tragic mis-

calculations and political opportunism. What had been seen as an attempt to give local communities control over their schools and wrench it away from the fossilized bureaucrats at the system's Brooklyn headquarters became in a few of the thirty-two new districts a tale of corruption and mismanagement that made the old system seem almost benign. See, e.g., James Traub, "A Lesson in Unintended Consequences," *New York Times Magazine,* Oct. 6, 2002, p. 70.

190. *CFE II,* trial transcript, p. 22920. DeGrasse acknowledged in passing that any solution might require major changes in the city's school governance system, but said that that, too, was the state's responsibility. *CFE II,* 190.

191. *CFE II,* trial transcript, pp. 15988, 15641.

192. Ibid., p. 22940.

193. *CFE III,* defendants' brief, pp. 44, 51.

194. *CFE II,* trial transcript, p. 140.

195. *CFE II,* testimony of David Rubenstein, trial transcript, pp. 11537, 11544–45, 11563–66.

196. *CFE II,* 185.

197. *CFE III,* defendants' brief, p. 82.

198. *New York: The State of Learning: Statewide Profile of the Educational System* (Albany: N.Y. State Education Department, 2001), p. 32; *CFE II,* 40; *CFE II,* testimony of James Smith, trial transcript, p. 20394; *CFE III,* defendants' brief, p. 75. The somewhat mystifying question of what makes a good teacher is discussed in the next chapter.

199. The most notorious are dropout data, which in most official reports include only students known to have dropped out; when students simply stop showing up, they are not counted as such. So while a state like Texas might report a dropout rate of 1.6 percent per year, when comparisons are made between seventh-grade enrollment and number of graduates and/or seniors six years later, the attrition is likely to be over 30 percent. For years, until states began to impose marginally tougher criteria, many districts would also report that their students were scoring above the national average, even as national tests had them far below.

200. *CFE II,* 51.

201. *CFE II,* trial transcript, 5434–5.

202. *CFE II,* trial transcript, 2266; *CFE II,* 52.

203. *CFE II,* defendants' trial evidence volume, 301.

204. Rossell phone interview, Sept. 18, 2002.

205. *CFE II,* trial transcript, Rossell testimony, pp. 16742, 16745, 16762, 16874, 16889; Rossell interview.

206. *CFE II*, 53.

207. *CFE III*, defendants' brief, p. 85.

208. "Citywide Reading Test Results, Spring 1997: A Report on the Results of the CTB Reading Test Administration in New York City," New York City Board of Education, n.d.; *CFE II*, defendant's exhibit 10104.

209. Anemona Hartocollis, "Results of New Reading Test Stir Debate," *New York Times*, June 11, 1999; Abby Goodnough, "After Disputes on Scoring, School System Switches Provider of Reading Tests," *New York Times*, Sept. 28, 2002. The irony in this drama, of course, was that through many of the disputes with CTB/McGraw-Hill, the district itself was complaining about inflated scores.

210. Interviews with two well-regarded national testing industry executives who were familiar with the New York process and who, while asking for anonymity, had no professional conflicts in their analysis. The New York report acknowledged that the state (and thus the BOE) had liberalized the rules for exempting students with limited English proficiency from the tests in such a way that any student falling below "specified language proficiency levels" was exempt.

211. "Percentage of Average Grade Enrollment Passing the Regents Examinations in New York City as Compared With the Rest of the State (1997–98)," in *New York: The State of Learning: Statewide Profile of the Educational System* (Albany: N.Y. State Education Department, 1999).

212. *CFE II*, trial transcript, p. 23019.

213. *CFE II*, 5; Rebell interviews, April 25 and July 1, 2002. The Court of Appeals had consolidated the Board of Education suit and the CFE case and heard them together in the proceedings that in 1995 allowed *CFE* to come to trial and threw the BOE case out of court. But in the process, the court itself seemed to narrow the issue in *CFE* to state financing. When Simpson Thacher was brought in, the case was already about finance and only incidentally about the state's responsibility to check the city's mismanagement.

214. Crew interview; *CFE II*, trial transcript, p. 22897; *CFE II*, defendants' findings of fact, pp. 300–31.

215. *CFE II*, trial transcript, p. 20405.

216. Lindseth phone interview, June 14, 2002.

217. Mark Gimpel phone interview, June 24, 2002.

218. Crew interview.

219. *CFE II*, trial transcript, pp. 23068–9.

220. *CFE II*, 103. Once the City University of New York began to tighten

its admission requirements and limited remedial programs, the remedial numbers declined from their scandalous peaks.

221. *CFE III*, 28–29.

222. "Carl McCall and Dennis Mehiel Blast CFE Ruling," McCall campaign press release, June 26, 2002.

223. Shaila K. Dewan, "Pataki Attacks June Ruling That 8th Grade Education Is Enough," *New York Times*, Sept. 13, 2002. See also Randi
Weingarten, "An Endorsement Well Earned," <www.uft.org/
?fid=198>.

224. Weingarten, "An Endorsement."

225. "Settlement Talks in Campaign for Fiscal Equity Case Reach Impasse," CFE press release, Dec. 2, 2002.

226. Greg Winter, "Regents Urge More Spending on Poorer School Districts," *New York Times*, Dec. 14, 2002.

CHAPTER 4

1. Coleman, E. Q. Campbell, C. J. Hobson, J. McPartland, A. M. Mood,
F. D. Weinfeld, and R. L. York, *Equality of Educational Opportunity*
(Washington, D.C.: National Center for Educational Statistics, 1966);
Gunnar Myrdal, *An American Dilemma: The Negro Problem and Mod-
ern Democracy* (New York and London: Harper, 1944).

2. George A. Clowes, "Incentives: The Fundamental Problem in Education, An Interview with Eric A. Hanushek," *School Reform News,*
January 2000.

3. Lawrence O. Picus, "Does Money Matter in Education? A Policy-
maker's Guide," in *Selected Papers in School Finance 1995*, NCES 97–
536 (Washington, D.C.: National Center for Education Statistics,
1997), http://nces.ed.gov/pubs97/97536-2.html.

4. Eric A. Hanushek, "Assessing the Effects of School Resources on Student Performance: An Update," *Educational Evaluation and Policy
Analysis*, summer 1997, pp. 141–64; Hanushek, "The Impact of Differential Expenditures on School Performance," *Educational Researcher* 18, 4 (1989), p. 49.

5. Brian M. Stecher and George W. Bohrnstedt, eds., *What We Have
Learned About Class Size Reduction in California* (Palo Alto, CA:
American Institutes for Research, 2002), www.classize.org; Christopher Jepsen and Steven Rivkin, *Class Size Reduction, Teacher Quality,
and Academic Achievement in California Public Elementary Schools*

(San Francisco: The Public Policy Institute of California, 2002). The numbers who transferred from inner-city schools to the suburbs were relatively small, but the shortage of qualified teachers for those new classes was, and remains, serious.

6. Eric A. Hanushek, "The Evidence on Class Size," Occasional Paper 98-1, W. Allen Wallis Institute of Political Economy, University of Rochester, 1998.

7. Eric A. Hanushek, *The Failure of Input-based Schooling Policies* (Washington, D.C.: National Bureau of Economic Research, 2002), p. 10.

8. Picus, "Does Money Matter?" p. 26.

9. *Digest of Education Statistics* (Washington, D.C.: National Center for Education Statistics, 2002), Tables 112, 124. See also David Grissmer, "Rand Responds," *Education Matters*, summer 2001, p. 4; Alan B. Krueger, "Reassessing the View That American Schools Are Broken," Working Paper #395, Industrial Relations Section, Princeton University, Nov. 16, 1998.

10. Eric A. Hanushek, "Efficiency and Equity in Education," *NBER Reporter*, spring 2001.

11. See, e.g., Eric A. Hanushek, "The Productivity Collapse in Schools," in William J. Fowler Jr., ed., *Developments in School Finance, 1996* (Washington, D.C.: National Center for Education Statistics, 1997), pp. 183–195.

12. Eric A. Hanushek, "Have New York City Children Been Saved?" *Hoover Essays*, May 30, 2002.

13. Picus, "Does Money Matter?" p. 30.

14. *Campaign for Fiscal Equity v. State of New York* (CFE II) (2001), Supreme Court, County of New York, Part 25, no. 111070/93, trial transcript, 22360.

15. Eric A. Hanushek, "A Jaundiced View of 'Adequacy' in School Finance Reform," *Educational Policy*, December 1994, pp. 460–69.

16. Allan R. Odden and Lawrence O. Picus, *School Finance: A Policy Perspective* (New York: McGraw-Hill, 1992).

17. Hanushek, "Efficiency."

18. Eric A. Hanushek, "Outcomes, Incentives, and Beliefs: Reflections on Analysis of the Economics of Schools," *Educational Evaluation and Policy Analysis*, winter 1997, pp. 301–8.

19. Hanushek interview, Aug. 27, 2002.

20. Arthur Jensen, *Genetics and Education* (New York: Harper and Row, 1972), p. 203.

21. Richard Herrnstein and Charles Murray, *The Bell Curve: Intelligence and Class Structure in American Life* (New York: The Free Press, 1994).

22. The definite work here is Christopher Jencks and Meredith Phillips, eds., *The Black-White Test Score Gap* (Washington, D.C.: Brookings Institution, 1998).

23. David Grissmer, Ann Flanagan, and Stephanie Williamson, "Why Did the Black-White Score Gap Narrow in the 1970s and 1980s?" in Christopher Jencks and Meredith Phillips, eds., *The Black-White Test Score Gap* (Washington, D.C.: Brookings Institution, 1998), p. 194.

24. Ibid., p. 211.

25. Hanushek interview, Aug. 27, 2002.

26. John U. Ogbu, *Black Students in An Affluent Suburb: A Study of Academic Disengagement* (Mahwah, N.J.: Lawrence Erlbaum Associates, 2003); Claude Steele, "A Threat in the Air: How Stereotypes Shape the Intellectual Identities and Performance of Women and African Americans," *American Psychologist* 52 (1997), pp. 613–29; Claude Steele and Joshua Aronson, "Stereotype Threat and the Test Performance of Academically Successful African Americans," in Christopher Jencks and Meredith Phillips, eds., *The Black-White Test Score Gap* (Washington, D.C.: Brookings Institution, 1998); Claude Steele, "Thin Ice: 'Stereotype Threat' and Black College Students," *The Atlantic*, Aug. 1999.

27. Alan B. Krueger, "Understanding the Magnitude and Effect of Class Size on Student Achievement," in Lawrence Mishel and Richard Rothstein, eds., *The Class Size Debate* (Washington, D.C.: Economic Policy Institute, 2002), p. 9.

28. Rob Greenwald, Larry V. Hedges, and Richard D. Laine, "The Effect of School Resources on Student Achievement," *Review of Educational Research* 66, 3 (1996), pp. 361–96.

29. Frederick Mosteller, "The Tennessee Study of Class Size in the Early School Grades," *The Future of Children*, 5, 2 (1995), pp. 113–27.

30. Barbara Nye, Larry V. Hedges, and Spyros Konstantopoulos, "The Long-Term Effects of Small Classes in Early Grades: Lasting Benefits in Mathematics Achievement at Grade 9," *Journal of Experimental Education*, spring 2001, p. 245; Debra Viadero, "Tenn. Class-Size Study Finds Long-Term Benefits," *Education Week*, May 5, 1999.

31. Alan B. Krueger and Diane M. Whitmore, "Would Smaller Classes Help Close the Black-White Achievement Gap?" Princeton University Industrial Relations Working Paper #451, March 2001, www.irs. princeton.edu/pubs/working_papers.html.

32. Eric Hanushek, "Evidence, Politics and the Class Size Debate," in Lawrence Mishel and Richard Rothstein, eds., *The Class Size Debate* (Washington, D.C.: Economic Policy Institute, 2002) p. 61.

33. Eric A. Hanushek, *Some Findings from an Independent Investigation of the Tennessee STAR Experiment and from Other Investigations of Class Size Effects* (Washington, D.C.: National Bureau of Economic Research, 1999), pp. 40–41.

34. Ronald Ferguson and Helen Ladd, "How and Why Money Matters," in Helen F. Ladd, ed., *Holding Schools Accountable: Performance-Based Reform in Education* (Washington, D.C.: Brookings Institution, 1996), p. 279.

35. Alex Molnar et al., "2000–01 Evaluation Results of the Student Achievement Guarantee in Education (SAGE) Program," Wisconsin Department of Education, Madison, January 2002, www.asu.edu/educ/epsl/sage.htm; "Burmaster: SAGE Bridges Achievement Gap," Wisconsin Department of Education press release, Jan. 21, 2002.

36. *CFE II*, trial transcript, 22386, 22399, 22426.

37. William L. Sanders and June C. Rivers, "Cumulative and Residual Effects of Teachers on Future Student Academic Achievement," Tennessee Value-Added Assessment System, Knoxville, 1996, www.mdk12.org/practices/ensure/tva/tva_2.html.

38. Ronald F. Ferguson, "Paying for Public Education: New Evidence on How and Why Money Matters," *Harvard Journal on Legislation* 28 (1991), pp. 465–97.

39. Steven G. Rivkin, Eric A. Hanushek, and John F. Kain, "Teachers, Schools and Academic Achievement," paper prepared for the National Bureau of Economic Research, July 2002, p. 3.

40. Ibid., p. 35; Hanushek interview, Aug. 27, 2002. The quote comes from Hanushek's unpublished summary of the findings in "Teachers, Schools and Academic Achievement," but closely corresponds to the conclusions in the published report.

41. Ronald F. Ferguson, "Can Schools Narrow the Black-White Test Score Gap?" in Christopher Jencks and Meredith Phillips, eds., *The Black-White Test Score Gap* (Washington, D.C.: Brookings Institution, 1998), pp. 351–57.

42. Ibid., p. 358.

43. Dan D. Goldhaber and Dominic J. Brewer, "Does Teacher Certification Matter? High School Teacher Certification Status and Student Achievement," *Educational Evaluation and Policy Analysis* 22, 2 (2000), pp. 129–45.

44. Linda Darling-Hammond, "Access to Quality Teaching: An Analysis of Inequality in California's Public Schools," unpublished paper prepared for plaintiffs in *Williams v. California*, 2002.

45. *Meeting the Highly Qualified Teachers Challenge* (Washington, D.C.: U.S. Department of Education, 2002), p. 14.

46. The debate is extensively aired on the respective Web sites of the two groups: http://credo.stanford.edu/working_papers.htm and www.teacherscollege.edu/nctaf/publications/FocusBulletin_Aug2001.htm.

47. *The Teachers We Need and How to Get More of Them* (Washington, D.C.: Thomas B. Fordham Foundation, 1999), www.edexcellence.net/library/teacher.html.

48. "Paige Releases Report to Congress That Calls for Overhaul of State Teacher Certification Requirements," U.S. Department of Education press release, June 12, 2002.

49. Abby Goodnough, "With New Rules and Higher Pay, New York City Gets Certified Teachers," *New York Times*, Aug. 23, 2002; Levine phone interview, Oct. 12, 2002.

50. Arthur Levine, "Rookies in the Schools," *New York Times*, June 29, 2002.

51. Darling-Hammond, "Access to Quality Teaching."

52. Interview with Darling-Hammond, April 1999. Peter Schrag, "Who Will Teach the Teachers?" *University Business*, July/August 1999, p. 33.

53. Liping Ma, *Knowing and Teaching Elementary Mathematics* (Mahwah, N.J.: Lawrence Erlbaum Associates, 1999). Liping Ma, who's studied math teaching both in her native China, where she taught herself, and in the United States, points out that the major problem in this country is not the teachers' lack of pedagogical training or their weak backgrounds in advanced math courses. It's that they don't comprehend the elementary math they're trying to teach, teaching it to emphasize procedures rather than conceptual understanding. Chinese teachers, often with no more than a high-school level education, understand the concepts and thus teach it much more successfully.

54. Goodnough, "With New Rules"; Peter Schrag, "California's 40,000 New 'Highly Qualified' Teachers," *Sacramento Bee*, Aug. 7, 2002.

55. In the past decade or so, the pendulum, particularly among policy makers and a growing number of researchers, has swung sharply toward phonics-based reading instruction, especially through text series such as Open Court, published by SRA/McGraw-Hill, which has been associated with significant reading improvements among young children in urban schools. It's the apparent success of programs such as

Open Court that, in considerable measure, is the basis for the requirement in federal law that federally funded reading programs be scientifically based.

56. KIPP, "The Basic Principles from the Five Pillars," www.kipp.org; Caroline Hendrie, "KIPP Looks to Recreate School Success Stories," *Education Week*, Oct. 30, 2002.

57. *Abbott v. Burke*, 119 N.J. 287 (1990), 367–368. Actually the number is $972,000, not counting benefits.

CHAPTER 5

1. Peter Schrag, "Too Good to Be True," *The American Prospect*, Jan. 3, 2000, p. 49.

2. Michael A. Rebell, "Education Adequacy, Democracy and the Courts," paper prepared for the National Academy of Sciences, 2001.

3. Augenblick phone interview, July 22, 2002.

4. James W. Guthrie and Richard Rothstein, "Enabling 'Adequacy' to Achieve Reality: Translating Adequacy Into State School Finance Distribution Arrangements," in Helen F. Ladd, Rosemary Chalk and Janet S. Hansen, eds., *Equity and Adequacy in Education Finance* (Washington, D.C.: National Academy Press, 1999), p. 219.

5. Ibid., p. 252.

6. Florida Constitution Article IX, Section 1.

7. *Honoré v. Florida State Board of Education* (Leon County Circuit Court, filed January 1999).

8. *Quality Education Model* (Salem, Ore.: Quality Education Commission, 2000), p. 9.

9. "Survey of Finance Adequacy Studies," ECS StateNotes, Education Commission of the States, Denver, September 2001.

10. Thomas B. Timar, "You Can't Always Get What You Want: School Governance in California," paper prepared for submission in *Williams v. California*, San Francisco County Superior Court, No. 312236, March 2001.

11. The Edison story is a saga in itself. But the company's problems in Philadelphia may be as much a signal as any that the optimistic predictions of just a few years ago about the great possibilities of privately managed public schools have crashed. See, e.g., "Edison: An F in Finance," *Business Week*, Nov. 4, 2002.

12. Judith C. Cambria, *Take The Money and Run: How Fiscal Policy from*

the 90s to Now Threatens New Jersey's Future (Trenton, N.J.: New Jersey Policy Perspective, 2001).

13. *Leandro v. State,* 488 S.E. 2nd 249 (1997).

14. Eric A. Hanushek, "The Long Run Importance of School Quality," NBER Working Paper 9071, National Bureau of Economic Research, Cambridge, Mass., July 2002.

15. "Participation in Education: Racial/Ethnic Distribution of Public School Students," National Center for Education Statistics, http://nces.ed.gov/programs/coe/2002/section1/tables; sht03_1.asp.

16. In fourth-grade NAEP scores in the year 2000, for example, the average score for low-poverty schools was 236; for high-poverty schools, it was 191. The national average was 217. See http://nces.ed.gov/programs/coe/2002/section2/tables/t07_2asp.

17. Jack Norman interview, July 10, 2002; Norman, *Funding Our Future: An Adequacy Model for Wisconsin School Finance* (Milwaukee: Institute for Wisconsin's Future, June 2002). In 2001–2, the state was not only stuck in recession but mired in a set of political scandals touching both parties and both houses of the legislature. It was thus not a propitious time to move toward any sweeping reform in funding schools.

18. See Raymond E. Callahan, *Education and the Cult of Efficiency* (Chicago: University of Chicago Press, 1962). Efficiency and scientific management doctrines lent themselves nicely to dismissal of immigrant and minority children as worthy of major educational efforts.

19. Michael Rebell, "Education Adequacy, Democracy and the Courts." Paper prepared for a forthcoming Publication of the National Academy of Sciences and the National Research Council, 2001.

Sources and Acknowledgments

Much of this book is based on official documents—judicial orders, trial transcripts, depositions, motions, and other court papers; the records of legislative floor debates, committee hearings, and reports; and the records of the political campaigns that drive those legislative proceedings—as well as several hundred interviews with educators, lawyers, legislators, scholars, and activists engaged in school policy issues. It also draws on the increasingly rich data banks of the state departments of education and the major school districts in the states this book deals with and, of course, on the great lode of information at the National Center for Education Statistics, the Census Bureau, and other federal repositories. More generally, the book relies on some forty years of visiting schools; talking with teachers, students, administrators and community leaders; studying American education policy and history; reading the reams of research on which much of that policy is supposedly based; and writing about the complex relationship between what goes on in American classrooms and the school policy, politics, and cultural controversies that surround them.

In this electronic age, the texts of many court decisions and legislative acts can be found on the Internet, as can many of the countless reports and studies that proliferate in this field. Where they are conveniently on-line, the Web addresses are listed. But for court transcripts and similar documents, for the details of the legal and legislative work behind those official acts, and for an understanding of the strategies and motivations of the players, journalists and historians are as dependent on the participants and firsthand visits as they ever were.

On that score I'm indebted to countless people and organizations—lawyers, legislators, state and local officials, community activists, academic researchers, parents, teachers, students—who provided information and insights and stood (or more often sat) still for endless questions, sometimes in long or multiple interviews, about what they did and why. Many are quoted by name and/or cited in the endnotes. But for various reasons some are not quoted or are not credited sufficiently for the help they provided.

Among them: Michael Rebell, Jessica Garcia, and their colleagues at the Campaign for Fiscal Equity in New York; Alfred Lindseth of the Atlanta firm of Sutherland, Asbill and Brennan; Robert Blum and Mark Gimpel of the New York State Attorney General's Office; former New York City Schools Chancellor Rudolph Crew; Mark Rosenbaum and Catherine F. Lhamon of the American Civil Liberties Union of Southern California; Michael Jacobs, Jack Londen, and Leecia Welch of the San Francisco firm of Morrison and Foerster; Joseph Wayland of Simpson Thacher and Bartlett in New York; Hilary McLean and Drew Mendelson at the office of Governor Gray Davis of California; Robert Tiller of the Raleigh (NC) law firm of Parker Poe; Steven Block and Paul Tractenberg of the Education Law Center in Newark, NJ; Sheria Reid of the North Carolina Education and Law Project; William Phillis of the Ohio Coalition for Equity and Adequacy of School Funding; Debra Dawahare of Wyatt, Tarrant & Combs in Lexington, KY; Robert Sexton and Cindy Heine of the Prichard Committee for Academic Excellence, also in Lexington; Jack Moreland, superintendent of schools in Covington, KY; Lisa Gross of the Kentucky State Department of Education and David Holwerk, long-time editorial page editor of the Lexington, KY *Herald-Leader*, who now sits in my old chair as the editorial page editor of the *Sacramento Bee*.

Also, Cathy Gassenheimer of the A+ Foundation in Montgomery, AL, Jim Williams of the Public Affairs Research Council of Alabama; former Alabama supreme court justice Ralph Cook; Sally Howell of the Alabama School Boards Association; Karen Royster, executive director, and Jack Norman, research director, of the Institute for Wisconsin's Future in Milwaukee; Mike Griffith, Bob Palaich, and former executive director Frank Newman of the Education Commission of the States; Steve Smith of the National Conference of State Legislators; John Oswald of Educational Testing Service; Wayne J. Camara and Janice Gambs of the College Board; Jeannie Oakes and Michelle Renee of the University of California at Los Angeles; Eric Hanushek of the Hoover Institution at Stanford; Kati Haycock and Jeanne Brennan at the Education Trust in Washington, D.C., and Russlynn Ali at the Education Trust West; Todd Silberman of the *Raleigh* (NC) *News and Observer*; Elizabeth Hill and many others at the California Legislative Analyst's Office; David Lyon, Mark Baldassare, Julian Betts, Abby Cook, Joyce Peterson, Hans Johnson, Deborah Reed, Kim Reuben, Heather Rose, Fred Silva, Jon Sonstelie, and Michael Teitz of the Public Policy Institute of California; Bob Blattner, Paul Goldfinger, and their colleagues at School Services, Inc.; Bob Schaefer at FairTest; Dean Misczynski at the California Research Bureau; Walter Haney and George Madaus of Boston College; former acting U.S. Deputy Secretary of Education Marshall Smith; Hamilton Lankford of the State University of New York at Albany; Bebe Verdery of the American Civil Liberties Union of Maryland; state senator Robert Neale and former state senator Barbara Hoffman of Maryland; Donna Cooper of Good Schools Pennsylvania; state senator Dede Alpert and assemblyman Darrell Steinberg of California; Stephen Levy, director of the Center for Continuing Study of the California Economy; Rich Savors of the Ohio School Facilities Commission; Robert Balfanz of Johns Hopkins University; Linda Darling-Hammond and Mike Kirst of Stanford University; Marguerite Roza and Paul Hill of the Center for Reinventing Public Education at the University of Washington; Arthur Levine and Henry Levin of Teachers College, Columbia University; Jim Guthrie of Vanderbilt University; Allan Odden of the University of Wisconsin; Tom Goldstein, former dean of the journalism schools at both Berkeley and Columbia; Lawrence Picus of the University of Southern California; Bella Rosenberg, Mary Bergan, and the late Albert Shanker of the American Federation of Teachers; John Hein of the California Teachers Association; Bob Chase, former president of the National Education Association; Representative George Miller of California; and John Coons, John Ellwood, David Kirp, Eugene Smolensky, and Steven Sugarman of the University of California at Berkeley.

I also appreciate the help of John Affeldt, John Augenblick, Steve Bachrach, Ann Bancroft, Kathryn Baron, Stephen Blake, Linda Bond, George W. Bohrnstedt, Cathleen Boucher, Pat Callan, Davis Campbell, Carl Cohn, Jack Coons, Patricia DeCos, Delaine Eastin, Ken Epstein, Mary Pat Fannon, Chester Finn, Warren Fox, Alice Furry, Kenneth Futernick, Patricia Gandara, Phil Garcia, Margaret Gaston, Margaret Goertz, Patricia Gray, Elizabeth Guillen, Murray Haberman, Ena Harris, Gary Hart, Jerry Hayward, Bill Honig, Harvey Hunt, Susie Lange, Ted Lobman, Jerry Lubenow, Bill Lucia, Bill McCann, Kerri Mazzoni, John Mockler, Stan Murphy, Bill Padilla, Susan Phillips, Mary Ellen Raab, Diane Ravitch, Constance Rice, Jean Ross, Richard Rothstein, Shane Safir, Lois Salisbury, Jonathan Schorr, Jay Schenirer, Jim Smith, Doug Stone, Steven Sugarman, Suzanne Tacheny, Thomas Timar, Ron K. Unz, Michael Usdan, and Harold Williams.

I'm particularly indebted to Marion Joseph and Maureen DiMarco for their very generous help and counsel on complex education and testing issues over the years; to Judith Brown, Claire Cooper, Susanna Cooper, the late Edie Decker, John Hughes, Debbie Meredith, Bob Mott, Mark Paul, Tom Philp, Jewel Reilly, Ginger Rutland, Jim Sanders, and my other friends and former colleagues at the *Sacramento Bee*; to Bruce Cain and Nelson Polsby of the Institute of Governmental Studies at Berkeley for their political wisdom and for allowing me the run of the place as a visiting scholar; to Susan Rasky for her warm encouragement and colleagueship through many years of journalism; to Trish Williams, Mary Perry, and others on the wonderful staff at EdSource in Palo Alto, CA, for their constant help on education data beginning long before this book was started. Special thanks also to Richard Colvin of the Hechinger Institute on Education and the Media at Columbia, Phil Daro, Delaine McCullough of the California Budget Project, and my longtime friend and colleague Rhea Wilson for reading various drafts of the manuscript and their helpful suggestions for it; to the Rockefeller Foundation for supporting the research that led to this book; and to André Schiffrin at The New Press, a wise and loyal editor who keeps the flame burning against the icy chill of big-bucks publishing. Finally, there was the constant encouragement and help of Trish Ternahan, who read the manuscript two or three times and provided no end of support and insights; the inspiration of the late Alan Hight, a teacher in the highest sense of that word; and the shining example of David Schrag, who, as a wise and dedicated fifth-grade teacher in a challenging urban school, practices every day what his father only preaches.

Index